DATE DUE

AG 1 '02			
3-16.06			
OCT 23 2007			
OCT 25 2007			

Demco, Inc. 38-293

Culture and Customs of the Philippines

Culture and Customs of the Philippines

Paul A. Rodell

Culture and Customs of Asia
Hanchao Lu, Series Editor

GREENWOOD PRESS
Westport, Connecticut • London

Library of Congress Cataloging-in-Publication Data

Rodell, Paul A.
    Culture and customs of the Philippines / Paul A. Rodell.
        p. cm.—(Culture and customs of Asia, ISSN 1097–0738)
    Includes bibliographical references and index.
    ISBN 0–313–30415–7 (alk. paper)
    1. Philippines—Civilization.   2. Philippines—Social life and customs.
3. Philippines—History.   I. Title.   II. Series.
DS664.R63   2002
959.9—dc21   2001023338

British Library Cataloguing in Publication Data is available.

Library of Congress Catalog Card Number: 2001023338
ISBN: 0–313–30415–7
ISSN: 1097–0738

First published in 2002

Greenwood Press, 88 Post Road West, Westport, CT 06881
An imprint of Greenwood Publishing Group, Inc.
www.greenwood.com

Printed in the United States of America

The paper used in this book complies with the
Permanent Paper Standard issued by the National
Information Standards Organization (Z39.48–1984).

10 9 8 7 6 5 4 3 2 1

This book is dedicated to the memory of my parents,
Gustave and Helen Rodell,
and my late wife,
Lee Gek (Jade) Tan Rodell

And to my adoptive Philippine parents,
Col. (ret.) *Juan B. and Resureccion Villanueva,*
living in Botolan, Zambales

Contents

Illustrations

Series Foreword

GEOGRAPHICALLY, Asia encompasses the vast area from Suez, the Bosporus, and the Ural Mountains eastward to the Bering Sea and from this line southward to the Indonesian archipelago, an expanse that covers about 30 percent of our earth. Conventionally, and especially insofar as culture and customs are concerned, Asia refers primarily to the region east of Iran and south of Russia. This area can be divided in turn into subregions commonly known as South, Southeast, and East Asia, which are the main focus of this series.

The United States has vast interests in this region. In the twentieth century, the United States fought three major wars in Asia (namely, the Pacific War of 1941–45, the Korean War of 1950–53, and the Vietnam War of 1965–75), and each had profound impact on life and politics in America. Today, America's major trading partners are in Asia, and in the foreseeable future, the weight of Asia in American life will inevitably increase, for in Asia lie our great allies as well as our toughest competitors in virtually all arenas of global interest. Domestically, the role of Asian immigrants is more visible than at any other time in our history. In spite of these connections with Asia, however, our knowledge about this crucial region is far from adequate. For various reasons, Asia remains for most of us a relatively unfamiliar, if not stereotypical or even mysterious, "Oriental" land.

There are compelling reasons for Americans to obtain some level of concrete knowledge about Asia. It is one of the world's richest reservoirs of culture and an ever-evolving museum of human heritage. Rhoads Murphey, a prominent Asianist, once pointed out that in the part of Asia east of Afghanistan and south of Russia alone lies half the world, "half of its people and far more than half of its historical experience, for these are the oldest living civilized traditions." Prior to the modern era, with limited interaction and mutual influence between the East and the West, Asian civilizations developed largely independent from the West. In modern times, however, Asia and the West have come not only into close contact but also into frequent conflict: The result has been one of the most solemn and stirring dramas in world history. Today, integration and compromise are the trend in coping with cultural differences. The West—with some notable exceptions—has started to see Asian traditions not as something to fear but as something to be understood, appreciated, and even cherished. After all, Asian traditions are an indispensable part of the human legacy, a matter of global "common wealth" that few of us can afford to ignore.

As a result of Asia's enormous economic development since World War II, we can no longer neglect the study of this vibrant region. Japan's "economic miracle" of postwar development is no longer unique, but in various degrees has been matched by the booming economy of many other Asian countries and regions. The rise of the four "mini dragons" (South Korea, Taiwan, Hong Kong, and Singapore) suggests that there may be a common Asian pattern of development. At the same time, each economy in Asia has followed its own particular trajectory. Clearly, China is the next giant on the scene. Sweeping changes in China in the last two decades have already dramatically altered the world's economic map. Furthermore, growth has also been dramatic in much of Southeast Asia. Today, war-devastated Vietnam shows great enthusiasm for joining the "club" of nations engaged in the world economy. And in South Asia, India, the world's largest democracy, is rediscovering its role as a champion of market capitalism. The economic development of Asia presents a challenge to Americans but also provides them with unprecedented opportunities. It is largely against this background that more and more people in the United States, in particular among the younger generation, have started to pursue careers dealing with Asia.

This series is designed to meet the need for knowledge of Asia among students and the general public. Each book is written in an accessible and lively style by an expert (or experts) in the field of Asian studies. Each book focuses on the culture and customs of a country or region. However, readers should be aware that culture is fluid, not always respecting national boundaries. While every nation seeks its own path to success and struggles to maintain its own identity, in the cultural domain mutual influence and integration among Asian nations are ubiquitous.

Each volume starts with an introduction to the land and people of a nation or region and includes a brief history and an overview of the economy. This is followed by chapters dealing with a variety of topics that piece together a cultural panorama, such as thought, religion, ethics, literature and art, architecture and housing, cuisine, traditional dress, gender, courtship and marriage, festivals and leisure activities, music and dance, and social customs and lifestyle. In this series, we have chosen not to elaborate on elite life, ideology, or detailed questions of political structure and struggle, but instead to explore the world of common people, their sorrow and joy, their pattern of thinking, and their way of life. It is the culture and customs of the majority of the people (rather than just the rich and powerful elite) that we seek to understand. Without such understanding, it will be difficult for all of us to live peacefully and fruitfully with each other in this increasingly interdependent world.

As the world shrinks, modern technologies have made all nations on earth "virtual" neighbors. The expression "global village" not only reveals the nature and the scope of the world in which we live but also, more importantly, highlights the serious need for mutual understanding of all peoples on our planet. If this series serves to help the reader obtain a better understanding of the "half of the world" that is Asia, the authors and I will be well rewarded.

Hanchao Lu
Georgia Institute of Technology

Acknowledgments

THIS BOOK IS THE product of my fascination with the Philippines, its history, culture, and social life, that has continued for over thirty years. To give proper acknowledgment to all of my Filipino friends who have shared their lives and their culture with me would require a full chapter. While such a listing is clearly impossible, I will note some of those experiences and people who were most influential in shaping my perspectives of this Southeast Asian nation's culture and those who helped produce this volume.

My introduction to the Philippines began as a Peace Corps volunteer in the town of Botolan, Zambales, where I worked in agriculture extension. There, I was introduced to the Villanueva family, who became, and remain, my second family. Being an adopted member of a Filipino family provided a wonderful life experience for which I will always be grateful. From my provincial roots, I continued for a third year in the Peace Corps working in the agency's Manila office. My job required that I travel throughout the country, visiting other volunteers, and helping define sites for future volunteer placement. In the process, my horizons expanded as I sampled the subtle variations of Philippine culture.

After the Peace Corps, I enrolled in a graduate program at the Asian Center, University of the Philippines. This was a critical and fortunate juncture, because I benefited from a first-rate faculty, who helped me analyze and interpret what I had only experienced and enjoyed as a volunteer. Just as important, were my fellow graduate students, who were from other countries in Asia, as well as from the Philippines. Today, many of these former fellow students remain friends and valued colleagues. My academic nurturing continued in the United States under the helpful guidance of John A. Larkin with whom I completed my dissertation on the Iglesia Filipina Independiente, the Philippine Independent Church of Fr. Gregorio Aglipay. Fortunately, my career allows ample opportunity to make frequent return trips to the Philippines for research and professional conferences, so my ties to friends and "family" continue.

The completion of this book was greatly assisted by two grants, which supported the additional library research I needed to explore areas outside of my principal fields of experience. The first was a research travel grant from the Faculty Research Committee of Georgia Southern University, while the second was an "academic sharing program grant" from the Center for South and Southeast Asian Studies of the University of Michigan, where I enjoyed access to the best Philippine studies library collection in the country. During the writing process, a number of friends contributed their thoughtful, and frequently critical comments on earlier drafts of some of my chapters. I specifically wish to thank Belen Calingacion and Laurice Guillen for their comments on my analyses of Philippine theater and film. Other friends, who either read various portions of this book or helped in many other ways, include, Gerardo Tan, who teaches art at the University of the Philippines; Carol Sobritchea, director of the university's women's studies center; Oscar Evangelista, now retired from the department of history; and Susan Evangelista, who taught in the department of English at the Ateneo de Manila University. I also wish to thank Vicky Belarmino, film archivist of the Cultural Center of the Philippines, who helped me in numerous ways, and indirectly introduced me to the noted film historian, Agustin "Hammy" Sotto. Many thanks go to writer and social critic F. Sionil "Frankie" Jose, for his graciousness.

I am grateful, as well, for the specific assistance and encouragement given to me at various points by Nicanor "Nick" Tiongson, College of Mass Communication, University of the Philippines; Ambeth Ocampo, whose insights put fun into the study of Philippine history; Corazon G. Inigo, vice president and artistic director, Cultural Center of the Philippines; Alice M. Esteves, officer-in-charge, library division, Cultural Center of the Philippines; Dominador Ferrer, Jr., administrator, Intramuros Administration; Armando Malay, Jr., dean, and Normita G. Recto, secretary, Asian Center, University of the Philippines; and Bernie S. Cervantes. I must mention, too, my mentors in Philippine politics, the Honorable Loreta "Etta" Rosales, Akbayan partylist representative to the House of Representatives, Republic of the Philippines, and Joel Rocamora, executive director of the Institute for Popular Democracy. While I profited from the kind advice and assistance these people gladly shared with me, it must be understood that the present book is the result of my efforts and all errors of fact and interpretation remain my sole responsibility.

I have the good fortune to be a member of a truly supportive department of superior scholar-teachers and I owe them a debt of gratitude for their support of all of my activities, including this one. Special thanks go to the folks who helped most directly in the preparation of this book, beginning with the series editor, Hanchao Lu, who first entrusted me with the task of writing the Philippine volume, and who offered numerous critical comments for helpful revisions all along the way. As well, I am indebted to my very patient Greenwood editor Wendi Schnaufer, and to the professionalism of production editor Betty Pessagno. Finally, it is my hope that this book will offer sufficient information and insight for readers unfamiliar with the Philippines.

Chronology of the History of the Philippines

100,000–60,000 B.C.	Australiod peoples inhabit island Southeast Asia
22,000 B.C.	Age of oldest skeletal remains found on Palawan Island
3,000–2,500 B.C.	Modern Malay peoples inhabit island Southeast Asia
10th–14th century	Chinese traders establish routes to island Southeast Asia
15th century	Muslim missionaries reach the southern Philippines from Indonesia
1521 A.D.	Ferdinand Magellan killed on Mactan Island
1565	Arrival of Miguel Lopez de Legazpi who begins Spain's colonization
1571	Legazpi expedition transfers to Manila
1593	Publication of the first book in the Philippines, *Doctrina Cristiana*
1615	Beginning of galleon trade between Manila and Acapulco
1645–1647	Naval battles between Spanish and Dutch warships for control of the islands

1762–1764	England occupies Manila during the Seven Years War, remaining beyond the end of the conflict
17th–19th century	Almost 300 acts of resistance against Spanish rule because of native dissatisfaction
1815	The galleon trade ends
1826	Filipino priests are removed from their parishes in favor of Spanish priests
1834	Opening of Manila to international trade and investment
1872	Mutiny of Filipino soldiers at naval arsenal in Cavite (Manila Bay) and execution of three Filipino priests marks the birth of modern Philippine national consciousness
1887	Publication of Jose Rizal's anti-Spanish novel *Noli Me Tangere*
1892	Rizal returns to the Philippines and is arrested. Andres Bonifacio founds the revolutionary society, the *Katipunan*
1896	*Katipunan* revolt against Spain in June; Rizal is executed in December
1897	Bonifacio loses control of *Katipunan* to Emilio Aguinaldo and is executed
1898	May 1: U.S. Commodore George Dewey captures Manila Bay; June 12: Aguinaldo proclaims Philippine independence; August 13: American forces capture Manila, excluding Filipino insurgents; and in December, Spain cedes the Philippines to the United States
1899	February 4: beginning of the Philippine-American War. After heavy initial losses, Filipino forces switch to guerrilla warfare
1901	Aguinaldo is captured, but many revolutionaries fight on
1902	July 4: President Theodore Roosevelt declares war ended

1907	The Philippine Assembly, the first popularly elected legislature in Asia, convenes
1909	Free trade created between the United States and the Philippines, firmly linking the colony's economy to America
1934	U.S. Congress passes Tydings-McDuffie Act creating Philippine Commonwealth and setting independence ten years later
1935	Philippine Commonwealth established with Manuel Quezon as president and Sergio Osmena as vice president
1941	Japanese forces attack the Philippines and Hawaii. General Douglas MacArthur orders a retreat to Bataan province
1942	Philippine-American forces in Bataan surrender on April 9, and are forced on a "death march" to their prison camp; defenders on Corregidor Island surrender in May
1944	U.S. troops land on Leyte Island begin to conquer the archipelago
1946	The United States gives the Philippines its independence
1947	The United States gains military bases and "parity" rights for U.S. citizens in the Philippine economy
1948–mid-1950s	Insurgency by communist Hukbalahap movement threatens government; American covert intelligence agents play key role in reversing the insurgency
1954	Newsman Benigno Aquino, Jr. meets with insurgent leader who surrenders a few months later
1964	Student demonstrations against U.S. military bases and parity rights
1965	Ferdinand Marcos wins presidential election
1968	Communist Party of the Philippines (CCP) is formed

1969	Marcos elected to a second presidential term; CCP forms New People's Army
1970	"First Quarter Storm" occurs whereby students and workers mount a series of massive demonstrations against the Marcos government
1971	Marcos decries the bombing of an opposition rally and claims Aquino is linked to the communist movement
1972	Libyan leader Muammar Qaddafi declares support for Philippine Muslim insurgents; severe typhoons devastate the country's rice crop; Manila is rocked by mysterious bombings, and the defense secretary's car is ambushed
1972	September 22: Marcos declares martial law, Congress is abolished, universities are closed, the media is silenced, and thousands of government opponents are arrested, the most prominent being Senator Aquino
1976	Tripoli Agreement ends fighting between the government and Muslim rebels
1979	Manila Archbishop Jaime Cardinal Sin appeals for the release of the long imprisoned Aquino
1980	Marcos releases Aquino to travel to the United States for heart surgery
1983	August 21: Aquino returns to Manila, and is assassinated leaving the plane under heavy military guard; his funeral is attended by millions, and sparks renewed massive protests
1984	Opposition candidates make significant gains in legislative elections. A government panel finds the military guilty of Aquino's murder
1985	Marcos announces "snap elections" in six weeks; Corazon Aquino announces her candidacy for president
1986	February 7–25, "People Power" revolution occurs; Massive civilian, religious, and military protests take place due to election fraud; Aquino swept into power; Marcos flees to the United States

1991	Long dormant volcano, Mt. Pinatubo, erupts burying the U.S. Clark Air Force Base in volcanic ash; the base is abandoned
1992	Fidel Ramos is inaugurated president; the Philippine Senate refuses to renew American rights to Subic Bay Naval Base
1994	Ramos government negotiates a cease fire with Muslim rebels, and offers amnesty to communist insurgents and military rebels
1996	Peace agreement between the government and Muslim insurgents
1998	Joseph Estrada inaugurated president; his attempt to amend the constitution is overwhelmed by public out-cry
2000	Former Estrada political ally accuses the president of massive corruption; the House of Representatives passes articles of impeachment
2001	January 16–20: "People Power II" erupts when Es-trada's senate allies keep bank records from being en-tered as evidence; Estrada's cabinet members, and the military join huge protest crowds; the Philippine Su-preme Court declares the presidency vacant and Vice-President Gloria Macapagal-Arroyo is sworn into office of president

Map of the Philippines.

1

Land, People, and History

TO THE FIRST-TIME American visitor the Philippines has a deceptively familiar Western feel to it. In Manila, the capital city's architecture is dominated by modern high-rise office buildings and condominiums. Its streets are clogged with cars taking their passengers to many stores that have familiar American chain store names, and the kinds of goods sold in local stores are easily identified thanks to the shop signs, all of which are in English. Though the local population is distinctly Malay (the dominant racial group in the island Southeast Asian nations of the Philippines, Malaysia, and Indonesia) in physical appearance, their manner of everyday dress is similar to that in virtually any American town or city, and their open friendship has made Filipino hospitality well known around the world. Filipinos are quick to point out that because of their colonial past they have spent 300 years in a Spanish convent and then fifty more years in Hollywood, so they are very aware of Euro-American culture.

The facile observation of the first-time visitor contains some truth. Many Filipinos are literate in English, since it is taught in schools as a second language, and they follow the latest American songs, movies, and novels, all of which are locally available. Philippine newspapers, magazines, and broadcast news devote at least some attention to American politics and social trends, and many Filipinos have relatives in the "states" and have visited the United States, sometimes frequently. Every year, many Filipinos leave their homes for work overseas where they are valued because of their English proficiency and general sophistication. But, the visitor who stays for more than a brief visit soon discovers that even Western foods do not taste quite like they do back home and that Filipinos really prefer their own foods to imported dishes, which are regarded as snacks rather than real food. It also becomes apparent that personal relationships are conducted in ways that are much closer to Asian rather than Western models. Soon, this comfortable Westernized Asian country becomes remarkably odd and difficult to understand in fundamental ways.

The truth is that Filipinos have a strong indigenous Asian culture that has incorporated many external influences and refashioned them according to its own standards. This book is intended to be a bridge between initial impressions and deeper understandings of the resulting cultural synthesis. The complex combining of cultural elements to create a uniquely Philippine culture is a major theme found in many of the following chapters whether the topic is architecture, music, literature, religion, family life, or fashion. This exploration of just what it is that constitutes Philippine culture is not only of interest to the foreign reader, but is also a major concern of Filipinos who must constantly define their national identity in response to foreign influences.

This chapter looks at the country's physical reality to determine the geographic and climatic impact of the archipelago on Philippine society. It also identifies the more important groups of Philippine minority peoples, as well as the major dialects and ethnic identities that differentiate various lowland, or majority, Filipinos from each other. Finally, the chapter reviews those historical patterns and influences that have shaped the present Philippine reality.

THE PHILIPPINE ARCHIPELAGO, CLIMATE, POPULATION, AGRICULTURE, AND RELIGIOUS COMPOSITION

The Philippine archipelago lies about 100 miles to the south of Taiwan and a few nautical miles from its Southeast Asian neighbors to the southwest, Malaysia and Indonesia. To the west is the South China Sea while immediately to the east is the undersea Philippine Trench of the Pacific Ocean, one of the deepest parts of any ocean in the world. The archipelago's location at the far southeastern edge of Asia has meant that many aspects of the region's religious and cultural influences could be selectively adopted into the pre-existing culture. So, for example, Hinduism and Buddhism left very little impression on the peoples of the Philippines while Islam did not reach the islands until the fourteenth century but was synthesized into the local cultural milieu. Similarly, cultural influences from China were taken into the country via the mediation of merchants from that country's southern provinces and were adopted slowly and selectively. This relative isolation and the freedom to pick and choose from other cultures have helped to produce the very unique amalgam that is the Philippines.

The archipelago is made up of over 7,100 islands of which only 460 are more than one square mile in area. The rest of the islands are uninhabitable and some disappear at high tide. The country's major islands include, first and foremost, the main island of Luzon that stretches from the far north to Manila and beyond to the southeast via a long arm forming the Bicol region. Luzon is ethnically and geographically divided into a number of subregions and is the home to three of the country's six major language dialects. To the far south is the large island of Mindanao that extends from a southwesterly arm known as the Sulu archipelago up to the main portion of the massive island that is home to an uneasily mixed population of non-Christian tribal groups, indigenous Muslims, and recent Filipino Christian migrants. Mindanao is very diverse geographically with a number of major river basins, gulfs, and bays, and it is home to a number of ethno-linguistic groups.

The islands in the center of the country are known as the Visayas and include the long thin island of Cebu, which was the 1521 landing spot for Ferdinand Magellan during his exploratory voyage around the world and where he lost his life in a battle with a local chieftain. Later in 1565, Cebu was again the initial landing area and colonial capital for Spain's founding expedition under the command of Miguel Lopez de Legazpi. Today, Cebu is the Philippine's second largest city and as such is a major port and industrial center. Immediately to the west lies the island of Negros (pronounced "Naygross" and in Spanish meaning "the dark island"). Though long underpopulated, the island rapidly filled in the nineteenth century when its fertile volcanic soils were tapped to grow sugar cane for a booming international market. The Negros sugar economy still plays a major role in the nation's economy and supports a number of major cultural activities. The next island to the west is Panay, which has long been inhabited and is a source of rich archeological materials. Its port city of Iloilo has a natural harbor and is at the base of a large agricultural flood plain that supports a substantial population. Other major islands in the Visayas include Samar, Leyte, Bohol, and Masbate, while other major islands of the archipelago include Mindoro and Marinduque and the Romblon group, all of which are just south of Luzon and the long island of Palawan, which seems to connect Luzon with the Malaysian state of Sabah to the southwest.

The country's total land area is 115,600 square miles, which is slightly smaller than the combined area of the states of New York, Illinois, and Maryland.[1] Though impressive, this figure does not convey how large a total surface area the country covers, since its islands are divided by substantial bodies of water, which are incorporated within its national boundaries. So, it is best to keep in mind that the Philippines stretches about 1,100 miles from north to south and some 650 miles across from east to west. This distance is almost equal to the distance from Duluth to New Orleans and from St. Louis to Washington, D.C., respectively. As well, the archipelago's irregular coastline stretches for approximately 14,000 miles or about twice that of the continental United States.

The archipelago's irregular coast offers a number of good harbors, protected straits and gulfs and many hundred rivers and bays. Manila Bay has an area of some 700 square miles and a circumference of about 120 miles, making it one of the best natural harbors in the world. Meanwhile, the smaller Subic Bay, west of Manila, has a well-protected harbor and until recently served as the home for a massive U.S. naval facility. Currently, Subic Bay is the port for a large export processing industrial zone that is playing a major role in the country's industrialization. Other major ports include those of Cebu and Iloilo in the Visayas and Zamboanga and Davao on Mindanao. The easy access to saltwater from most locations in the country, as well as freshwater rivers and lakes, accounts for the amount of fish, shellfish, and aquatic plants in the local diet. The country's fishing industry is largely a small-scale operation of individual boat owners whose easy access to a livelihood assures the country of a steady supply of fish.

A physical map shows that the archipelago has a number of prominent mountain ranges, many of which are volcanic. On Luzon, the most important ranges are the Central Cordillera in the north, the Zambales mountain chain to the west, the Sierra Madre along the eastern edge, and the Caraballo de Baler mountain chain extending along the southeastern arm of the island. On Mindanao, four distinct mountain ranges divide the island, while the highest peak in the country is Mt. Apo west of the city of Davao with an elevation of 9,692 feet. The most active volcanos include Mt. Pinatubo in the Zambales chain, which erupted with devastating impact in 1991, causing the departure of the U.S. military from neighboring Clark Air Base and nearby Subic Bay naval station. Also very active are the Taal volcano to the southeast of Manila and the perfectly cone shaped Mayon Volcano in the Bicol region. All of these mountains and volcanos are a part of the so-called Pacific Ring of Fire, a line of volcanic and seismic activity that occasionally causes great destruction. In the past century and a half, the Philippines has experienced three particularly severe earthquakes, in 1863, 1937, and 1968, as well as many hundreds of lesser quakes and tremors.

The Philippines has a tropical climate that averages eighty degrees Fahrenheit, though interior valleys and the leeward sides of the islands have warmer temperatures than the windward coasts, whose temperatures are moderated. Meanwhile, mountain areas can be substantially cooler such that light sweaters are required in the winter months. It was for this climatic reason that the U.S. colonial government built a summer capital in the town of Baguio in the central Cordillera Highlands in the early years of its rule. So desperate were the American officials to escape Manila's oppressive summer heat that they had construction crews cut a steep and winding road along the very face of the Cordillera's mountains. That road is still used today and offers travelers breathtaking scenic views from bus and car windows, while vehicle tires come dangerously close to the edges of steep cliffs along the narrow roadway.

There are three seasons in the year. The rainy season monsoon begins in late May or June and lasts until October, bringing winds and rain from the southwest and typhoons that can cause heavy damage. From the end of the rains until about late February, the temperatures moderate and become quite enjoyable, especially for the celebration of Christmas. The rather idyllic temperatures of winter become steadily hotter as the winds shift from the northeast, bringing dry conditions and thermometer readings that reach their zenith in late April and May. During these hot months, schools are on summer break until early June when returning rains make going to school bearable again.

The annual rains bring more than relief from the heat: They are critical for the nation's rice crop. At the first rain, farmers across the country prepare seedbeds, plow, and harrow the hardened soil and repair irrigation canals and the dikes of the rice paddies. Since the development of high-yielding hybrid seeds in the late 1960s by the International Rice Research Institute, located in Los Banos, Laguna, a short drive southeast of Manila, the nation's farmers have shifted from low-yielding native varieties to high-yielding hybrids. The country is now self-sufficient in this basic grain. In addition to rice, corn is raised in some of the Visayan Islands and Mindanao where the hardened grains are pulverized and mixed with rice or are consumed as a substitute for rice. The annual rains are also crucial for sugar grown on Negros Island and in provinces north and south of Manila. Meanwhile, the banana-like abaca plant, which produces high-grade natural cordage and coconuts, is grown in the Bicol region and depends on the annual rainfall. One other major crop of the country, tobacco, is not as dependent on the annual rains and is grown in the northern provinces of Luzon, where the rains are lighter and the soil not as rich.

In 1995, the Philippines population was almost 70 million of which 46 percent was classified as urban. At the beginning of the twentieth century, the population was only one-tenth its present size and stood at just slightly more than seven and a half million. The country's population is expected to continue to climb at its current high rate of 2.3 percent, since birth control has been strenuously resisted by the Roman Catholic Church, which represents about 80 percent of the total population. Another nine percent of Filipinos are Protestant, four percent are Muslim, and the remaining population are members of the country's animistic tribal groups.

In addition to formal opposition by the Catholic hierarchy, many Filipinos are reluctant to embrace birth control, since having a number of children is socially important. The desire for large families is less in urban areas, but even here Filipino urban families continue to be larger than their counterparts elsewhere in the world. The single largest urban area is the metropolitan district of Manila, which includes seventeen cities and towns and has a population of approximately ten million. This size makes metro Manila the eleventh largest urban area in the world. Other large provincial cities include Cebu, with a population over 600,000; Davao with over one million inhabitants; and Zamboanga, which claims over 500,000.[2]

PEOPLE

The majority of the population are the Christianized "lowland" Filipinos who are usually differentiated according to which one of the almost eighty dialect groups they belong. It is important to note that the Philippines has dialects rather than separate languages, the distinction being that the dialects are variations of a single linguistic root, since they all belong to the Malayo-Polynesian language family. Exceptions include the Filipino Christian population on Mindanao, who identify themselves by geographic residence; the Muslim peoples, who base their identity on religion; and the nation's indigenous peoples, whose pre-Christian and pre-Islamic religious beliefs and cultures give them distinct identities.

On Luzon, Tagalog speakers live in the metropolitan Manila area and the adjacent regions of Central Luzon to the north and the southern Tagalog provinces to the south. Tagalog forms the basis of *Pilipino*, which over the last few decades has made real progress in becoming a true national language, despite the resistance of other dialects whose speakers resent the Manila/Tagalog dominance of the nation's political, economic, and cultural life. *Ilocano* is the native dialect of Filipinos living along the coastal plains and agricultural valleys of northern Luzon. In the past two hundred years, Ilocano people have pioneered new settlements further south of their home base. In the early decades of the twentieth century, they comprised the bulk of Philippine immigrants who worked on sugar plantations and farms in Hawai'i and California. Ilocanos have a reputation for being very hard working and extremely frugal, which undoubtedly results from their difficult life on their ancestral farms, that have notoriously poor soil conditions. The people of the Bicol region on the southeastern arm of Luzon have their own dialect and cultural identity. Bicolanos are best known for their spicy foods that make abundant use of chili peppers and their consumption of the coconut vodka *lambanog*. The Bicol region is also solidly Roman Catholic and well known for supporting vibrant regional arts.

If the stereotype of the Ilocano is one of hardworking frugality, the Visayan is the archetypal opposite. The abundant marine resources and rich volcanic soils of the central islands has helped to produce a culture that values music, fun, and gregarious personal relations. A study in contrasts was the marriage of former president Ferdinand Marcos, an Ilocano of simple tastes and conservative personal spending, and his Visayan wife Imelda, whose personal collection of thousands of shoes, profligate shopping sprees, and impromptu singing at parties bespoke of her Leyte island origins. The Visayans have well-known local centers of art, especially on Negros Island, where the sugar planter elite has been generous in their support of local musicians, actors, and writers. Linguistically, the Visayan Islands are divided into a number of dialects: principally, Ilongo of Panay Island, Cebuano from Cebu, and Waray-Waray spoken on the islands of Leyte and Samar.

Most of Mindanao's Christian population is comprised of relatively recent migrants, who came from all over the Philippines to settle this second largest island of the country. Therefore, they do not have a distinct dialect of their own but speak the language of their original home provinces. However, an increasing number of these Christian residents are locally born, and their sense of identification is geographic rather than linguistic. If they share an ethic, it is that of the rugged and independent pioneer taming the wilderness and wide plains of this underpopulated virgin territory. As well, they believe, with some justification, that the national leadership, dominated by northern politicians, does not allocate suitable national resources to develop the island's potential. They resent attempts of the Manila government to create autonomous governmental structures for the region's Muslim population, since this limits their ability to further expand across the island.

The nation's Muslims resent Christian Filipinos for encroaching on their ancestral lands, and they believe that Manila consistently neglects the needs of the island. The Muslim population is divided into five ethnic subgroups, including the boat-dwelling Badjaos, who rarely set foot on land; the Tausugs of the Sulu archipelago, who have a well-deserved reputation of fighting prowess; the Samals of the Zamboanga peninsula of Mindanao; the Maranaos, who reside in the vicinity of Lake Lanao in the northwestern Mindanao; and the Maguindanaoans, who make their home to the south of the Maranaos. Religiously and culturally, the Muslims have much more in common with the neighboring Malaysians and Indonesians than they do with their fellow Filipinos against whom they have waged a brutal independence struggle for a number of years. In 1996, the main branch of the Moro National Liberation Front signed a peace accord with the government and was given a measure of self-rule through the creation of the Autonomous Region in Muslim Mindanao. More recently, Muslim dissatisfaction with the government and an aggressive military policy of Philippine President Joseph Estrada has led to a deadly resumption of fighting that is costly in lives and places an extreme burden on an already weak Philippine economy.

HISTORY

Pre-Contact Philippines

The diverse nature of the Philippine population, from the pygmy "negritos," scattered throughout the archipelago, to the peoples who compose the numerous non-Christian national minorities, to the majority lowland Filipinos, shows that the islands have always hosted immigrant groups. Exactly when these different peoples arrived and from where they originated is open to question. The oldest archeological evidence of human habitation in the Philippines is a 22,000-year-old skull found in 1962 on the island of Palawan. Much earlier fossil remains dating as far back as 300,000 to one million years ago have been found on the island of Java in Indonesia. The so-called Java man was followed by more modern skeletal structures of Australoid peoples dating to 100,000 to 60,000 years ago. These people were concentrated in the southern areas of Southeast Asia, Papua, and Australia and survive today as isolated populations of negritos throughout the region, including the Philippines. The pre-Neolithic period of approximately 13,000 to 4,000 B.C. saw the rise of Noabinhian culture in Vietnam and Thailand, whose characteristics are shared by many Philippine minority peoples. Finally, the majority Malay population of the Philippines, as well as of Malaysia and Indonesia, seems to have originated in present-day southern China and migrated into Southeast Asia between 2,500 to 300 B.C.[3]

Travel to and from the Philippines was easy, especially during the last ice age when the already shallow South China Sea receded by about 150 feet, creating land bridges between the Asian mainland and the islands. Even after the water returned to earlier levels, travel within Southeast Asia was easy because of the short distances involved, mild weather conditions, and the numerous islands and atolls that provide rest along the open waterways. Popular Philippine mythology claims that the country's Malay ancestors came as families and even as whole communities in vessels called *barangay*. This name is currently used for the country's neighborhood political structure at the municipal level. Continuing in historical times, the ease of travel also facilitated contacts between early Filipinos and their Asian neighbors. There is ample archeological evidence in the form of pottery and other trade items indicating extensive early links with Thai, Vietnamese, Taiwanese, and Chinese merchants. There is even linguistic evidence embedded within the languages of the Philippines indicating at least indirect contact with India.

Despite these contacts, the Philippines was on the periphery of the region, and this limited the impact of Asia's major empires and civilizations. While the archipelago's indirect contact with India left little mark, Chinese influence was greater thanks to its merchant visitors who acted as cultural emissaries. Chinese influence had its greatest impact on the Filipino diet and the general material culture because of the goods that the traders brought to exchange for local forest and agriculture products. Despite Indian and Chinese influences, Filipinos never adopted either Hinduism or Buddhism. Confucian philosophy never entered the archipelago, and women retained a level of social equality unknown in either India or China. Only Islam eventually gained acceptance among the peoples in the southern islands, and even here, the religious practice of Philippine Muslims has, until recently, been markedly more relaxed than elsewhere in the Islamic world, indicating the relatively casual Philippine approach to foreign influences.

While many of the details of the pre-European life of Filipinos remains unknown, it is nonetheless apparent that this early culture continues to serve as the foundation for the culture and customs of contemporary Filipinos. Before the arrival of the first Spaniards, Filipino religious beliefs, social organization, gender relations, and material culture were already well developed and exhibited strong similarities among all groups in the islands. Whether in music, literature, dress, architecture, gender relations, or political practices, the indigenous culture continued to shape Filipino sensibilities and guided the adoption of external influences.[4] While each succeeding chapter in this book will elaborate various individual cultural topics more fully, suffice it to say that aspects of Spanish and American culture were selectively integrated into the cultural fabric based upon their acceptability to the pre-existing culture.

Under Spanish Colonialism

Spanish colonization had the twin goals of profit and religion. The first Spaniard to arrive in 1521 was Ferdinand Magellan, who came to the Philippines as part of his attempt to circumnavigate the globe for Spain. Unfortunately the explorer's journey ended on the island of Mactan near the larger island of Cebu when Magellan allied himself with one local ruler versus

Puerto Real, or main gate, to the old Spanish walled
city of Manila. Photo by the author.

another and was killed in a violent encounter. In 1565, an expedition of
colonization comprised of four ships and almost 400 men arrived under the
command of Miguel Lopez de Legazpi and his court-appointed priest and
ship pilot Father Andres de Urdaneta.

After first establishing themselves on Cebu island, this founding Spanish
expedition eventually discovered a prosperous Muslim kingdom in Manila
Bay, which they conquered in 1571. Because the food supply in the Manila
area was better than in Cebu, the Legazpi expedition decided to transfer to
this new location on Luzon Island. Very soon a number of government
buildings were constructed, along with churches, houses for the religious
missionary orders, and a cathedral for the bishop. In due course, a wall was
constructed around the city that faced both the open bay and the Pasig River.

Thus, Manila was a protected port city for international trade and a secure colonial headquarters that dominated the important island of Luzon.

Although Manila was won and protected by Spanish arms, the rationale for the colony's existence was not simply military and strategic. Spain hoped to secure a source of spices as rich as that controlled by the Portuguese in the nearby "spice islands" in present-day Indonesia. While these hopes were never realized, Manila's port instead began to serve as a conduit for the "galleon trade" that exchanged Mexican silver and gold for goods from south China. A special area of the city, the Parian, was set aside for the city's growing Chinese merchant population, which was forbidden to venture beyond the city. This restriction was imposed for both commercial and strategic reasons, since it was intended to limit Chinese influence among the native population. Until its demise in 1811, the Galleon Trade never completely fulfilled the hopes of the Spanish king in Madrid, but it did bring immense profits to the Spanish residents of Manila who invested heavily in it.

At its peak, the exchange of Spanish silver for Chinese luxury goods created profits that supported the construction of schools, charitable hospitals, and societies and made Manila the "Pearl of the Orient." The easy profits of the galleon trade also served as a deterrent to Spaniards who might otherwise have ventured into the Philippine countryside to seek their fortune. Except for a few officials appointed to administer nearby provinces, the bulk of the Spanish civilian population lived contentedly in Manila, borrowing money and speculating on the annual galleon shipment.

The country's hinterlands, meanwhile, were left to the priests who fanned out across the archipelago to secure the second goal of Spain's colonization, the conversion of the native population to Christianity. The missionary priests, commonly referred to as friars, brought the dispersed native population into towns so they would be within the sound of church bells and could receive religious instruction. To support their work, the religious orders had an annual subsidy from the Spanish crown, and in exchange, the local *padre* (priest) served as the government's representative overseeing municipal affairs. Due to the efforts of generations of friars, the number of converts reached almost one million by the middle of the eighteenth century and constituted over 80 percent of the population in 1898.[5] Only the Muslims to the south and isolated minority peoples in difficult-to-reach mountain areas successfully resisted the missionary impulse.

The genuine hospitality shown to individual Spanish friars and the nominal acceptance of Spain's authority did not always mean that Filipinos were happy with foreign rule. From 1565 to 1898, there were hundreds of revolts and individual acts of defiance against Iberian rule. The causes of these rebellions ranged from simple antiforeignism to revenge against individual abusive government officials or friars, to revolt against excessive taxation. The largest uprisings took place in special circumstances, such as during the brief British invasion of the Philippines in 1762, which occurred in conjunction with the Seven Years War (1756–1763). In this instance, large numbers of insurgents were active across wide areas of the country under the banner of a variety of rebel leaders. Most often such uprisings were short lived and took place in isolated areas where Spanish forces had difficulty reaching. In these cases, once royal troops arrived, and the insurrection's leader was captured or killed, the insurgent forces melted back into the general population. Peasant rebellions often left great damage in their wake, but they rarely constituted a serious threat, since they lacked organizational strength and did not provide an ideological alternative to foreign domination.

Instead, it was a number of fundamental nineteenth-century social-economic changes that eventually undermined Iberian rule of the colony. Principle among these changes was the decline of the galleon trade, as silver supplies from the Americas declined and as competition for the China trade, especially from England, intensified. At the same time, the country's Chinese "mestizos," born of Chinese merchant fathers and local women, began to develop their fortunes in the country's hinterlands.[6] These mestizos integrated themselves with the local population and occasionally joined with local native elites in export commercial agriculture ventures such as sugar and hemp.[7] This economic shift soon had profound social implications as well.

After mestizo and native elites acquired wealth by transforming the hitherto neglected economic potential of the Philippine countryside, and soon thereafter Spanish social dominance was challenged. The newly wealthy mestizos purchased large Spanish-style homes and became consumers of luxury items and local patrons of the arts and religion. Meanwhile, their sons attended the country's best schools, and some even went to Europe for advanced education. Many of these new graduates went into business with their families, but many sought careers in the priesthood, an arena jealously guarded by the friar orders. When eventually the new elite attempted to participate in local political affairs, they often ran afoul of Spanish officials and friars who did not appreciate what they thought was a dangerous and subversive influence. So, despite their obvious upwardly economic mobility, the new mestizo elites found their way stalled by Spanish government officials and religious authorities who clung to power. Even more galling, as the new elites acquired wealth and social standing, these same government and religious officials made racist attacks on their character and abilities.

Nationalism and the Philippine Revolution

The spark that ignited feelings of nationalism and broke sentimental ties to Spain came in January 1872 with a mutiny by Filipino workers and soldiers at the Spanish navy yard in Cavite across the bay from Manila. The actual revolt was quickly crushed but was then turned into an excuse to round up prominent Filipinos whose loyalty to Spain was questioned. All the arrested civilians were banished to the island of Guam, but three prominent Filipino priests, noted for their efforts to improve the lot of the native priesthood, Fathers Jose Burgos, Mariano Gomes, and Jacinto Zamora were executed. Instead of intimidating the population, the executions had the opposite effect and served as the principle turning point in Philippine national development. Thus, the economic development of the colony and the rise of a new class of economic elites had the ironic result of creating the condition for the destruction of Spanish regime when the regime's cruelty revealed itself in 1872. Soon, ideas from the Enlightenment and the French Revolution began to resonate among Filipinos, especially among students in Europe who also began to rediscover their racial and cultural roots. For example, students in Madrid universities created an association called Los Indios Bravos (The Brave Indians) defiantly embracing the term *indio*, or Indian, which Manila Spaniards used to ridicule the native population.

In addition, the students issued blistering critiques of Spanish colonial practices, especially the dominance of the religious orders who had made the country into a "friarocracy." Their principle voice was the newspaper *La Solidaridad*, whose issues were smuggled into the Philippines. The most prominent of these Filipino students was Jose Rizal, whose two novels, *Noli Me Tangere* (1887) and *El Filibusterismo* (1891) and numerous essays did more than anything else to critique the colonial order. As a result of the efforts of Rizal and his compatriots, the idea of a Philippine nationhood separate from the Spanish mother country became possible, and Spain's hold on the colony was doomed.[8]

In 1892, Rizal returned to the Philippines, and on July 3, he and a number of patriots formed a civic society, *La Liga Filipina* (The Filipino Union). Three days later, he was arrested and sent into exile to the southern province of Zamboanga. A little known member of the *Liga*, Andres Bonifacio, promptly rejected any lingering thoughts of working peacefully and gathered others of similar thinking. The resulting organization they formed was a secret society called the *Katipunan*, which was dedicated to gaining independence from Spain by any means necessary. From its founding until its exposure by a Spanish priest on August 19, 1896, the *Katipunan* rapidly

Contemporary diorama depicting the execution of national hero Jose Rizal. Notice the friar on the right witnessing the killing. Photo by the author.

expanded its membership, created flags and secret codes, gathered weapons, and drafted patriotic writings to indoctrinate its members.

Caught off guard by the sudden exposure of their secret society in 1896, Bonifacio and his fellow *Katipuneros* desperately attempted to fight superior Spanish troops but after losing battle after battle, the rebel leader and some of his followers retreated to Cavite province, southeast of the capital. That province was under the control of the able *Katipunan* leader, Emilio Aguinaldo, who initially welcomed the leader from Manila. Soon, however, their mutual good feelings deteriorated, resulting in a tragic falling out that created a temporary split in the leadership and led to the murder of Bonifacio by Aguinaldo's men.[9] In the meantime, the Spanish government executed Rizal, a cruel act of vengeance that only fed the rebel fighting spirit.

Eventually, however, in the early months of 1897, Spanish forces concentrated on Cavite, forcing Aguinaldo to shift his field of operations to a mountainous area north of Manila. Safe in his new mountain redoubt, Aguinaldo and the Filipino insurgents formed a republican government and drafted a constitution based largely on an earlier one written by rebels in Cuba, whose defiance of Spanish colonialism had already attracted the attention of the United States. To quell its own festering rebellion, Manila's Spanish officials worked out an agreement with the rebels offering them safe passage to Hong Kong and a substantial monetary compensation in exchange for a cessation of hostilities. Assessing his situation, Aguinaldo decided to accept the offer, and in late December, he and a select number of his leadership departed for Hong Kong, where they attempted to purchase arms and planned for a return to continue the fight.

International events soon projected the revolution in ways that Aguinaldo and his followers did not anticipate. On February 15, 1898, the U.S. battleship *Maine* exploded in Cuba's Havana Harbor, killing 266 men and eventually leading the U.S. Congress to declare war on Spain on April 19. The Philippines was soon thrown into the firestorm of the Spanish-American War, when on the morning of May 1, Commodore George Dewey and his "Asiatic Squadron" entered Manila Bay, quickly destroying the defending Spanish fleet. While Dewey enjoyed an easy naval victory, he did not have the necessary troops to capture Manila and found himself in need of the Filipino rebels. Aguinaldo was provided U.S. naval transportation to return to the Philippines on May 19 and was immediately taken to Dewey's flagship where he was given honors due the general of an army. Dewey is said to have assured the Filipino rebel that the United States had no desire for colonies and urged him to renew his interrupted rebellion. The Filipino leader needed no further assurances or urgings. Aguinaldo quickly issued a call to arms that aroused the nation, and in a short while, most of the country, with the exception of a few isolated Spanish military outposts, and the capital of Manila were under Filipino control. On June 12, Aguinaldo declared Philippine independence, a functioning Filipino government was created, and a constitution, was promulgated on January 21, 1899.

Tragically, Asia's first democratic government would not exist very long. As the nascent Filipino government began to take shape, U.S. army troop ships also began to arrive and relations between the two sides steadily deteriorated. On August 13, 1898, American and Philippine forces attacked Manila, and by a prior secret agreement, the defending Spaniards allowed themselves to be defeated by the Americans so they would not have to surrender to the "Indios." The Spanish surrender of Manila to American forces also gave the United States an international legal right to the islands that was confirmed by the Treaty of Paris on December 10. Filipinos were outraged by the clear American duplicity. Relations continued to deteriorate until, literally, the very eve of the U.S. Senate's vote on whether or not to confirm the treaty with Spain. On the night of February 9, 1899, fighting between American and Filipino forces suddenly erupted under suspicious circumstances as American forces quickly advanced against unprepared Filipino defenders. When informed of the "treacherous Filipino attack," the Senate quickly ratified the treaty.

As American troops advanced to the north and south against the retreating Filipinos, they sustained some casualties, but Filipinos suffered shockingly heavy losses. Aguinaldo moved his government steadily northward through Central Luzon to avoid the American advance and eventually ordered his troops to shift from regular military to guerrilla warfare tactics. At Christmas, his wife and other women in the Aguinaldo entourage surrendered to American forces. Freed from family obligations, Aguinaldo became a guerrilla leader, and by September 1900, he reached the remote location of Palanan near the northeast coast of Luzon in Isabela province.[10] Despite some notable defections by Filipino elites, who did not have the stomach for a sustained struggle, Aguinaldo continued to direct an effective campaign against the American invaders until March 23, 1901, when an American-directed party of Filipino traitors captured him and his bodyguard of soldiers. Despite the capture of their leader, a number of rebel leaders continued the struggle, but their efforts were increasingly futile. By the summer of 1902, war was effectively over such that on July fourth, the United States could claim hostilities at an end.[11]

The American and Japanese Interregnum

The United States was an ambivalent colonizer. At the peak of the fight against the Filipino government, the American public was upset about reports of mistreatment of the local population, especially instances involving the use of torture on prisoners. In fact, opposition to the war and imperialist expansion became the central issue of William Jennings Bryan's unsuccessful 1900 presidential campaign. Even the colonial administration under a re-elected President William McKinley incorporated prominent Filipinos, and the island's first American civil governor, William Howard Taft, spoke of eventual independence, although at some distant point in the future. Despite continued crackdowns on irreconcilable nationalists, *Filipinization* of the colonial government continued until the election and convening of a Philippine Assembly in 1907. This legislative body would then become the training ground for a future generation of political leaders who used their skills to lobby for independence.[12]

The U.S. colonial period also saw the infusion of American investment capital and a series of trade policies that locked the Philippine's export agricultural economy to the United States and flooded the Philippines with American manufactured goods. By the 1920s, approximately 75 percent of Philippine trade was with the United States. Domestically, American entrepreneurs were active in everything from the Manila Electric Company, to newspapers, to food processing, and Manila soon became one of Asia's economic powerhouses. Meanwhile, public health and sanitation projects brought health care beyond the major cities. Public works projects were responsible for the construction of modern government buildings in many towns even as the country's road system extended to most provinces. The prosperity of the American period also witnessed the beginnings of a true Filipino middle class even if it was only a small percentage of the overall population.

The American impact was especially strong on Philippine cultural life. Educators from the United States designed the country's educational system that even today still follows the basic patterns they laid down, including the use of English as the principle language for education, business, and government. Soon widespread knowledge of English facilitated the intrusion of popular American culture into the colony. The earliest Americans brought vaudeville and musical theater to the Philippines; later came Hollywood movies and dance crazes, while popular songs flooded an eager Philippine market. The American influence also spread to a variety of other aspects of culture including popular dress, art, and architecture such that, at its height, American influence seemed more likely to eliminate all aspects of Filipino culture than had the efforts of the Spanish friars, who had controlled the country for hundreds of years. Musicians, singers, writers, and theatrical artists who attempted to retain vernacular dialects and local cultural sensibilities in their works appeared to be swimming against the tide. Despite the odds, however, Philippine culture continued to make its presence felt by incorporating new American influences and refashioning them to local tastes, thereby laying a firm foundation for the emergence of Filipino culture in the post–World War II era.

All the while, however, Filipino aspirations for independence remained strong. The first step on the road to independence came in 1916 under the Democratic presidency of Woodrow Wilson with the passage of the Jones Law, which committed the United States to eventual Philippine independence. Filipino nationalists soon found allies in American agricultural interests, especially sugar. In 1934 the lobbying efforts of Philippine legislators and American vested interests secured passage of the Tydings-McDuffie Act. Under provisions of this legislation, the Philippines promulgated a new constitution and formed a Commonwealth government in 1935 under President Manuel L. Quezon to prepare for independence, which was scheduled for 1946.

Despite the American period's general prosperity, new cultural influences, and political advances, the era did not witness a significant narrowing of the social divide between rich and poor. Wealth remained concentrated in the hands of the mestizo landed elite who built strong ties with the new American rulers. Dissatisfaction among the poor rural tenants and the newly emergent urban working class appeared in the form of a rural socialist movement and the founding of strong labor unions linked to the Communist Party of the Philippines (CCP), inaugurated in 1930.[13] Then, in the mid-1930s, a major peasant uprising, the *Sakdals*, broke out in Central Luzon, clearly showing that resentment of the rich was reaching dangerous levels. Especially upsetting was that the *Sakdals'* leader looked to the emerging Japanese military powerhouse to help the Philippine poor.

Even though class tensions were building to dangerous level in 1930s Philippine society, the Second World War did not disrupt the amicable bond that had developed between the United States and its Asian colonial possession. In fact, the war actually strengthened those ties. In 1941, while other nations in the region used the Japanese advance to throw off their colonial masters, most Filipinos rallied to defend the American colony against the Japanese attack. During the wartime occupation of the country, there was a collaborationist government that worked with the Japanese military, but most Filipinos hated the Japanese and actively supported guerrilla bands, as well as supported the Philippine government-in-exile in Washington, D.C.[14]

At the outbreak of fighting on December 8, 1941, General Douglas MacArthur declared Manila an "open city" (i.e., excluded from combat) and ordered his Philippine and American troops to the Bataan peninsula and Corregidor Island to fight until reinforcements could arrive. Unfortunately, the United States was not in a position to send reinforcements after the devastating Japanese attack on Pearl Harbor. In March 1942, MacArthur left Corregidor for Australia along with Philippine Commonwealth President Quezon and Vice President Sergio Osmena, promising the Philippines that "I Shall Return." In early April, the Bataan peninsula fell to the Japanese and 36,000 Filipino and American defenders were subjected to a forced "death march" to a prison camp in Central Luzon. Early the next month, the island of Corregidor also fell after holding out under conditions that defy imagination. During the war, thousands of Filipinos, and some American soldiers who had been cut off from their units at the outbreak of the invasion, formed guerrilla units that harassed the enemy. These forces swelled and in 1944 welcomed returning U.S. forces that were led by a triumphant MacArthur, who kept his promise to return.

New Republic and New Society

The euphoria of victory was soon replaced by the need to rebuild the shattered country. The retreating Japanese did not reciprocate MacArthur's designation of Manila as an open city, and in their battle against the returning Americans, the capital became the third worst struck city in World War II, after Tokyo and Dresden. There were also Filipino collaborators who had to be dealt with and an economy that had to be restored. In 1945, in exchange for desperately needed American assistance, a reluctant Philippine Congress accepted the terms of the Bell Trade Regulations Act, which gave American citizens "parity rights" with Filipinos for the ownership and exploitation of all Philippine natural resources. This act was despised at the time and became a major nationalist issue in later years. April 1946 saw elections and a new president who supported MacArthur but was also tainted by his wartime relationship with the Japanese occupation government. Thus, when independence was formerly granted on July 4, 1946, not all was well in the newly freed nation.

Violence erupted in early 1948 when the *Hukbalahap*, a peasant organization based in the Central Luzon plain and in the provinces south of Manila that was allied with the CCP and had fielded a major anti-Japanese guerilla movement during World War II, rose against government corruption and landlord excesses.[15] The revolt quickly spread beyond the government's capacity to contain it, despite the arrest of the Huk (short for *Hukbalahap*) leadership in late 1950. In 1952, the former Secretary of Defense Ramon Magsaysay became president in an election heavily influenced by American money and Central Intelligence Agency operatives. In addition to this outside help, Magsaysay enjoyed substantial popular support. He was an extremely effective political leader who had been a guerrilla fighter during the world war.[16] The tide of battle began to turn as Magsaysay shook up the military and instituted a number of land reform measures. The revitalized campaign against the insurgents soon had an impact when Luis Taruc, the *Huk* Supremo, surrendered. Still, the Huks remained active for many years, and the Supremo's successor was not captured until 1964. More ominously, significant imbalances between rich and poor remained.

It is within this context of an incompletely recovered economy, lingering social economic disparities, and the failed Huk movement that a young congressman, Ferdinand Marcos, from the northern Ilocano province of Ilocos Norte emerged on the national political scene. In 1965, Marcos's popularity increased to the point that he easily won the presidency. In his first term of office, he seemed to make substantial progress in programs to increase food production, advance land reform, and stimulate community development projects. However, his 1969 re-election campaign emptied the national treasury and was widely believed to be the most corrupt in history, despite the fact that he could have easily defeated his weak rival without such measures. At the same time, the moribund leftist opposition was reignited by a young University of the Philippines professor of English, Jose Maria Sison, who formed a new Communist Party of the Philippines, took its inspiration from Mao Zedong's People's Republic of China. The party soon attracted the allegiance of a new generation of activists, students, and a few remaining leaders of the old Huk movement.

The start of a new and different era of dissent broke out after Marcos's State of the Nation address to the Philippine Congress on January 26, 1970, where he appeared as the nation's first popularly re-elected president. When he emerged from the Congress building, Marcos was confronted by a huge throng of protesters that attacked him and his wife, Imelda. The protests continued with an attack on the presidential palace that was turned back by a brutal police counterattack. This initial confrontation was followed by one student demonstration after another over a period of months and became known as "The First Quarter Storm." In the street demonstrations, students were joined by organized labor. Meanwhile, in the countryside, former Huk fighters and poor peasants joined Sison's new Communist Party to form an armed wing, the New People's Army (NPA), which rapidly gained adherents among the country's rural poor.

Conditions continued to deteriorate for the rest of the year and into 1971, when there were elections for the Philippine House of Representatives and Senate. In late August, during a major rally of Marcos's Liberal Party opponents, a bomb exploded killing a number of people in the audience and seriously wounding some of the opposition senatorial candidates. Most people assumed Marcos was behind this bombing, along with a number of others that rocked the city. Suspicious seemed confirmed when Marcos used the violence to temporarily suspend the writ of *habeas corpus* and arrest a number of opposition figures. Confrontations between protesters and the nation's military continued unabated. To make matters worse, in June the following year, the country experienced one of the worst typhoons in memory causing tremendous hardship and economic deprivation.

When Filipinos woke up on the morning of September 21, 1972, they found almost all radio stations silent while television stations broadcast only cartoons. In the evening, President Marcos spoke to the nation announcing that he had issued Proclamation 1081, declaring martial law in response to what he claimed was the threat from Communists and a growing separatist Muslim movement in the south. Initially, Marcos had the support of a sizable portion of the population, which was tired of violent confrontations and worried about armed insurrection and the country's economic future. This group of support was pleased when thousands of unregistered guns were confiscated, private armies beholden to individual politicians were disbanded, and a sweeping series of reform decrees poured out of the presidential palace.

Still, it was disquieting that the Philippine Senate and House of Representatives and all local governments were disbanded and the country's free media and major universities were shut down. It also seemed that martial

law was used as an excuse to arrest hundreds of prominent democratic critics
of the Marcos presidency. The most important of these critics was Senator
Benigno "Ninoy" Aquino, a popular political leader, who, it was widely
assumed, would succeed Marcos as president. Gradually, too, a new and
disturbing pattern began to emerge. Many prominent businessmen linked to
opposition politicians were forced to sell their investments at substantial
losses to individuals who were friends of the president and first lady. Soon a
new elite of presidential "cronies" emerged, who gained substantial government contracts and favors.[17] As well, the simmering, resistive Muslim population on Mindanao and the Sulu archipelago broke out into a full-blown
armed secession movement that quickly consumed the military even as the
NPA continued to operate with impunity and grow in strength.[18]

The People Power Revolution and Beyond

The Marcos regime eventually fell for a variety of political and economic
reasons, but the catalyst that ignited the popular outrage against the regime
was Senator Benigno Aquino, who in death became a martyr whose memory
catapulted his widow to the presidency. Arrested the night of the martial
law's imposition and kept under arrest in secret locations for years, Aquino
was released in 1980 and allowed to go to the United States for a heart by-
pass operation. After the surgery, he remained in the United States, where
he had an appointment at Harvard University, until the fall of 1983, when
he decided that he had to return and face Marcos. On August 21, the plane
carrying Aquino touched down at the Manila International Airport, but he
did not live to greet the huge crowds that were waiting for him. His plane
was diverted from its scheduled arrival gate, and military officers immediately
entered the passenger cabin to provide an armed escort for the former senator.
Moments after leaving the plane and while walking down a ramp brought
up exclusively for Aquino's use, he was shot in the back of the head at close
range. His dead body fell the remaining distance to the ground. Lying next
to him was the body of a second man, a common criminal the military
gunned down claiming he had infiltrated the security group and assassinated
Aquino.

The nation was united in its horror, and no one believed the official story.
Especially poignant was the return of "Ninoy's" wife Corazon, or Cory, and
her children from their exile home in Boston. Cory refused to allow under-
takers to "touch up" her husband's body and insisted on an open casket
funeral. Uncounted thousands of Filipinos, rich and poor alike, filed past the
coffin as the nation's outrage continued to mount. The funeral cortege became the largest gathering in the nation's history and was a powerful testa-

Statue of Ninoy Aquino in 1983 being forced off the plane moments before his assassination, which set off the chain of events that by 1986 resulted in the overthrow of the government of Ferdinand Marcos. In the background are the ultra-modern business buildings of the wealthy Manila suburb of Makati. Photo by the author.

ment to the government's loss of popular confidence. After the funeral, the protests continued and reached levels not seen before. Significantly, the wealthy financial and business suburb of Makati, home to scores of Philippine and international corporations, saw almost as many massive marches and rallies as were held in the university district in downtown Manila. Over the next two years, as rich and poor marched side-by-side, capital flight, raging inflation, and the loss of confidence by international lending institutions resulted in a virtual halt in the economy. In the countryside, the NPA grew dramatically in manpower, geographic scope, and military daring.

Under pressure from the political opposition and at the urging of U.S. President Ronald Reagan, who sent Senator Paul Laxalt to talk to the Philippine leader, Marcos announced a "snap" presidential election to be held in just sixty days, the first week of February 1986. Marcos expected to win because of his absolute control of the government and because his opposition had always been divided in the past, but this election was different. The Archbishop of Manila, Jaime Cardinal Sin, brokered a truce among opposition leaders, who then supported Cory Aquino on the single party ticket. Her campaign ignited the nation and in her support, thousand of ordinary Filipinos volunteered to become poll watchers and ballot box guards for the non-governmental organization NAMFREL (National Citizens' Movement for Free Elections), an extremely risky thing to do.

What happened next seems to defy credibility. Filipinos poured out to the nation's polling booths in record numbers, and common citizens, seminarians, and nuns kept ballot boxes from gangs of armed thugs. In the crucial tabulation, NAMFREL's "operation quick count" differed widely from the official count. The election corruption was exposed definitively when a group of women clerks in the government's counting center staged a walk-out to protest the fraudulent count. They carried computer discs with the true count with them as they deserted to the opposition. Despite the public outcry and the condemnation of a number of nations, Marcos's rubber-stamp legislature declared him the winner.

Even while the election tragedy was unfolding, another scene in the final act of the Marcos drama began. On February 22, the nation's minister of defense, Juan Ponce Enrile, and the armed forces vice chief of staff, General Fidel V. Ramos, learned that Marcos had ordered their arrest and that of other military reformers. They withdrew their allegiance to the president and barricaded themselves at their headquarters in suburban Quezon City. Initially, the two men were only joined by a handful of soldiers and their imminent arrest was expected. It was at this point that Archbishop Sin called on the people of Manila to rally around the besieged military leaders.

The popular protest over Marcos's presidency shifted to protecting the dissident military leaders. Hundreds of thousands of people poured into the streets completely halting all traffic by creating roadblocks and setting human barricades. When government tanks and troops advanced, they found their way closed off by a wall of their fellow citizens, including old men and women, people in wheelchairs, and nuns praying on their knees. This example of "People Power" soon emboldened other military units to defect, including an Air Force helicopter unit sent to attack the dissidents, and the tide of battle shifted rapidly. In the meantime, Cory Aquino and her running mate took their oaths of office in an alternate ceremony covered by the international media and held with as much solemnity as the "official" swearing-in of Ferdinand Marcos days earlier. With Marcos thoroughly isolated from his countrymen, U.S. President Reagan offered the beleaguered Filipino leader safe haven in the United States, which he eventually accepted. The hated Marcos years were over.[19]

Cory Aquino was faced with the daunting task of returning the country to its former democratic roots, reviving a moribund economy, and quelling a large armed leftist insurgency. Her success during her six-year term came from her massive popular support, the financial backing of international lending institutions, and the unwavering loyalty of the new armed forces chief-of-staff, General Ramos. As president, she survived six coup attempts by unrepentant Marcos loyalists and dissident military officers who resisted the return of the nation to civilian control. Although she introduced a new democratic constitution, halted the economic downturn, and undercut the insurgent's appeal, the country remained in bad economic shape, and human rights abuses against suspected insurgents seemed to continue unabated.[20]

Aquino's most important failure concerned the issue of U.S. military bases which she wanted to retain contrary to increasing popular nationalist calls for their removal. Aquino's failure was, in a sense, double sided because she lost the senate vote and she was out of touch with national sentiment. After World War II, the United States was granted a large number of military bases throughout the Philippines, some of which were substantial, such as the huge Clark Air Base. Eventually the post-war euphoria that existed when the Philippines first granted basing rights to the United States wore thin, and the base concessions to the former colonial ruler became a thorn in the national pride. Additionally, U.S. military personnel frequently enjoyed immunity from local laws when off the base, especially in the instance of capital crimes, which many Filipinos found extremely galling. In addition, lawlessness and prostitution flourished near the bases and corrupted adjacent communities thereby adding to the nation's woes. With the end of the Marcos regime, the country wanted change which also included the exit of the American military. Ultimately, the fate of the bases was sealed by the fearsome eruption of Mt. Pinatubo in 1991 just as the senate debate concerning the bases raged. With virtually all of its buildings and hangars crushed under tons of volcanic ash, the U.S. Air Force announced that it would abandon the site. The fate of the United States' remaining bases was sealed shortly thereafter by the Philippine Senate's vote not to renew the post-war agreement.[21]

Despite this one setback, the democratic stability that Aquino's presidency brought to the nation became the base upon which her chosen successor, former general Ramos, built his successful term of office. During his six years in office (the new constitution allows only one presidential term), Ramos continued the policy of reasserting civilian rule over the military and reached out to Communist and Muslim insurgents. However, his most strenuous efforts went toward restoring the country's economic vitality. The times favored Ramos's economic development agenda as the early years of his administration coincided with the dramatic growth years of the Asian economy. The Philippine's growth rates picked up dramatically, even though some discordant voices warned of the unhealthy nature of the country's economic development policies.[22] Still, the collapse of the Asian growth bubble in the summer and fall of 1997 did not affect the Philippines as dramatically as it did neighboring Thailand and Indonesia, but the downturn was enough to undercut most of the progress of Ramos's first four years in office.

The 1998 election witnessed a fundamental change in the political landscape with the election of the popular Joseph Estrada, who swept into office thanks to a huge majority of the country's poor who voted for him in record numbers. Before entering politics, Estrada was a popular movie star whose roles saw him as the friend of the downtrodden, and he parlayed that image into unbeatable political capital. Unfortunately, the new president quickly committed a number of errors that resulted in the rapid erosion of his popularity. Even before taking office, Estrada announced that he would allow the remains of former president Marcos to be buried in the country's hero's cemetery. This proposal so enraged the country that the plan was eventually dropped.

Once in office the Estrada administration did virtually nothing for the poor who swept him into office, negotiations with communist insurgents stalled, and talks with Muslim rebels collapsed when Estrada ordered the military to seize Muslim rebel bases. Most distressing to many Filipinos was the return of many of Marcos's former "cronys" to positions of influence. Estrada also pushed for a new constitutional convention, which concerned many people who feared that he might use such a convention to destroy the legal safeguards Aquino put into place to prevent a future power grab. In 1999, demonstrators led by Cory Aquino and Archbishop Sin again took to the streets amidst increased political polarization. The low point of the Estrada administration was reached in the fall of 2000 when he and one of his political cronys, Governor Chavit Singson of Ilocos Norte province, had a falling out. Singson thereupon presented testimony and documents showing that Estrada received hundreds of millions of pesos in bribes from national gambling syndicates and was the recipient of many more millions of diverted tax revenues. In addition, substantial investigative reports showed that the president and his family and some women friends had recently moved into some of the largest mansions in the country. In November, articles of impeachment were passed by the Philippine House of Representatives and sent to the Senate for full impeachment proceedings. Meanwhile, anti-Estrada demonstrations grew larger and more vocal in their demand for his resignation, even as members of his cabinet resigned their positions. Despite the gravity of the charges against him, Estrada had a sufficient bloc of supporters in the Senate to defeat the charges against him, but events did not follow their expected course. On January 16, 2001, Estrada's supporters made a serious error when they defeated a prosecution attempt to introduce potentially damning evidence. Suddenly, the legal proceedings lost all credibility, and hundreds of thousands of Filipinos in metro Manila and throughout the country took to the streets once again as they had in 1986. The Philippine president was swiftly deserted by his cabinet and the armed forces who joined the "People Power II" throngs. The drama ended in a few days when the Philippine Supreme Court declared the presidency vacant and Vice President Gloria Macapagal-Arryo was sworn into office. Though pleased with the outcome of the recent popular movement, thoughtful Filipinos are questioning their culture's political values and are seeking a new set of political values that will make a future "People Power III" unnecessary.[23]

NOTES

1. See Luis Francia, *Passport Philippines* (San Rafael, CA: World Trade Press, 1997), 6.

2. Republic of the Philippines, National Statistical Coordination Board, *1999 Philippine Statistical Yearbook* (Makati, NSCB, 1999), tables 1.1, 1.3, and 1.6.

3. D. R. SarDesai, *Southeast Asia: Past and Present*, 4th ed. (Boulder, CO: Westview Press, 1997), 7–10.

4. For a description of Philippine life at the time of Spanish contact, see William Henry Scott, *Barangay: Sixteenth-Century Philippine Culture and Society* (Quezon City: Ateneo de Manila University Press, 1994).

5. See the study of the dynamic between the missionaries and their Philippine converts by Vicente Rafael, *Contracting Colonialism: Translation and Christian Conversion in Tagalog Society under Early Spanish Rule* (Ithaca, NY: Cornell University Press, 1988).

6. A crucial pioneering work is Edgar Wickberg, *The Chinese in Philippine Life, 1850–1898* (New Haven, CT: Yale University Press, 1965).

7. For the impact of the sugar and hemp industries, see John A. Larkin, *Sugar and the Origins of Modern Philippine Society* (Berkeley: University of California Press, 1993) and Norman G. Owen, *Prosperity without Progress: Manila Hemp and Material Life in the Colonial Philippines* (Berkeley: University of California Press, 1984).

8. For a set of readings, see John Schumaker, S.J., *The Making of a Nation: Essays on Nineteenth-Century Filipino Nationalism* (Quezon City: Ateneo de Manila University Press, 1991).

9. For a first-hand account of the revolution, see Santiago V. Alvarez, *Recalling the Revolution: Memoirs of a Filipino General*, trans. by Paula Carolina S. Malay (Madison: Center for Southeast Asian Studies, University of Wisconsin, 1992).

10. An excellent overview is given in Stuart Creighton Miller, *"Benevolent Assimilation" The American Conquest of the Philippines, 1899–1903* (New Haven, CT: Yale University Press, 1982), while an in-depth study for one province was made by Glenn A. May in his book, *Battle for Batangas: A Philippine Province at War* (New Haven, CT: Yale University Press, 1991).

11. In the early 1980s, American journalist David Haward Bain retraced the route of Aguinaldo's retreat and that taken by his captors as he combined history with a look at modern society in *Sitting in Darkness: Americans in the Philippines* (New York: Penguin Books, 1984).

12. For the country's political life in the late Spanish period through the later American commonwealth government, see Ruby R. Paredes, ed., *Philippine Colonial Democracy* (New Haven, CT: Yale Southeast Asia Studies, 1988).

13. The memoirs of a Communist Party-U.S.A. liaison to the Philippines, James S. Allen, were published in 1993 by MEP Publications of Minneapolis as *The Philippine Left on the Eve of World War II.*

14. For a comparative study of reactions to the Japanese, see Theodore Friend, *The Blue-Eyed Enemy: Japan Against the West in Java and Luzon, 1942–45* (Princeton, NJ: Princeton University Press, 1988).

15. Benedict J. Kerkvliet presents the perspective of the average peasant who joined the Huk guerrilla organization in *The Huk Rebellion: A Study of Peasant Revolt in the Philippines* (Berkeley: University of California Press, 1977).

16. The degree to which the Magsaysay and other Philippine administrations attempted to cultivate autonomy despite strong postwar American influence is well argued by Nick Cullather, *Illusions of Influence: The Political Economy of United States-Philippine Relations, 1942–1960* (Stanford, CA: Stanford University Press, 1994).

17. The underside of the Marcos years until its collapse in 1986 and its connection with the United States have been thoroughly examined by such popular authors as Sterling Seagrave, *The Marcos Dynasty* (New York: Harper & Row Publishers, 1988) and Raymond Bonner, *Waltzing with a Dictator: The Marcoses and the Making of American Policy* (New York: Times Books, 1987).

18. Thomas M. McKenna, *Muslim Rulers and Rebels: Everyday Politics and Armed Separation in the Southern Philippines* (Berkeley: University of California Press, 1998) examines the Philippines resilient Islamic culture that continues to resist Christian domination, while Benjamin Pimentel, *Rebolusyon! A Generation of Struggle in the Philippines* (New York: Monthly Review Press, 1991) presents the story of the left opposition to Marcos's rule and beyond.

19. There was a veritable flood of popular literature about the People Power revolution; among the best book-length accounts are Bryan Johnson, *The Four Days of Courage* (New York: The Free Press, 1987) and Lewis M. Simons, *Worth Dying For* (New York: William Morrow and Co., 1987).

20. An early assessment of her presidency was given by a long-time Philippine specialist and former American colonial official, Claude A. Buss, in *Cory Aquino and the People of the Philippines* (Stanford, CA: Stanford Alumni Association, 1987). A less sanguine analysis is found in David G. Timberman, *A Changeless Land: Continuity and Change in Philippine Politics* (New York: M. E. Sharpe, 1991). For an assessment of the human rights condition during the Aquino administration, see Lawyers Committee for Human Rights, *Out of Control: Military Abuses in the Philippines* (New York: LCHR, 1990).

21. The question of U.S. bases was the single most contentious issue between the Philippines and its former colonial master. The U.S. position followed the cold war analyses of global politics and security as in A. James Gregor and Virgilio Aganon, *The Philippine Bases: U.S. Security at Risk* (Washington, D.C.: Ethics and Public Policy Center, 1987). Meanwhile, the antibases position is represented by Lolita W. McDonough, ed., *United States Military Bases in the Philippines: Issues and Scenarios* (Quezon City: International Studies Institute of the Philippines, Law Complex, University of the Philippines, 1985).

22. See Paul D. Hutchcroft, *The Philippines at the Crossroads: Sustaining Economic and Political Reform* (New York: Asia Society, 1996).

23. See especially the newspaper commentary of Isagani A. Cruz, "The Gathering Storm," *Philippine Daily Inquirer*, January 19, 2001; Bambi I. Harper, "Quo Vadis, Filipinas?" *Philippine Daily Inquirer*, January 19, 2001; and Rigoberto Tiglao, "A Better People Power, Yes But . . . ," *Philippine Daily Inquirer*, January 21, 2001.

SUGGESTED READINGS

Brands, H. W. *Bound for Empire: The United States and the Philippines.* New York: Oxford University Press, 1992.

Karnow, Stanley. *In Our Image: America's Empire in the Philippines.* New York: Random House, 1989.

Schirmer, Daniel B. and Stephen R. Shalom. *The Philippine Reader: A History of Colonialism, Neocolonialism, Dictatorship and Resistance.* Boston: South End Press, 1987.

2

Thought and Religion

TO THE CASUAL OBSERVER, the Philippines is an overwhelmingly Christian country. The country's apparent uniformity, however, obscures the complexity and uniqueness of its religious life. Though overwhelmingly Roman Catholic, the nation's religious diversity also includes two major indigenous Christian churches, the Muslim population of the southern islands, and minority peoples scattered throughout the archipelago. Beyond questions of religious affiliation, Filipino religious thought has an immediacy based on a perceived close relationship between the supernatural and daily human life that is uniquely Asian and is not present to the same degree in the religious mentality of Western Christians. This perceived relationship predated Islam and Christianity and actually guided the process whereby these world religions were selectively adopted and domesticated. As a result, much of Philippine religion can thus be called "folk," since many beliefs are at variance with strict interpretations of the adopted religions.

Despite the Roman Catholic church's predominance, the twentieth century witnessed the emergence of two substantial indigenous churches, the nationalistic Iglesia Filipina Independiente (IFI, or Philippine Independent Church) and the rapidly growing Iglesia ni Cristo (INC, or Church of Christ). Still other Filipinos have shifted their allegiance to a variety of mainline Protestant churches and the Mormon church. Even within the Roman Catholic church the semiautonomous charismatic El Shaddai movement claims eight million members, and its dynamic leader Mariano "Brother Mike" Velarde frequently upstages the formal church leadership.

In addition to reviewing the country's contemporary religious landscape, this chapter examines indigenous Philippine beliefs and the process by which they modified the world religions of Christianity and Islam. The political role of religion in the Philippine's historical context is reviewed to show how Filipinos have connected religion and politics. As the institutional religion of the colonizer, the Roman Catholic church played a key role in affairs of state and later in the development of Philippine nationalism. Though relatively quiescent during the American colonial period, the church has recently returned to its earlier tradition of political involvement and played a leading role in the overthrow of the Marcos regime in 1986. Even today, different churches and movements are heavily involved in questions involving the political destiny of the country and how modern, largely American, notions of democracy, egalitarianism, and social justice will be adopted to the local scene.

CONCEPTS OF NATURE AND THE SUPERNATURAL

Until the arrival of Islam in the latter years of the fourteenth century, the Philippines had remained peripheral to major Asian religions, although some archeological evidence of Hindu influence has been discovered in the southern islands. Instead, the dominant religious characteristic of the archipelago's scattered communities was animism (the worship of spirits in nature) and deism (a vague belief in numerous gods). While known by a variety of names, the islands' inhabitants generally believed in the dominance of a single powerful deity supplemented by a pantheon of lesser gods and an active spirit world. One of the earliest Spanish priest chroniclers wrote that the Tagalogs spoke of *Bathala* as their principle god, while other peoples around the archipelago had other terms for this same concept of an all-powerful deity. Since this supreme god was remote and inaccessible, his powers and presence was complemented by lesser deities to whom Filipinos made offerings and prayers to gain immediate benefits.

The most common of these lesser deities were the *anitos*, who were usually good if properly appropriated. The *anitos* could be the spirits of deceased ancestors who were supplicated in exchange for help in times of stress. Other *anitos* were spirits who lived in special natural objects such as old majestic trees, powerful rivers, or awe-inspiring rock outcroppings. Sacrifices were also made to these spirits to gain favor and to ward off any angry influence. Sometimes idols or images were crafted to represent these spirits, and the images then gained supernatural power as a result of their representation of the spirit reality. Even today, images in Roman Catholic churches are sometimes said to be invested with special powers and have miraculous stories ascribed to them that are reminiscent of the tales accredited to images of *anitos.* It is to the *anitos* that the farmer will make a small sacrifice as he prepares his fields for planting and to which other people will offer small gifts for any of a number of specific requests or occasions. Even the act of having the parish priest bless a new house for its occupants is laden with meaning that predates Christianity.

In addition, there is a special class of malevolent spirits known generally as *asuangs* and by other more specific names according to their specialized type. These spirits are outside the normal range of social control that normal people and *anitos* inhabit. The *asuang* is usually a nocturnal creature and is responsible for a variety of evil activities, including attacks on pregnant women, people out alone at night, and the sick. The *asuang* are variously vampires, viscera-suckers, weredogs, ghouls, or witches and can take a variety of forms, such as that of a beautiful woman who will lure a man to his demise. Their existence performs the social function of explaining otherwise confounding issues of the unknown associated with illness, miscarriages, and death. Numerous Filipinos from a range of social-economic backgrounds readily talk about their own sighting of one or another of these creatures.

When either plagued by an offended *anito* or attacked by an *asuang*, the victim might seek relief either from the local expert in medicine, the *herbolario*, or the local shaman who will perform a seance in an attempt to find the means necessary to placate the *asuang*.[1] These ceremonies are still practiced among Philippine minority hill tribes. In the mountains of Zambales province, most ceremonies were held in the evening after the day's work. The shaman, who was frequently an elderly woman, would dance in a rapid spinning motion to the rhythm of a guitar until eventually collapsing to the floor at which time she would speak in tongues. The seance would result in a command by the aggrieved spirit, speaking through the shaman, that the afflicted human had to obey before relief would be granted. On rare occasions, much more elaborate ceremonies were held that could take as many as three days. These would be community events and required the continuous feeding of guests, ritual dancing, and chants and offerings to placate the angered spirit, whether *anito* or *asuang*.[2]

The Filipino concept of the natural and the supernatural worlds and one's relationship to them is thus immediate, since the trees and rock outcroppings in one's own community may house powerful spirits. Furthermore, because one's own ancestors might be *anitos*, there is a heightened sense of intimacy in the Filipino's relationship to the hereafter. Most often, the supernatural world is benign as long as the spirits are appropriated with suitable prayers and offerings that are given for a variety of reasons. It is only the *asuang* who constitutes a deadly threat and often cannot be controlled, since they act capriciously and cannot be appropriated by the usual offerings and social techniques. Instead, they take the lives of innocent children and pregnant women and give fatal illnesses to even the strongest men.

A "FOLK" CHRISTIAN COUNTRY IN ASIA

Christianity came to the Philippines as the religion of the conqueror and clashed with the influence of Islam in the south and the beliefs of non-Islamic Filipinos throughout the rest of the country. Although Spain's motives for exploring the Pacific Ocean beyond Mexico included its rivalry with Portugal and the lure of wealth, religion also played an important role. In fact, it is difficult to overestimate the importance of religion during the Philippine colonial experience as it shaped the nation's culture and political life. Missionary priests accompanied Miguel Lopez Legaspi's founding expedition in 1565, and soon priests had spread throughout the hinterlands to bring the local population into the Roman Catholic community. A clear indication of the importance of the Spanish missionary impulse is found in the annual subsidy that the government of Madrid provided for the maintenance of parish priests. In turn, the priests became *de facto* representatives for the Spanish crown and supervised the affairs of towns throughout the colony.

Just as missionary parish priests were the true authority figures at the local level, so too were their superiors in Manila the masters of the colony. Because Spanish civil officials rotated in and out of office with some regularity, their knowledge of the country's political life was sketchy, especially when compared to that of a long resident and politically savvy head of a monastic order. It was not very long, therefore, before the heads of the monastic orders were considerably more powerful than many of the king's own appointed representatives. Early in the Spanish colonial period, a few governor-generals attempted to operate independently of monastic approval and were very sorry for the experience. As well, on four different occasions when a new governor had not arrived from Spain, or was otherwise absent, the archbishop of Manila actually served as the interim governor. Thus, whether at the local or national level, the monastic orders had a unique degree of political importance far beyond what might have been expected.

Ironically, while the influence of the parish priest over community affairs was unrivaled, his mastery of the religious experience of the local population was not always as complete. Though Filipinos converted in great numbers, it soon became apparent that the depth of their religious allegiance was not as thorough as the missionary priests wished. Many of the natives had converted without an ideal level of conviction or even an adequate understanding of Christian beliefs. In part, this inadequacy resulted from the fact that only a few Spanish priests were in charge of the national conversion process and

Santo Nino of Cebu, the image of the Christ child believed to have been brought by Ferdinand Magellan and given to native allies shortly before his death in battle in 1521. Courtesy of the Cultural Center of the Philippines Library Collection.

were hard pressed just to fulfill their daily duties. In addition, there were language difficulties and cultural differences that biased ways of understanding theological concepts, presenting difficulties for the natives to comprehend basic distinctions between their prior beliefs and the new messages. These difficulties were sometimes even reinforced by missionaries who attempted to use prior concepts and adopt them to Christian teachings, often getting them wrong in the process or failing to get the proper message across to the convert. The result was the development of a folk tradition in Philippine religious thinking that united the foreign ideology with local perceptions and values.

The missionary priest, for example, would try to make the concept of the Christian God familiar to the local population and used the name *Bathala*, the Filipino name for a powerful god. The local population hearing *Bathala* would imagine that the priest was referring to their local god and saw no inconsistency in attending a mass on Sunday even while retaining their earlier beliefs. Thus, no matter how rigorously the priest might attempt to end beliefs in pre-existing gods and supernatural beings, the Filipino response to the missionary enterprise became a complex layering of both submission and resistance.[3]

Filipino Catholics conceptualized the Christian God as a wise and powerful peasant father and the Virgin as an ever-indulgent mother while Christ as savior was the personal link to the remote father figure. As a personal savior who sacrificed his own life and who continues to give favors (*puhunan*), Christ was owed a perpetual debt of gratitude (*utang na loob*) that is so great that it can never be repaid. In the face of such enormous power, the Filipino cleaved to the worship of saints, the apostles and martyrs, and even of local natives who had led exemplary lives. Sometimes this worship led to clashes with the church that views any such worship outside the hierarchy's control as heresy. Meanwhile, the church building became the representation of authority, with the priest as the spokesperson and the human medium to the spiritual world. The mass in Latin was as mysterious as the shaman's speaking in tongues, and communion at mass served as the link to the blood life force of the remote God. Recitations of the *pasyon* (the story of the life and death of Christ) at Easter, and even brutal acts of flagellation, became a way for the believer to enter into a direct relationship with Christ.

From the colony's founding until the French Enlightenment reached Spain during the Bourbon monarchy in the mid-eighteenth century, the missionary priests, or friars, were unchallenged. At that time, approximately three-fourths, and virtually all of the best and wealthiest, of the country's parishes were held by the friars. Meanwhile, native clerics and Spanish secular priests (priests who were not members of one of the monastic orders and who reported directly to diocesan bishops) were given the poorest of parishes in remote locations. The Bourbon kings made a sincere effort to train as many Filipinos as possible to become members of the secular priesthood, but this initiative floundered because it was pushed too fast, and many of the new priests were so incapable that the program became discredited. Later, by the early decades of the nineteenth century after Spain lost much of its colonial empire in the Americas, criticism of Filipino priests took on distinctive racist tones supplemented by expressions of an ill-defined fear that native priests would become the leaders of an anti-Spanish nationalist revolution.

The increasingly virulent anti-Filipino attitudes held by the Spanish clerics became a self-fulfilling prophecy, although not in quite the manner that the friars feared. With a few notable exceptions, native priests did not lead the revolt against Spain, but their cause became a principle rallying cry of the revolution. By 1871, only 181 of the country's 792 parishes were under the control of *mestizo* and native *indio* priests, and religion had become the focal point of the earliest forms of an emergent nationalism.[4] Because of the ostracism heaped upon the Filipino *indios* and even the *mestizos*, it was among these abused priests that concepts of national and racial identity were most sharply brought into focus. Events took a tragic but defining turn in 1872 when three prominent Filipino priests, Fathers Jose Burgos, Jacinto Zamora, and Mariano Gomez, were executed for their alleged role in a mutiny by native troops assigned to the Spanish naval station in Cavite along the shore of Manila Bay southeast of the capital. There is little doubt of their innocence of the charges brought against them by Spanish authorities who were searching for scapegoats and for a reason to silence these articulate leaders of the Filipino priests. But much more important was the impact that their executions had on the young educated elite Filipinos of the period, the *ilustrados*, including Jose Rizal. From this point onward, the issue of monastic supremacy, the cause of native clergy, and nationalism were inextricably entwined.

Meanwhile, the peasant majority continued to interpret Christian doctrine through their folk or indigenous Filipino perspective of worship. It is, in fact, through folk worship that the native culture preserved itself from being subsumed by the dominant foreign culture. Especially important, even today, is the Holy Week of Easter, since that is the given time to reflect on the meaning of the Christ story. The principle method for the faithful is the recitation of the story, the *pasyon*, of Christ. The text of the story is sung in houses, not just in church, and is a shared communal activity because of the length of the story. But the *pasyon* text encompasses more than only Christ's story; it begins with the creation of the world. As such, the *pasyon* remains a powerful instructive instrument in which cultural as well as religious values are transmitted and reinforced. So, too, is the *penitencia* (physical flagellation) a reinforcement calling to mind, through the bloody self-wounding of the believers, of Christ's compassion (*damay*). As believers fully develop themselves, their *loob* (inner self) is strengthened in goodness of the light (*liwanag*) of Christ.[5]

Some aggressive folk religious movements incorporated the language of the church and the *pasyon* into their ideology and ritual and then turned

Group reciting the story of the *Pasyon* (Passion) of the life and death of Christ at Easter. Courtesy of the Cultural Center of the Philippines Library Collection.

them against the colonizer and local landlords. In 1841, an uprising by failed seminary student Apolinario de la Cruz laid waste to provinces southeast of the capital while folk millenarian leader and sometime revolutionary leader Papa Isio and his followers held portions of the island of Negros in terror until his surrender during the early days of the American regime. During the revolt against Spain, much of the language of the *pasyon* also found its way quite naturally into the propaganda of the *ilustrado* rebel leaders in their appeals to the peasant followers of the movement. The vitality of the folk religious tradition has been kept alive by a variety of more recent peasant movements.[6] For example, in 1967, a march into Manila by followers of Valentin de los Santos and his organization the Lapiang Malaya ended tragically with a massacre of the peasants who thought that their blessed amulets with holy scriptures would protect them from the bullets of government soldiers. In the 1980s, peasant religious groups reappeared in Negros to challenge the government and the island's sugar hacienda elite until they too were brutally suppressed by the military.

During the revolt against Spanish rule, many friars fled their provincial parishes for the safety of Manila while others were intercepted and taken prisoner by the revolutionaries. Considering the level of animosity, it is surprising that very few priests suffered physical harm but, rather, were sent to Manila and from there departed for Spain. At the same time, the Filipino revolutionary government adopted a constitution that embraced the idea of separation of church and state and appointed an excommunicated native priest Father Gregorio Aglipay, to be the vicar general of the Philippine revolutionary army. When the United States later suppressed the Filipino revolt, it inherited this volatile religious, anticlerical, and nationalistic tradition. The response of the new American colony's first governor-general, William Howard Taft, was to reinforce the notion of the separation of church and state as he attempted to remain neutral in the nation's religious controversies. While accepted by many Filipinos, the separation doctrine ran counter to deeply ingrained Spanish practices and could not be implemented overnight, which sometimes led to clashes between Roman Catholics and adherents of the nationalistic church, the Iglesia Filipina Independiente, founded by Father Aglipay in 1902.[7]

In response to its losses, the Roman Catholic church reintroduced as many missionary priests as it could from a number of countries, especially the United States, even as it sought to affirm the loyalty of as many of its native priests as possible. A vigorous program to train Filipinos for the priesthood was begun in an attempt to make up for centuries of Spanish neglect. This strategy soon had an impact, and in 1907, the first Filipino was invested with the robes of a bishop. Despite this massive effort, the country still had to depend upon foreign priests for many decades. While there was somewhat less than 1,000 parishes for a Philippine population of approximately seven and a half million at the turn of the century, the population and the number of parishes grew rapidly during the American colonial period and after. The country's rapid growth meant, in effect, that the church was barely able to keep pace with the expanding population's spiritual need for more priests, much less could the native priesthood take over the reigns of the country's hierarchy. It was not until after the Second World War that there was a majority of Filipino priests at the parish level and among the nation's hierarchy. Even today the Philippines remains a center of missionary activity for a number of foreign religious orders.

Indigenous Christian Churches

Primary among mainstream indigenous religious movements is Father Aglipay's church, the Iglesia Filipina Independiente (IFI) which in a real sense was the fruition of the friar prejudice against Filipinos, especially the native priests. The IFI's roots were planted in a bedrock reaction against the execution of the three martyr priests in 1872 and were nurtured in the soil of Philippine nationalism. In the spiritual vacuum created by the forced and abrupt departure of the Spanish friars, the schism grew rapidly, especially because in its earliest days the new church made no claim to a radical theology but simply separated the Philippine church from the authority of Rome. While most native priests were hesitant to affiliate with the schismatic movement and feared being accused of heresy, Aglipay was joined by some clerics, especially those from his native region of the Ilocano provinces to the north. The schism then spread rapidly across the nation with centers in various areas of Luzon, in the islands of Iloilo and Negros in the Visayas, and in a scattering of towns on other islands including Mindanao. Only the Bicol area of Luzon, that long arm extending far to the southeast, remained relatively free of the schism.

Aglipay was also supported by a number of secular nationalist leaders who had been involved in the failed fight against the United States, so the IFI became a conduit channeling the smoldering embers of the lost nationalist cause. Soon, however, the new church introduced practices within the culture's folk tradition, such as formally making Jose Rizal and the three martyr priests from 1872 saints of the new church. To this day, nationalist icons of various sorts are displayed in many IFI churches. Also problematic was its later publication of an official book of doctrine that made statements of beliefs that were at distinct variance with established Roman Catholic theology. Yet, in its first days, the biggest problem for the new church was training a sufficient number of priests rapidly enough in new seminaries to supply the demand. In this sense, the indigenous church and its Roman Catholic rival shared the problem of a scarcity of qualified priests.

Census records from 1903 are vague on the question of popular religious affiliation, and estimates of the growth of the schism vary widely from one and a half to three million. In fact, the true figure might have been at some midpoint between the two claims as indicated by the next census made in 1918. By this time, the IFI was in serious decline after losing the legal right to occupy the country's churches that had been abandoned by the Spanish priests. As well, a resurgent Roman Catholic church actively trained new priests and challenged the nationalist church. According to this later census, the IFI retained a membership of about one and a half million adherents even after significant losses. This is an important point because it indicates clearly that anywhere from one-fourth to one-third of the population joined the nationalist schism from Rome in 1902, even after being loyal Roman Catholics for hundreds of years.

Over time Father Aglipay's personal theological beliefs became identified with Unitarianism even while the majority of his priests and followers remained firmly in the Roman Catholic tradition. After Aglipay's death in 1940 and the conclusion of the Second World War, a struggle broke out within the IFI over its theological direction. Eventually, those priests identified with mainline Christian values emerged supreme, and by 1960, the church had reformed its doctrinal beliefs to a sufficient degree so that it entered into an alliance with the American Episcopal Church. This alliance signified the IFI's acceptance into the World Anglican Union, and the IFI began to receive an annual subsidy from the Episcopal church of the United States to help the Filipino church survive into the next century. Today, the IFI's cathedral and the residence of its chief bishop are located in the Ermita area of Manila, and there are approximately thirty bishops to service its membership. The church is an accepted part of the Protestant group of churches in the country, and its clergy frequently engage themselves in issues of local and national importance just as do their Roman Catholic counterparts. Although IFI membership declined seriously by the 1970s and 1980s, it seems to have rebounded in the past decade, which augers well for its long-term standing.

A second indigenous Christian church is the Iglesia ni Cristo (INC) founded in 1914 by Felix Manalo, a man who led an extremely interesting and varied religious life. Born in 1886, Manalo was raised Roman Catholic, but his poor parents could not afford to give him much of an education. He could, however, read the Bible, which led him to question the consistency with which Catholicism preached its message. Manalo then joined a *Colorum* peasant religious group until discovering that the supposed voice of God was really only that of the group's leader. Under the open religious atmosphere of American colonialism, Manalo joined a succession of Protestant churches beginning in 1904 with the Methodist Episcopal Church, then the Presbyterian church, which he left in 1909 to enter the Disciples of Christ in America, where he was introduced to the practice of baptism by immersion, a practice of the INC today. Two years later, he became a member of the Seventh Day Adventists, but he soon had as many doubts about this sect as he had with the others.

Finally, in 1913 he began to preach his own religion to whoever would listen, and the following year he formally incorporated his religious organization. Though enthusiastic, his efforts only slowly showed results, and his first bamboo chapel was not constructed for two years. By 1920, he had assembled a small group of followers plus a few fellow priests, and he proclaimed himself to be an "angel of revelation" sent by God.[8] He also came to the conclusion that Jesus Christ was not a deity, but was only a man, even if a very special one, who was the head and savior of his church. In addition, he stressed that the only true source of religious knowledge was found in the Bible and that anything that did not come from the Bible had to be false. He, therefore, rejected the worship of images and the veneration of saints as pagan appropriations of the Roman Catholic church. So, too, was the practice of confession and the belief in purgatory eliminated from the INC's doctrine.

However, Manalo did stress that salvation could only come to those who joined his church, since his was the true church created by Christ from which the Roman Catholic church severed itself.[9]

Until the Second World War, the INC expanded slowly from one province to another from its Manila roots. The conversion process was usually aided by a member who converted while living in the national capital and then brought the new religion back to his home province with the assistance of one of Manalo's missionary priests. The church expanded and gradually established a credible national network even before the Second World War, reaching Cotabato province in Mindanao in 1941. In general, the INC's converts came from among the poorest of Philippine society, and even basic literacy among the membership was rare. The INC has placed great emphasis on the physical attraction of its church buildings, and their tall spires and dramatic pseudo-Gothic lines are instantly recognizable and a source of pride. Despite its humble beginnings, Manalo's efforts began to pay off in the postwar period as the congregation grew from approximately 85,000 in 1936 to 200,000 in 1954 and rising to about 500,000 in 1970 with congregations established in almost every province.[10]

In the late 1950s, as Felix Manalo's health failed, his son Erano began to assume control of the organization, so the founder's death in 1963 did not cause a disruption in the church's activities. By the late 1960s, Erano had proven himself a worthy successor to his father and began a number of initiatives, including the establishment of branches of the church in the United States and other countries. Today, Erano Manalo is still the head of the church that in the early 1990s had somewhere between one and three quarter to two and one quarter million adherents. The INC's administrative headquarters are located in a large complex that includes their Central Tabernacle, a seminary, the New Era University, and, most recently, a hospital. Since 1969, the church has operated its own radio station with regionally syndicated programs, and it started television programming with national syndication in 1983.[11]

In addition to its evangelical work, the INC has also continued the Philippine tradition of uniting religion and politics. Felix Manalo had political clout greater than the size of his church would otherwise suggest because he would instruct the faithful about how they should vote, and his directions were followed. The INC's endorsement was, therefore, especially important in races where the church was particularly strong and even in national contests, since he commanded a solid bloc of voters. Manalo was courted by politicians of all parties. This wielding of political influence was continued under Erano Manalo, who was a well-known supporter of Ferdinand Marcos. Despite the collapse and discredit of the Marcos regime, the INC continued to play a visible role in Philippine politics, giving its support to President Joseph Estrada. Against this reality, the changing social-economic demographics of the INC membership may be affecting the degree to which the church can continue to control a solid bloc of voters. Though still a working class phenomenon, the INC has attracted an increasing number of middle-class converts, and many of its formerly poor members, especially in Manila and other urban areas, are bettering their lot in life. This increase in status seems to be weakening the control that church officials formerly held.

The Contemporary Activist Roman Catholic Church

Because the Roman Catholic church implanted itself in the Philippines in cooperation with the Spanish colonial government, it suffered when Iberian rule was ejected and had to go through an extended period of rebuilding. In the end, however, the church may have become stronger because while it is still criticized for catering to the elite, it can take pride in its activist role in Philippine society. The church's interest in social and political causes has roots that go back to the pre-World War II era and received its initial impetus from the idealism of American missionary priests. But it was not until the 1950s, especially as Filipinos took control of most of the country's parishes and rose in the hierarchy, that the call for social justice truly began to emerge, even if slowly. One watershed event was the hierarchy's opposition to a strike by unionized workers at the Dominican-run University of Santo Tomas in 1956 that elicited opposition within clerical ranks even though the leaders of that opposition were foreign missionaries.

The papal leadership of John Paul and his liberalization of the worldwide Catholic community was soon reflected in the Philippines. In 1962, Manila's Rufino Cardinal Santos founded the Asian Social Institute, which soon initiated a research program into the country's social and economic inequalities and began training a cadre of idealistic young professionals who wanted to work for social justice. Five years later, the hierarchy created the National Secretariat for Social Action, and the church began to immerse itself in a range of community development projects as more and more priests and even a few bishops began to view addressing temporal needs as an extension of their religious duty. By the late 1960s, a number of young Filipino priests led by Fathers Edicio de la Torre and Luis Jalandoni began to raise serious questions about the meaning of the priesthood and its social role that went far beyond issues of development and questioned the structure of the Philippine social order.[12] It should be noted that while some in the Catholic church were moving in this radical direction, the nation's youth were also becoming more socially aware and beginning to critique the country's inequalities. Activist student organizations were already forming, and even a group of young dissidents within the country's old Communist Party was beginning to question the hierarchy.

Ferdinand Marcos's September 1972 declaration of martial law was a turning point for the church as well as for the nation. While conservative elements in the hierarchy cautioned restraint, the more socially active and critical members of the church were not long in criticizing the regime.[13] Leading the way was the Association of Major Religious Superiors and its Task Force on Detainees, which was created to monitor the rapidly deteriorating human rights condition under the martial regime. In addition to raising specific concerns over the regime's excesses, the impact of the principled Catholic stance against martial law was to counter the nationalistic facade that Marcos and his propagandists attempted to build in justification for his rule. Meanwhile, some of the young socially concerned priests joined Father de la Torre in founding the Christians for National Liberation, while a few, such as Father Jalandoni left the church altogether and joined the new radical underground Communist Party of the Philippines and its New Peoples' Army.

Eventually, religious and secular opponents of martial law were united by the tragic August 1983 assassination of Marcos foe Senator Benigno Aquino. In death, Aquino rose from being Marcos's principle political enemy to a martyr of folk proportions, gaining a permanent place in the country's pantheon of national heroes. His widow, Corazon Aquino, is an extremely devout Catholic whose piety in the face of her personal tragedy captured the imagination of the nation. She was cast in the role of the grieving Mary Magdalene whose calm opposition to the Marcos evil instantly lifted her high above the usual elite politics. The presidential call for a "snap" election in early 1986 thus set the stage for a *pasyon* play of epic proportions when Corazon Aquino was nominated to run against Ferdinand Marcos.

Normally non-confrontational Filipinos, including almost all the country's seminary students and many of its priests and nuns, volunteered to protect ballot boxes. When Manila's Jaime Cardinal Sin appealed to the citizenry to protect anti-Marcos military mutineers, throngs of common citizens responded to the religious leader's call.[14] Clearly good had triumphed over evil, and the pious grieving widow and the entire nation were redeemed by their courage and sacrifice. Noteworthy is the Tagalog word for political independence, *kalayaan*, which also translates as religious redemption. Corazon Aquino was thus the living reality of both meanings.[15]

Since 1986, the Catholic church has remained a vigilant champion of democracy and social justice. Cardinal Sin publicly criticized Aquino's presidential successor, Fidel Ramos, when it was rumored that he was considering supporting a movement to amend the new constitution to allow for a second six-year presidential term of office. More recently, the cardinal and Aquino led massive rallies in opposition to former president Joseph Estrada. While the public still supports the cardinal and the former president, criticism of the church is occasionally expressed by those who claim that Cardinal Sin's involvement in political affairs is weakening the country's twentieth-century tradition of separation of church and state. Another important criticism of the church and the cardinal is that for all of the church's stated concern for the poor, little seems to be done.

It is within the context of this latter criticism that the phenomenal rise of Mariano "Brother Mike" Velarde must be understood. Velarde was a poor but intelligent young man from the Bicol region of Luzon who worked his way through college in Manila and then made a fortune in real estate with the help of powerful political friends. His close connection to Marcos's allies led to his economic downfall in 1986, at which point, he turned to religion and founded the El Shaddai movement as a radio ministry. Currently, the movement claims eight million members and assets in the billions of pesos. Velarde's message is geared specifically to the poor who attend his all-night open-air prayer rallies and to whom he offers not only redemption but also tremendous wealth here on earth.

In 1998, he campaigned for winning presidential candidate Joseph Estrada and was then named the president's new spiritual advisor. A number of questions concerning his doctrinal purity have been raised by some bishops, who are calling for an examination of his pronouncements. These calls reached a peak after Velarde held a huge rally to counter a large anti-Estrada gathering in August 1999 led by Cardinal Sin and Corazon Aquino. Velarde's rally was billed as his birthday celebration but was graced by then President Estrada and many members of his cabinet and party so the event had clear political overtones. Perhaps more crucial than the embarrassment of having a charismatic leader such as Velarde attempt to upstage the cardinal is the fact that he leads a popular movement that is in keeping with the country's folk religious tradition. Any attempt to censure Velarde may, in fact, only increase his strength and weaken the authority of the church.

REBELLIOUS FOLK ISLAM

Since the creation of the Sultanate of Sulu, which preceded the introduction of Christianity in the Philippines by only one century, Islam has also undergone a process of indigenization that has given it a folk dimension contrary to the teachings of Islamic purists.[16] Until recently, the converts of the country's southern islands were at the periphery of the Islamic world, and there has never been a single strong Islamic state that could promote the religion. Rather, for hundreds of years, the Muslims of the Philippines have either been under Christian rule or were members of small, weak, and ethnically defined states. Since national independence in 1946, and with the increased intrusion of Christian Filipinos into traditional Muslim areas, the Islamic peoples have responded by more fully developing their religion and by mounting armed resistance to the national government. The latter led to an outbreak of fierce fighting in 1972 that still continues today by small armed bands even after the main Muslim armed organizations made peace with the government in exchange for a system of regional autonomy.

Although Islam offers a connection to a vibrant world religion, its Philippine converts continue to cling to pre-Islamic beliefs similar to those found among their Christian neighbors. Like the Christian, the Muslim Filipino pays attention to the local spirit world even while praying in the great tradition of his adopted religion. So, for example, he will make an offering to his pre-Islamic rice spirits before planting a crop, but later give a portion of the profit to the mosque to support the *zakat* (religious tithe). Important are the *awliya* (early mystics) as well as rituals and rites given to spirits (*diwatas, tonongs,* and *hantus*) and powers quite outside of the Islamic belief system. These include the *lalabutan* (food offerings), the *duwaa* (thanksgiving rites), the *kalilang* (ceremony to appease an angered spirit), and various *binangbinang* (special ceremonies). More specific examples are the rituals that the Muslim seafarer has developed to calm angered spirits of the sea, the *tawal* and the *duwaa,* that are quite foreign to traditional Islam. Even the design of early houses of worship, the *langgal,* was architecturally different from the usual Islamic mosque found elsewhere and is more in keeping with typical Southeast Asian houses of prayer.[17] As late as the early 1960s, most Filipino Muslims knew their religion through oral traditions linked to folk beliefs, and *adat* (customary law) was more important than religious teachings.

For much of the Spanish colonial period, the Muslim area was effectively autonomous from Manila's control, and flotillas of raiders from the southern islands frequently plundered Christian areas for loot and slaves. So commonplace were their attacks that the architecture of many churches and the layout of many towns were designed defensively to thwart these depredations. In turn, the sultanates of the southern islands looked upon the Spanish pretense of overlordship as nothing less than crass imperialism. For most of the Iberian regime's rule, each side was equally matched against the other such that the tide did not begin to turn in Spain's favor until the middle of the nineteenth century thanks to steam-powered naval vessels and better weaponry. As well, the assignment of Jesuit priests to Mindanao also aided in the conversion process and increased local security. But, it was left to the American regime to complete the conquest of the Muslim areas. The United States took over the area with superior military technology and offers of generous stipends to Islamic leaders willing to make peace. Just as important was the U.S. army's use of force in a manner similar to that applied to native American peoples in the western United States. In one such "battle" some 600 Muslims, mostly women and children, trapped in a valley were slaughtered by American soldiers who shot them from the ridges above.

During the American colonial period and since independence in 1946, Christian Filipino national governments have actively developed the southern islands as a frontier area. Homestead land grants were offered to Christian Filipinos willing to resettle to Mindanao, and large tracts of cheap agricultural property were sold to agricultural corporations. By the 1950s, as a result of these government programs, Mindanao had a majority Christian population who controlled the social and economic life of the island and the region.[18] Then, in 1968, an alleged massacre of thirty Muslim soldiers on Corregidor Island for a supposed mutiny was the spark needed to inflame a revolt. By the next year, the Moro National Liberation Front (MNLF), headed by former University of the Philippines professor Nur Misuari, began training a guerrilla force. This local movement soon gained support from the Islamic world, including Malaysia, Libya, and Saudi Arabia. When President Marcos declared martial law in 1972, Philippine troops were countered by a large and well-trained army of Muslim adversaries who were fighting for their religion and way of life. In the ensuing struggle, MNLF guerrilla tactics soon bogged down the technologically superior Philippine army.

The government was eventually able to use divisions among the Muslims to disintensify the movement and sign a weak peace agreement with the MNLF in 1982. Nevertheless, the resistance movement has continued and even grown under the influence of fundamentalist religious revivalism currently sweeping the Islamic world. As a result, even the use of the word "Moro" for the separatist struggle is important because it comes from the dismissive Spanish term "Moor" used to belittle Muslim Filipinos. The idea is to adopt the derisive terms of the oppressors and turn them into terms of liberation.

Many young Muslim clerics (*ulemas*) have studied at Al-Azhar University in Cairo, Egypt, famous for its influence on Islamic reform, and their message is now spreading among the faithful. A number of Islamic religious schools (*madrasas*) for children have been built thanks to support from Saudi Arabia, and these serve as an alternative to the government's secular public schools. More young Filipino Muslims are going on the annual *hajj* (the pilgrimage to Mecca) than ever before, and Muslim scholars and teachers are including the Philippines in their itineraries. As a result of this religious resurgence, a new, more radical political leadership is beginning to emerge. Even older conservative and secularist Muslim leaders must now appear in traditional clothing for ceremonial occasions and adopt some of the new rhetoric. Ironically, in terms of gender relations, the separatist struggle has actually increased the active role that Muslim women play in their society. Whether women will continue to enjoy autonomy as peace returns and religious strictures increase is open to question.[19]

Despite the appearance of being an overwhelmingly Roman Catholic nation, the Philippines has a remarkable degree of religious diversity, with an underlayer of earlier indigenous beliefs that have moderated the intrusions of world religions. Further complicating the religious picture is the political nature of religion, since both Christianity and Islam have entered with a political mandate, and their political as well as religious agendas have shaped events and religious institutions. This latter point is especially apparent in the twentieth-century creation of the two major domestic Christian churches.

NOTES

1. See Richard Lieban's classic study of the role of sorcery, healing and society, *Cebuano Sorcery* (Berkeley: University of California Press, 1967).

2. Author's observations while living with the Pinatubo Aeta people of Botolan, Zambales, 1968–1970.

3. For a recent interpretation of this phenomenon, see Vicente L. Rafael, *Contracting Colonialism: Translation and Christian Conversion in Tagalog Society under Early Spanish Rule* (Ithaca, NY: Cornell University Press, 1988).

4. This statistic is given in David Joel Steinberg, *The Philippines: A Singular and Plural Place*, 4th ed. (Boulder, CO: Westview Press, 2000), 82.

5. See Jose de Mesa, "Holy Week and Popular Devotions," in Rene Javellana, S.J. ed., *Morality, Religion and the Filipino* (Quezon City: Ateneo de Manila University Press, 1994), 220–233.

6. Reynaldo C. Ileto, *Pasyon and Revolution: Popular Movements in the Philippines, 1840–1910* (Quezon City: Ateneo de Manila University Press, 1979).

7. Paul A. Rodell, "The 1909 Escalante Murder Case and the Politics of Religion in Negros Occidental," *Pilipinas: A Journal of Philippine Studies* no. 28 (Spring 1997), 61–78.

8. For a well-balanced study by a Roman Catholic theological writer: see Fernando G. Elesterio, *The Iglesia ni Kristo: Its Christology and Ecclesiology* (Manila: Cardinal Dea Institute, Loyola School of Theology, Ateneo de Manila University, 1997, 6–12.

9. Bienvenido C. Santiago, "Brother Felix Y. Manalo Remembered," *75 Blessed Years of the Iglesia ni Cristo*, Diamond Jubilee program (Quezon City: Iglesia ni Cristo, 1989), 49–50.

10. Elesterio, 14–27.

11. Bienvenido C. Santiago, "Brother Erano G. Manalo at the Helm," in Bienvenido C. Santiago, ed., *75 Blessed Years of the Iglesia ni Cristo, 1914–1989* (Quezon City: Iglesia ni Cristo, 1989), 51–57.

12. See the comprehensive study by Wilfredo Fabros, *The Church and Its Social Involvement in the Philippines, 1930–1972* (Quezon City: Ateneo de Manila University, 1988), 66–86, 94–106, 146–155.

13. An early and well-informed analysis is Alex Pescador (pseud.), "An Overview of Philippine Church-State Relations since Martial Law," in David A. Rosenberg ed., *Marcos and Martial Law in the Philippines* (Ithaca, NY: Cornell University Press, 1979), 298–309.

14. An excellent comprehensive analysis of the question of the role of religion and politics during the Marcos era is Robert L. Youngblood, *Marcos Against the Church: Economic Development and Political Repression in the Philippines* (Ithaca, NY: Cornell University Press, 1990).

15. Steinberg, 89–90.

16. For a thoughtful commentary on the arrival and initial adoption of Islam in the Philippines, see Oscar L. Evangelista, "Some Aspects of the History of Islam in Southeast Asia," in Peter Gowing, ed., *Understanding Islam and Muslims in the Philippines* (Quezon City: New Day Publishers, 1988), 16–25.

17. See Peter G. Gowing, *Muslim Filipinos: Heritage and Horizon* (Quezon City: New Day Publishers, 1979), 64–69, and Samuel K. Tan, *Internationalization of the Bangsamoro Struggle* (Quezon City: Center for Integrative and Development Studies, University of the Philippines, 1993), 25–27.

18. Samuel K. Tan, *The Socioeconomic Dimension of Moro Secessionism* (Quezon City: Center for Integrative and Development Studies, Mindanao Studies Reports no. 1, University of the Philippines, 1995).

19. A brief and insightful summary of these reformist developments is found in Jacqueline Siapno, "Gender Relations and Islamic Resurgence in Mindanao, Southern Philippines," in Camillia Fawzi El-Solk and Judy Mabro, eds., *Muslim Women's Choice: Religious Belief and Social Reality* (Providence, RI: Berg Publishers, 1994), 187–191.

3

Art and Literature

PHILIPPINE ART is an amalgamation of indigenous traditions, adopted Western forms, and a vibrant contemporary folk art. The older artistic forms still exist among the country's many minority peoples, although these traditions are disappearing at an increasing rate. Western-influenced art can be found at two cultural levels. At the high end of culture, artists produce sophisticated works comparable with any others on the international modern art scene. A number of these artists have used their imagination and skill to produce works on themes of national identity and social commentary. More broadly, Filipinos delight in bright colors and artistic exuberance that enlivens everyday life. This art at the mass or folk level of Philippine culture is seen in resplendent decorations for religious occasions and festivals, in urban popular art, and on the brightly decorated jeepneys (mass transit passenger vehicles first made from post-World War II U.S. army surplus) that ply the nation's roadways.

INDIGENOUS TRADITIONS

Pre-colonial Filipinos used art to represent religious notions of the hereafter and their relationship with their physical environment. Archeological evidence from burial jars indicates an elementary level of technical sophistication in the construction of pottery, with the frequent representation of figures in a boat, suggesting the need to cross a body of water to reach the afterlife. Decorative patterns for other types of pottery used geometric designs and nature motifs. Pottery for everyday use was made in a variety of functional styles, occasionally in the shapes of animal and human figures. In addition to domestic manufactures, Filipinos also used Chinese and Vietnamese pottery that was of higher quality and artistic design. Chinese pottery was copied and continues to be made in Vigan, Ilocos Sur province. Also surviving are woodcarvings of grainary gods and human figures. Most of these wooden representations have been found either in the northern mountains of Luzon island or among the Muslim peoples of the south. In the latter case, since Islam discourages the artistic reproduction of the human form, the stylized *naga* serpent; the *okir* curvilinear design; a variety of vine and leaf patterns; and the stylized sculpture of the *sarimanok*, a legendary bird with a fish in its beak, were produced instead.[1]

Personal adornment was also an outlet for indigenous Philippine artistic ingenuity. A few pieces of clothing from cave site explorations reveal that many pre-colonial patterns are still echoed in the patterns woven by today's minority peoples. Natural materials from simple barkcloth to fibers made of pineapple, *abaca* (a hemp), and other plants were used for clothing, while indigo and other natural agents, including ginger, colored woods, and mud with high iron content, were used to dye the material in a range of subtle colors and shadings. To supplement clothing, many early Filipinos made extensive use of tattooing. Sometimes a tattoo was added as a mark of a man's ability as a warrior, but among lowland Filipinos tattoos were adopted simply as beautification. This latter practice was especially true of the inhabitants of the islands of the Visayas who decorated themselves with a wide variety of geometric and floral designs. This practice led the early Spaniards to refer to Filipinos as *los pintados*, or the painted ones. Hats, meanwhile, were either made of gourds or were woven of rattan or certain substantial leaves. Woven cloth, as well as mats and baskets, were decorated with floral designs and imaginative multicolored geometric patterns, some of which created optical illusions.

It appears that jewelry was first adopted for use as amulets and charms to ward off evil spirits and later assumed an ornamental role. Multicolored beads, tusks, and water buffalo horn were combined with brass chains and bells to make necklaces, rings, earrings, bracelets, and anklets and were sometimes worn in conjunction with elaborate tattoos as part of one's permanent body design. In some areas of northern Luzon and Mindanao, gold and silver were fashioned into disk neckpieces. Other metal pieces were made into forms of stylized animal figures, and precious metals were supplemented by brass and coiled copper wiring. Local metalworking was adopted by the residents of Luzon's Central Cordillera and the Muslims of the south to make brass gongs. Meanwhile, a few groups developed a lost-wax technique of sculpture to create a mold of wax that was melted away by molten brass to create human figurines. The most ambitious metalwork was reserved for weaponry, such as the tips of spears carried by warriors of the Central Cordillera region and the ornately decorated iron *kris*, a wave shaped sword, carried by the Muslim men of the south. Metals were worked in a crude forge that consists of hollow bamboo tubes with plungers to create a blower sufficient to melt metal into workable forms for the craftsmen.

THE HISPANIC ARTISTIC TRADITION

The arrival of Spanish colonizers introduced a strong tradition of religious art that persisted until the nineteenth century.[2] This religious emphasis was not entirely alien to the Filipino, but the new European artistic mediums were different and revolutionary in their impact. Filipinos soon learned engraving, sculpture, oil painting, and architecture because their skills were needed to build and decorate churches and produce religious publications. Meanwhile, traditional skills in woodcarving were pressed into service to produce figures of saints and decorate altars and floats for religious processions. While hints of pre-existing native sculptural styles incorporating spirits such as the *anito* occasionally appeared in the works of native craftsmen, their labor was usually supervised quite closely and displayed little individuality or innovation.

Metalwork advanced since all churches needed bells and the Spanish military needed cannons, while fancy grillwork was used for the windows on the ground floor of prestigious homes. Finer metalwork was reserved for crucifixes and various religious pendants that served as amulets of the Christian faith just as earlier amulets protected pre-Christian Filipinos. Gold and silver from the galleon trade that was not transshipped to China was often made into fine women's jewelry and for the adornment of religious images. Whatever medium employed, Filipino artistry advanced very little until the nineteenth century because of the strict formulaic religious constraints set by the Iberian tradition. By the latter period, a wealthy clientele of Spanish and Chinese *mestizo* elite customers began to patronize secular art for the construction and adornment of their new masonry homes, and this elite group was not as constrained in their artistic traditions.

The one basic requirement for homes in the Spanish Philippines was furniture for storage, since houses were not designed with closets. Just as large finely carved cabinets, or *aparadores*, kept the priest's vestments safe and clean, so, too, were a variety of cabinets required for the cloths, table linens, bedding materials, and tableware in the homes of wealthy *mestizos*. As the *mestizos* increased their wealth, simple crude benches were replaced by more elaborately designed ones and finely crafted chairs, of which the most prestigious was the *butaca*, or planter's chair, with its woven rattan mesh cradle for the sitter and flat armrests extending far beyond the chair for use as a foot and leg rest. Gradually, too, beds replaced mats that had formerly been spread on bamboo floors. The graceful *Mariposa* (butterfly)-style rattan sofa appeared in the living rooms of the better homes, and the European-style high table for dining surrounded by sets of simple straight-back chairs made their appearance in more and more homes. All of these and other pieces of furniture gave secular work to Filipino artisans whose mastery of woodwork soon created some exquisite, though fully functional, pieces.

In addition to household furniture, nineteenth-century Filipino artists gained a new secular market for art representing everyday Filipinos. Whether small wooden statues or oil paintings, these *tipos del pais* (types of the place) were purchased by nineteenth-century visitors to the colony, who had come on business and were interested in taking home a souvenir. Also of increased popularity among the new *mestizo* wealthy were portraits that could be hung in their homes and displayed their wealth and social status. This increased demand for something other than formulaic religious art supported the most famous artist of the period, Damian Domingo, whose paintings and lithograph reprints still command high prices.[3] In 1821, Domingo opened the country's first art school, and it was eventually under the influence of this school that Philippine painting turned even more to landscapes and everyday scenes.

By the second half of the century, a few Filipino artists went to Europe to study, and some even won high praise. In 1884, Juan Luna won a gold medal at Spain's national arts festival held in Madrid for his massive painting *Spoliarium*. Interestingly, this work, depicting the body of a Roman gladiator being dragged off a stone floor of combat, was actually a subtle critique of the colonial experience, revealing the artist's true feelings. In Luna, the colonial subject had absorbed and even perfected the artistic culture of the master well enough to win fame even while using his art to critique the Iberian master.

TWENTIETH-CENTURY ARTISTIC DEVELOPMENTS

Art in the early American period was dominated by two men, the painter Fernando Amorsolo and sculptor Guillermo Tolentino. Amorsolo's rustic landscapes of bountiful harvests, contented farmers, and smiling young women framed in warm tropical sunlight speaks of a nation at peace and enjoying life. His work set the tone and the standard of the pre-World War II era. Quite different was the sculpture of Tolentino that was based on the restrained classical forms he mastered as a student in Rome, but whose energy seems ready to burst forth in emotion. Among his most important works is the monument to assassinated revolutionary hero Andres Bonifacio, which is a landmark in the Manila suburb of Caloocan City, where the *Katipunan* leader first assembled his followers to rise up against Spain. Tolentino also sculpted the *Oblation*, a naked male figure looking into the sun with outstretched arms, which serves as the symbol for the University of the Philippines.[4]

Even during the American period, but especially after World War II, the dominance of Amorsolo's school of painting was challenged by a group of modernists led by Victorio Edades, who believed that the subject of art should include the ugliness of life as well as the beautifully idyllic. What he and his fellow artists introduced were some of the major trends then being developed in the United States and Europe. Edades sought to introduce a full range of feelings and passion to the canvas as well as modern styles of art such as cubism, abstraction, and figurative expressionism.[5] Especially after the trauma of Japan's wartime occupation, Edades's modernist school reigned supreme, and two of its members, Vicente Manansala and its lone woman member Anita Magsaysay-Ho, became prominent. Manansala, especially, captured the mood and social concerns of the times with his cubism and neo-realist works of urban life, such as *Madonna of the Slums*, and his paintings of shanties and poverty. While these trends were introduced in the capital, regional centers of art also survived and continued to thrive. Especially noteworthy are the artists of the towns along the shore of Lake Laguna (Laguna de Bay) to the east of Manila. In Angono town, the folk tradition was first developed by modernist Carlos Francisco and has since been kept alive by Jose Blanco and his talented children, whose realist genre of large paintings featuring the actual residents of their town brings national and international praise.

The 1960s witnessed a further turn toward social realism in art, especially during the two elected presidencies of Ferdinand Marcos. The young artist Ben Cabrera represented the new style of artist, using a number of mediums, such as painting, printmaking, and etching as well as the mixed media of photography and painting to present his social statements most effectively. Cabrera uses historical allusions from the revolution to illuminate contemporary political issues, especially those dealing with the complexity of Filipino identity, Christian and Muslim, urban and rural. His works, and those of others who have followed in his style, have a strong nationalist theme mixed with folk aspects and surrealism.

The declaration of martial law in 1972 was matched by a rise in social realists who resumed the postwar trend of "proletarian art" and built on the nationalist themes that were already defined in modern Philippine art. Among their contributions was the further expansion of artistic mediums in

Madonna of the Slums, social realist art of Vicente Manansala
(1910–1981). Reproduction from the Cultural Center of the
Philippines Library Collection.

an effort to transcend the gap between the artist and the general public. So,
for example, they would use editorial cartoon and Philippine *komik* (comic
book) style of drawings, as well as posters and portable murals to reach a
larger audience and increase the political impact of their artistic statements.

At the same time, explorations of social symbols and feminist issues were
undertaken by Brenda Fajardo, who examined the role of women through
time and in the Filipino psyche. She and others attempted to incorporate
indigenous materials, such as bamboo, coconuts, vines, seeds, and rattan,
into their work to increase native authenticity and lend a more accurate
depiction of local Philippine society. Combining indigenous and folk materials to make modern statements on the international scene are the country's up and coming modern artists such as Gerardo Tan, who has exhibited

Artist Ben Cabrera's *Brown Brother's Burden* "photo" painting showing the colonized view of his relationship to the white colonizer. Courtesy of the Cultural Center of the Philippines Library Collection.

in the United States and Melbourne, Australia.[6] Manila's artists have also received a wider audience than ever before, since many of the capital's new shopping malls are also home to a number of art galleries. While the gallery-in-the-mall concept does not extend to malls catering to the city's less well-off clientele, malls in a number of middle- as well as upper-class portions of the metropolitan area have galleries. Now Filipinos who would never venture into an upscale downtown gallery are exposed to quality artwork at affordable prices.

FOLK ART OF THE PEOPLE

In addition to the high end of the Philippine's art culture, there is a dynamic folk art tradition that displays itself in the country's religious festivals, in the urban pop art scene, and on the innovative jeepneys that serve the transportation needs of the country. Philippine towns are at their most colorful during annual fiestas when bamboo arches embellished by palms or paper ornaments mark the main thoroughfares for celebrants, and paper and cloth bunting are strung between houses and poles or trees. Even food becomes art during the feast of San Nicolas de Tolentino, when special cookies with the image of the saint are given out. In the town of San Miguel in Bulacan province, dried milk confections known as *pastillas* are wrapped in colored paper with fine cut lace-like tails depicting fruits, flowers, and even greetings. During Christmas, the five-pointed star, the *parol,* is made by covering a frame of thin bamboo strips with translucent colored paper and then attaching intricately cut paper tails to the tips of two points of the star. The *parol* is hung from house windows to welcome visitors, and some large ones are fitted with small colored electric bulbs that have replaced tiny candles used in the past.[7]

The town of Paete in Laguna province is the unofficial national center for the making of paper-mâché fiesta figures, the most popular of which are horses painted red and decorated with elaborate saddles covered with floral designs. First made in the early twentieth-century, this folk art innovation has now spread, and the Paete figurines can be found at many fiestas in Laguna and neighboring provinces. Mention has already been made of the decorative fronds used during the Palm Sunday festivities. These fronds may only be decorated by a small attached bouquet of flowers, but more elaborate ones will have colorful leaves plaited into patterns and attached to them with, perhaps, some additional colored crepe flowers.[8] These decorated fronds are blessed in the church and hung in the house over doorways to ward off evil.

Mention must again be made of the mid-May *Pahiyas* harvest festival in the Quezon province towns of Lucban and Sariaya, where brightly colored rice wafers called *kipig* are dyed in a range of primary colors and used in a variety of forms, most frequently hung as chandeliers or fashioned into flowers. Other festivals such as the *Moriones* in Marinduque and the *Ati-Atihan* in Iloilo also give the opportunity for local residents to express their folk artistic preferences in costuming as they prepare their decorative attire to parade through the streets as Roman gladiators or fierce mountain warriors with darkened skins. All Filipinos everywhere will dress the town's image of the patron saint in the best of clothes so the *santo* (saint) will be resplendent.

As well, the country's urban areas are home to an underground economy of pop art assembled by talented but poor and untrained Filipinos, who use their artistic creativity to supplement their meager incomes. Their materials come from factory discards and junkyard scraps that are refashioned by hand to make products such as rugs from cloth remnants of clothing factories, feather dusters from chicken feathers, plaster-of-Paris figurines, children's toys from discarded tin cans, and coin banks from polished and painted coconut shells and a variety of products from sea shells. These products demonstrate the creativity of the Filipino and bespeak of the folk artistry of the common man and woman who make practical goods with an artistic quality.

Somewhat more sophisticated are the numerous art studios in Manila's old tourist district, which produce scores of stereotypic paintings of idyllic rural scenes that emulate Amorsolo's superior works. These sentimental renderings of a rural Philippines that never existed are made for the aspiring middle class who believe that a piece of artwork is needed for the space above the sofa or the new piano.[9] A more substantial form of artistry that is gaining in importance both locally and internationally is the Filipino artist who works for the comic book industry. The Filipino *komik* is a popular form of literature and the artistry that goes into these books demands the skill of a number of illustrators. In addition to the substantial domestic market, many American and Japanese comic book companies subcontract their work to Filipino artists. For example, more than 60 percent of the Disney Company's cartoon features have been made in the Philippines, not Hollywood.

Finally, the most obvious form of Philippine folk art is the ubiquitous jeepney, that product of World War II found on virtually every major street and road in the country.[10] The first jeepneys were quite literally U.S. army surplus vehicles that were refashioned for passenger use by extending the frame backward so that facing rows of bench seating could be installed. The jeepney holds about seventeen people—the driver and two passengers in the front and then seven, or more, passengers on each of the two long bench seats. After the original jeeps went the rusty way of all vehicles, Filipinos continued to make their own by importing the engine and building a local body. As Filipinos began to make their own vehicles, the need for a decorative panache for the jeepneys asserted itself, and the jeepney became mobile billboards for Philippine folk art. Each jeepney is specially painted and further individualized with additional lights; mirrors and reflectors; plastic streamers hung from antennae; hood decorations, such as standing chrome horses; letterings of favorite song titles; paintings of rural scenes or women in erotic poses; extra decals and chrome strips everywhere; the name of the manufacturer (usually Sarao Motors); and the proud nickname of the driver, "Lover Boy," "Jeepney King," "Action Kid," etc. In addition to its customizing, the jeepney will also display a license plate on the front bumper and a signboard across the top of the windshield giving the jeep's route for potential passengers to see.

The jeepney's interior is like no other vehicle on the planet. Curtains are hung along the open sides of the passenger compartment, the ceiling of which

A jeepney. Photo by the author.

may also be a canvas upon which additional paintings are found. In the front, the driver will frequently have a small shrine that includes a plastic icon of a saint, most often St. Christopher or Our Lady of Perpetual Help, upon which might be hung a sacrificial garland of the strong sweet smelling *sampaguita* flowers. Often, too, the driver will have miniature beer bottles glued to his dashboard along with a cassette recorder and a box for the tapes. Some drivers even install a small electric fan to lessen the city's oppressive heat and foul exhaust gases that constantly invade the jeepney, since the vehicle is completely open to the hostile environment except for its windshield. Important, too, is the wooden moneybox holding the driver's earnings, and the change needed for his customers. Somewhere among the driver's collection of icons and personal amenities are the actual gauges for the vehicle, but these often do not work and are irrelevant.

The passengers and driver enter into a communal relationship during a trip, with passengers helping each other on the jeep, passing fares up to the driver and repeating a request for a stop in case the driver did not hear the passenger who asked to get off. Thus, in microcosm the jeepney displays the communal nature of Philippine society. Unfortunately, the jeepney is a communal form of transportation in decline. At its height in the early 1980s, there were almost 30,000 jeepneys in Manila, but the need to conserve fuel and space on crowded city streets has led to a sharp restriction of jeepneys in favor of larger, more fuel efficient buses, especially those that feature air conditioning. Recent, too, is the appearance of an enclosed air conditioned sport utility-type vehicle, which holds only nine passengers but travels with limited stops thus offering a significant saving of time for the harried commuter. As the economic viability of the jeepney has declined so too has the artwork, at least in major cities. In the countryside, however, the jeepney's art continues to represent Philippine culture.

Firmly based in indigenous and vibrant folk traditions, the Filipino artist and writer have also fully mastered the international genres of their arts. Whether in literature or art, Filipinos continue to draw from their native traditions and use their skills and creativity to shape the cultural future of their people. In this evolving process, foreign artistic and literary forms are incorporated to strengthen the vibrancy of the country. In these areas, as in other aspects of Philippine culture, such as music and film, the adaptive process works to the benefit of the whole.

LITERARY TRADITION

Unlike music and other forms of art and culture, Philippine literature remained relatively free of colonial influence until the nineteenth century, which allowed it to retain its indigenous character as an oral tradition for a relatively long time. Philippine literature, especially poetry, was relatively unaffected by Spanish colonial influence because the Spaniards were not interested in passing along their language to Filipinos. Spaniards in the Philippines did not instruct the natives in their language, unlike their policy in South America, but, rather, kept knowledge of the language from the natives to limit their ability to challenge colonial authority. Thus, Filipino literature remained largely an oral tradition relatively unaffected by Iberian culture until the nineteenth century when changes in the international economy saw the emergence of a class of native and *mestizo* elites who gained access to the colonizer's language.

Once Filipinos gained a working knowledge of Spanish, indigenous oral traditions were modified by Iberian and European cultural infusions. In effect, Spanish finally became the unifying *lingua franca* for the archipelago, which otherwise has a large number of dialects. Use of the colonizer's language permitted a cross-fertilization of knowledge and accelerated the breakdown of regional differences. The somewhat ironic result of this linguistic adoption was that by the latter decades of the nineteenth century, Spanish, rather than an indigenous national language, became the language of Filipino nationalism. The national hero Jose Rizal was a medical doctor, essayist, poet, and amateur folklorist, but he is best known for his novels, which were written in Spanish and criticized the ruling Spaniards and their native sycophants. Philippine literature in Spanish was thus the single most powerful weapon in the nationalists' arsenal.

Although the literary tradition of writing in Spanish continued during the American period, the new North American colonial ruler actively promoted public education and the English language. The short-term impact of this American education and language policy was dramatic, and its long-term influence cannot be overestimated. In the short-term, education became something of an obsession with Filipinos, while in the long-term, English replaced Spanish as the nation's common and ethnically neutral language. Now, much of the nation's business and political life is conducted in English. In fact, the inauguration of President Joseph Estrada in June 1998 was especially noteworthy because Estrada became the first Filipino president since independence in 1946 to deliver his address entirely in Pilipino, the official national language. Meanwhile, visitors can still find English speakers in almost any town, and the nation's media continues to feature programs in English. In literature, too, as generations of Filipinos passed through the country's school system, the nation's novels, short stories, poetry, and literary criticism gradually became molded by American sources. As a result, Filipino literature and poetry written in English appeared relatively early and continues as a strong tradition today.

At the same time, however, the country's major dialects did not disappear and actually grew in strength thanks to the spread of basic literacy and benign American policies toward the media. While talk of revolutionary nationalism and a few other sensitive topics were forbidden, local publishers and writers were at liberty to explore the facility of their local languages. In a relatively brief time a number of weekly and monthly dialect magazines such as *Liwayway* and *Bulaklak* appeared and gave authors a forum for their work. Despite the spread of English, these magazines became and remained popular, since not everyone was skilled in the foreign language, and even English-educated Filipinos enjoyed stories written in the familiar dialects of their youth. In addition, the often overlooked, but important, phenomenon of the *Pilipino Komik* should not be forgotten in a literature survey. For many Filipinos, the lowly *komik* has served as a powerful medium of entertainment and as a bellwether for social values and societal change. While *komik* books have been stigmatized as escapist reading for the uneducated lower class, the *komik* has a general popularity, especially among teenagers and housewives, that is akin to the popularity of comics in Japan. Finally, beginning in the American colonial period, the deliberate non-use of English became a mark of integrity for some writers who developed the national language and local dialects. Many of these vernacular writers selected topics of social concern and nationalism for their writings and became leading social critics and activists. In retrospect many of these socially conscious writers produced some of the best pieces of Filipino literature in the 1930s and 1940s even though their English-writing colleagues were winning all of the accolades.

More recently, the Philippines has seen a strong increase in the use of Pilipino among the country's writers, poets, and literary critics. This resurgence is closely tied to two developments: the increasing sense of national identity and pride that accelerated rapidly in the late 1960s and the use of Pilipino as the medium of instruction, which is replacing English in the elementary and secondary school levels. It is an interesting and exciting time for Philippine literature.

Pre-Spanish Oral Traditions

Riddles, proverbs, and aphorisms were the basis of the Philippine's oral literary tradition, and collectively they served as the foundation of native poetry.[11] These forms were created in villages and were either spoken around a fire after an evening meal or put into song for entertainment. Most of this oral tradition spoke of daily life, such as working in the fields, fishing, and hunting, as well as love, marriage, sickness, and death. Much of the oral tradition also included folk stories about amusing characters whose tales imparted lessons of behavior for young and old. Some of these stories, such as the popular Tagalog folktales about Juan Tamad, live on in contemporary popular culture. Sometimes these oral recitations included verbal jousts between friends and young lovers and provided a means of education and entertainment. Even on present-day Philippine radio and television programs, the *balagtasan*, or contests in verse or prose, are a popular means to debate a variety of facets of daily life and personal relationships. Other tales involved animals, such as the mythological bird, the *Sarimanok*, and the story of "The Tortoise and the Monkey," a pedagogical story popularized by Jose Rizal.

A more complex form of oral tradition were epic stories, which passed on a group's creation myths and basic social values through tales of the supernatural or of heroic deeds. As is true of many other cultures in Southeast Asia, these epics told stories of heroes and gods whose exploits and foibles serve as models of behavior and cherished values, and their tales were carefully crafted by gifted storytellers. Undoubtedly, these stories shifted over time to address, in allegorical form, matters of concern to the community. While many of the epic stories, such as the tale of the first Filipino man and woman, *Malakas at Maganda* (*The Strong and the Beautiful*) are nationally known, others such as the Ilocano story *Biag ni Lam-ang* (*The Life of Lam-ang*) are specific to an ethnic group.

While folklore, creation myths, epics, proverbs, and literary forms from the pre-colonial period might at first glance seem obscure, they are still relevant to modern Philippine society and form a literary core that contains the culture's social beliefs and values. They also provide the basic framework for more than a few contemporary stories, modern dance productions, plays, and poetry that continue to enrich Philippine life. As such, the pre-Hispanic oral tradition is a genuine literary expression of the people and has grown to suit the needs of the nation.

Spanish Colonialism and Philippine Literary Growth

While the first materials printed in Manila were Spanish doctrinal religious tracts for the Spanish colonial population, the vast majority of the output by the religious orders consisted of publications in many local dialects. In addition to dictionaries and grammar books that were beneficial to the missionary effort, the religious presses also printed catechisms, prayer books, confessional manuals, and hymnals. As part of their missionary efforts, Spanish priests used local traditions and adapted them, so the native song, the *dalit*, for example, quickly became a form of religious lyric poetry. In fact, poetry and songs from the pre-colonial oral tradition were the earliest Philippine literary forms to be printed.[12]

The most complex and important of the lyric poetry was the *Pasyon*, or the story of the life and death of Jesus Christ. The earliest version of the *pasyon* was published in 1704 by Gaspar Aquino de Belen but that was later eclipsed by another version in 1814. Both versions were written in Tagalog and became the basis for the practice of public recitations called *pabasa*, which are performed during the Lenten season, while a staged version of the *pasyon*, the *sinakulo*, is performed throughout Holy Week. The popularity of the Tagalog *pasyon* soon spread throughout the colony and was translated into other Philippine dialects.[13] While the dominant social values of humility and submission to authority were clear in all versions of the *pasyon*, in fact, other social values such as honor and goodness are also present in the story. A prominent historian of the Philippines, Reynaldo Ileto, has argued that the social-religious values widely disseminated through the annual recitations of the *pasyon* actually formed the ideological message that linked the well-educated elites of the anti-Spanish revolutionaries of the late nineteenth century with the broad base of their uneducated fellow countrymen and women.[14]

Beyond the Spanish era, the basic storyline of the *pasyon* continues to lend itself to modern use when adopted by creative writers. In 1935, Pascual Poblete wrote *Patnubay ng Binyagan* (*Guide for the Baptized*) a *pasyon* for the Iglesia Filipina Independiente (IFI), a nationalist Filipino church created by a nationwide schism from the Roman Catholic Church in 1902. In this work, Poblete compares the *pasyon* of Jesus Christ to the struggle of the Philippines to gain independence from the United States. Another example from the 1930s is Lino Dizon's *pasyon*, which has Christ as a socialist while peasants are crucified by the vicious hacienda system. A more recent social revolutionary portrayal of Christ is Francisco Rodrigo's 1970 *Pasyon Si Kristo ay Rebelde* (Christ Is a Rebel), which critiqued the pre-martial law regime of Ferdinand Marcos. Finally, the recent *Pasyon nang Bayan* (*Passion of the Nation*) by Joaquin Malibo has served to inspire a number of social protest poems by some of the country's top writers.[15]

It was from this base of religious poetry that secular poetry began to emerge in the early to mid-nineteenth century. At first this secular poetry was set to the musical forms of the *awit* and the *korido* (romance songs of love and adventure) and consisted of little more than Filipino versions of European stories of kings, queens, and courtly love and were consistently from the perspective of the Spanish colonizer. However, by mid-century as native frustration with Spanish excesses accumulated, this new secular literature began to find a political use. Francisco Baltazar was especially proficient in this new use of literature and writing. Under the pen name of "Balagtas," his 1838 narrative poem *Pinagdaanang Buhay ni Florante at Laura sa Cahariang Albania* (*An Account of the Life of Florante and Laura in the Kingdom of Albania*) became the first entry in a literature of protest. In this narrative poem, the oppressive nature of the kingdom of Albania is a clear metaphor for the excesses of the Spanish regime in the Philippines, and the pure-of-heart lovers Florante and Laura must overcome the evil designs of King Adolfo.[16]

A significant break with the literary past occurred in the latter decades of the nineteenth century as the colony became drawn into the world's economic system. The opening of the Suez Canal in 1869 and the adaptation of the steam engine for ships drastically reduced the time and hazard involved in traveling to the Philippines. As well, the first decades saw the decline of the Spanish galleon trade and the development of a colonial export agriculture economy. Integral to this development was the transfer of economic power from Manila's Spaniards to *mestizo* agriculture landlords who pioneered the new export crops.

With knowledge of Spanish no longer denied them, young *mestizos* began to produce a literature of reform using Spanish as their medium. The educated *mestizos*, referred to as *Ilustrados*, attended universities in Spain and began a Propaganda Movement that was responsible for searing indictments of the Spanish colonial regime published in their newspaper *La Solidaridad*.

Jose Rizal best epitomized the young *Ilustrado* group, and it was he who brought the literary efforts to the greatest height. Although a masterful essayist and poet, Rizal's best known works are his novels *Noli Me Tangere* (*Touch Me Not,* 1887) and *El Filibusterismo* (*The Subversive,* 1891), both of which use realism rather than religious or folk allegory.[17]

In the first novel, the young hero Crisostomo Ibarra returns home from Europe filled with hope of serving his people as a school teacher and using education to liberate his native land from the hand of colonial oppression. He also returns to court his childhood friend and sweetheart, the beautiful Maria Clara. The lives of these two attractive, intelligent, and pure young people are then destroyed by the colonial oppression that strangles their country, portrayed by the Spanish friars Padre Damaso and Padre Salvi. The first novel concludes with Maria Clara's suicide and the revelation that she is actually the illegitimate daughter of the priest Padre Damaso and with Ibarra's escape from the authorities after having been falsely accused of conspiring against the state. In *El Filibusterismo,* Ibarra returns, and using the pseudonym of Simoun, he attempts an elaborate plot to overthrow the hated colonizer, but his conspiracy fails and the conspirator hero dies a sickly failure.[18]

While the message of Rizal's two novels is ambiguous at best, they nevertheless served to crystallize popular opinion about the legitimacy of Spanish rule. It remained for other nationalists such as Andres Bonifacio and Emilio Aguinaldo to raise the standard of revolution and free the country from Spanish rule. Meanwhile, Rizal paid dearly for his writings. Arrested and tried on dubious charges, he was executed by a Spanish firing squad on December 30, 1896, even as those who advocated a violent overthrow of the colonial regime were already engaged in battle. The committed nationalistic prose of the pre-revolutionary Propaganda Movement continued during the fight against Spain and then against the United States. The generation of *Ilustrados* writing in Spanish published a small number of newspapers for the Aguinaldo government and produced essays, manifestos, and poetry denouncing the Yankee imperialists. Meanwhile, theatrical authors wrote and helped stage popular Spanish *zarzuela* style plays, with lines that used allegory and double-entendre to maximum subversive effect.

By the end of the Spanish colonial regime, Philippine literature had grown from its roots as an oral tradition found in individual communities. By adopting the language of the colonizer, various dialectic and regional differences were transcended and a modern national consciousness was created. Thus, the creation of a modern nation went hand-in-hand with the creation of a modern national literature, which would remain true to its indigenous origins.

From American Conquest to 1960

Despite the American emphasis on education in English and the rapid construction of schools during the first decades of the American regime, Spanish continued to be used in government, academia, and business circles and was considered the prestige language of the "old rich." This section begins with the American occupation when English was first introduced, but carries its discussion beyond the Second World War and into the independence period, since the American impact on language and literature has lasted for far longer than its colonial dominance.

The first two decades of the American era saw the literary fruition of the Hispanic period such that a full listing of the noted authors of the period would be overwhelming. However, chief among this era's writers in Spanish was Fernando Maria Guerrero, who first wrote for nationalist newspapers during the war against the United States and continued to work on Spanish-language newspapers after hostilities even while he perfected his poetry. Meanwhile, writing under the pen name "Batikuling," Jesus Balmori wrote four volumes of verse as well as three novels and a number of essays. One of those essays was *Aves de Rapina* (*Birds of Prey*), which was published in the Spanish-language newspaper *El Renacimiento* in 1908. This satirical essay pilloried American colonial official Dean C. Worcester, who promptly sued the paper for libel. The case was especially important because of the chilling effect it had on the Philippine press that had just been freed from a number of wartime constraints. The case became well known on both sides of the colonial political divide.[19] In addition to the writers already mentioned, it is necessary to cite the nationalist and post-World War II Philippine Senator Claro M. Recto, who was also well noted for his essays, plays, and poetry, which he produced in a beautiful, flowing Spanish.

While Spanish continued to leave its mark on Philippine literature in the twentieth century, English gained ascendance under the enthusiastic promotion of the American regime, and it was not long before a number of talented Filipino writers in English emerged. Again, a complete listing of these authors would be far beyond the scope of this essay, but there are certain notable individuals who deserve recognition and whose work reflected the times in which they lived and the richness of Philippine culture that still shone through the medium of English. In poetry, Jose Garcia Villa stood out for his ability to use English to create a new style of poetry. Villa also represented the continual international searching of the Filipino intellectual for stimulus. His literary collaborators and friends included such celebrities as Gertrude Stein and e.e. cummings, but his participation in the "art for art's sake" intellectual movement of the time and his poetry also showed his cultural alienation while working in a foreign language.[20] Meanwhile, other writers in English sought a more socially responsible art. These talented writers, many of whom were associated with the University of the Philippines, included essayist Salvador P. Lopez and short story authors Arturo Rotor and Manuel Arguilla. By 1939, the Philippine Writers' Club declared the need for the writer to join in the struggle against social injustice and oppression. Especially important in this movement for social responsibility was Lopez's 1940 collection of critical essays and reflections *Literature and Society*.[21]

These writers not only found work at the national university, but were able to publish in a number of English-language magazines such as *The Philippines Free Press* and the *Philippines Herald Magazine* so that by the end of the 1920s there was already a sizable corpus of Filipino short stories in English. Most notable were Rotor's "The Wound and the Scar" (1937), Arguilla's "How My Brother Leon Brought Home a Wife" (1941), and N.V.M. Gonzalez's memorable "Bread of Salt" and "A Warm Hand." Another notable writer of the pre-war period was Carlos Bulosan, a poor immigrant farm worker in America who rose to substantial literary success through his short stories that were collected in *The Laughter of My Father* (1944).[22] Shortly before the Second World War, the Filipino novel in English emerged with the publication of Juan Laya's *His Native Soil* (1940) and N.V.M. Gonzalez's *The Winds of April* (1940), which clearly showed that the Filipino writer had not only mastered but internalized the new language.

While Japan's wartime restrictions temporarily suspended publications in English, the postwar period was marked by an explosion of high quality literature that frequently concerned itself with issues of cultural identity, since Filipino writers were attempting to communicate in what was a foreign language.[23] Gonzalez's novels *A Season of Grace* (1956) and *The Bamboo Dancers* (1959) were at the forefront of this advance in English as was his collection of short stories *Children of the Ash-Covered Loam and Other Stories* (1954). Meanwhile, the prolific writer Nick Joaquin's poetry and short stories were collected in various anthologies, but it was his novel *The Woman Who Had Two Navels* (1961) that best displayed his talent and subtlety. Also active in the postwar period was Benvenido Santos, who produced a volume of short stories entitled *You Lovely People* (1955), important, too, were Kerima Polotan-Tuvera's *The Hand of the Enemy* (1961) and Edilberto Tiempo's works, especially the 1947 wartime novel *Watch in the Night*.[24]

Although writing in English gained a solid foundation during the American period and remains a potent force in present day Philippines, it is the use of the vernacular that has proven to be the stronger force in the nation's literature. In actuality, the resilience of Philippine languages, especially the national language Pilipino, should not be surprising, since English was always a secondary foreign language to the vast majority of the Filipino people, and the innermost thoughts and longings of a people will always be best expressed in the native tongue. The utility of the vernacular was especially important for the socially committed writer who sought to address the basic issues and concerns of the average Filipino. The use of Pilipino was intimately linked to nationalism, especially in the face of the American cultural onslaught. Even during the American colonial period, publishing in the vernacular increased markedly as did its appreciative audience.

Writers in the vernacular enjoyed the advantage of being able to build upon the culture's pre-Hispanic oral tradition and were especially accomplished at poetics. Using the chanted verse, many talented Tagalog poets were soon producing a number of volumes. Especially prolific was Jose Corazon de Jesus, who produced a number of poems, *balagtasan* verses, satirical pieces, and songs, such as the beautiful nationalist hymn *Bayan Ko*, which is discussed further in Chapter Eight on music. At the same time, the socially committed writer Lope K. Santos wrote verse narrative in addition to his newspaper columns and satirical commentaries. The oral tradition also served as the basis for the short story, and a number of writers around the country soon became known as the fathers and mothers of the literature of their local dialect. Assisting the growth of vernacular literature was the founding of a series of regional magazines, many named after the dialect they were printed in, that carried the fiction of these writers, serializing their novels as well as publishing poetry and short stories.

The growth of vernacular literature, especially in Tagalog, was further spurred in the 1930s as the Philippine film industry was established and quickly gained popularity. Shortly before the Second World War, vernacular writers were already tapping into a very large market. There were over fifty vernacular magazines by 1940, with the industry leader being Liwayway Publications founded by Ramon Roces in 1922. The four magazines of the Liwayway chain catered to the nation's major dialects and had a weekly circulation more than five times greater than the English language *The Philippines Free Press*. Beyond sheer numbers, these magazines translated novels from one dialect to another to tap additional readers and thereby created a mass market chain that was a powerful influence on the emerging national vernacular literary style. The vernacular was given a further boost in the late 1930s as Filipino political leaders anticipated an eventual break from American rule and the need to develop a national language. In 1937, Commonwealth President Manuel Quezon proclaimed this need and proposed a national language based on Tagalog.[25] The increases made by local literature were further reinforced during the Pacific war when the Japanese occupation government outlawed English language publications, and many writers in

English began to experiment with their native languages. With the prewar development of a solid base, vernacular literature held its own during the immediate postwar period, when the use of English returned and reached its apex.

In the early American period, the most notable contributor of the vernacular writers was Lope K. Santos, the "Father of the Tagalog novel." Santos not only developed that language's literature, but he provided a bridge between the romanticism of the Spanish era and the social realism of the American period that has continued to characterize the best of vernacular literature. Building on the Spanish tradition, Santos combined his activism in journalism, labor unions, and socialism with literature to great success in his startling 1905 novel *Banaag at Sikat* (*Glimmer and Light*). Santos' pioneering efforts were followed by other socially committed writers, such as the accomplished Faustino Aguilar who also concerned himself with issues of foreign domination and agrarian exploitation. An early work of Aguilar is *Pinaglahuan* (*Eclipsed,* 1907), which used a love triangle to deliver a stunning socialist critique of society. This theme was further developed in his 1926 novel *Lihim ng Isang Pulo* (*Secret of an Island*). Another socially committed writer of the 1930s was Lazaro Francisco, whose novels explored Central Luzon's tenancy system, which sapped the life out of the farmers. Francisco's interest in social responsibility helped him produce especially good works after the war with *Maganda Pa Ang Daigdig* (*The World Is Still Beautiful*) in 1956 and the sequel *Daluyong* (*Tidal Wave*, 1962).[26]

The socially relevant terrain was dominated in the postwar period by Amado V. Hernandez's 1959 novel *Mga Ibon Mandaragit* (*Birds of Prey*) and two years later with his *Luha ng Buwaya* (*Crocodile Tears*). A winner of the 1938 Commonwealth Literary Award for his narrative poem "Pilipinas," Hernandez served as a guerrilla fighter during the war. With the return of peace he went back to journalism and labor activism, becoming the national chairman of the Congress of Labor Organizations (CLO). In 1951, the CLO's headquarters was raided by the military, and Hernandez was arrested and charged with rebellion. A legal struggle for his bail lasted almost six years, until Hernandez was freed from a sentence of "reclusion perpetual." It was during this time that he wrote *Mga Ibon Mandaragit* and a massive autobiographical narrative poem *Bayang Malaya* (*Free Nation*). Eight years later, the Philippine Supreme Court acquitted him of all charges. Until his death in 1970, Hernandez continued to write poetry and essays, and his example still serves as inspiration to socially committed young writers.[27]

Contemporary Literature: From the 1960s

Although precise dating is difficult, the contemporary period of Philippine literature can be said to have begun in the 1960s during the rule of President Ferdinand Marcos. In keeping with its oral and poetic origins, the contemporary period was initiated by poets who wrote in Tagalog, but who are equally versatile in English. Additionally, some younger writers began to experiment with Taglish, a hip urban mixing of English and Tagalog that gives the writer additional linguistic complexity to craft double meanings and situations of social satire. One group of these young university educated writers compiled *Manlilikha, Mga Piling Tula: 1961–67* (*Creator, Selected Poems: 1961–67*, 1967) that aspired to an international "modernismo" and was dense in its intellectualism. Meanwhile, another group of poets emerged from the country's premier Jesuit university, the Ateneo de Manila, and included Rolando Tinio who used Taglish in *Sitsit sa Kuliglig* (Calling The Cricket, 1972) and *Dunung-Dunungan* (Know-It-All, 1975). These young writers began the *bagay* (thing) movement that sought to free poetry from excessive emotionalism. All of these new poets and other writers of the 1960s, were greatly affected by the activism of the latter years of the decade, especially the rise of the new Communist Party of the Philippines under the leadership of University of the Philippines English professor Jose Ma. Sison. In 1971, a radical writer's group PAKSA (*Panulat para sa Kaunlaran ng Sambayanan* or Literature for the Advancement of the People) united many of these writers in discussions of social conditions and explorations of Marxism, especially those developed during China's Cultural Revolution.[28]

This early literary experimentation in poetry and the subsequent turn to socially relevant and protest literature had parallels among the nation's young short story writers and novelists. The early 1960s saw the development of two mutually exclusive approaches among short story writers, the realists and the existentialists. The former group sought alternatives to romantic and escapist literature while their stories sometimes employed a stream of consciousness technique as they described everyday characters who usually lived in contemporary urban settings. At the same time, the Philippine literary scene was heavily influenced by European existentialism, the ideas of which allowed writers to break with existing formalism and find shelter from the threatening real world. Western notions of angst and ennui typified the works of many writers who followed this latter philosophy of literature.

Meanwhile, among novelists, a faith in the possibility of social change was kept alive by one of the country's most accomplished writers in English, F. Sionil Jose, whose social and political vision is clearly laid out in his five-part Rosales Saga (*The Pretenders*, 1962; *Tree*, 1978; *My Brother, My Executioner*,

1979; *Mass*, 1982; and *Po-on* [*Dusk*], 1984). Each of the novels is set in Jose's hometown of Rosales, Pangasinan, and confront issues of national identity and the exploitation of one Filipino by another. Jose's work is a true saga, taking a family through the turmoil of history such that they are sometimes even torn from each other as even brother exploits brother while fighting oppression and landlordism. Despite the trials the family is put through, there is a theme of social justice as the antidote needed for Philippine society. Jose's works have attracted greater international attention than many other Philippine authors, and his books are available from foreign popular presses.[29]

Jose's underlying hope for the future and his faith in the Filipino's potential was not always shared by his contemporaries. In the early 1960s, many writers seemed to despair after the death of president Ramon Magsaysay and the defeat of the Communist-led Huk movement. Pessimism is clearly evident in Kerima Polotan-Tuvera's *The Hand of the Enemy* (1961) and Andres Cristobal Cruz's *Ang Tundo Man May Langit Din* (*Tondo Has a Heaven Too*, 1960). By the end of the decade, the deterioration of the nation's political life and the resulting social crisis re-energized these short story and novel writers. Many writers were affected by the student activism of the "First Quarter Storm" of 1970, and cause-oriented and politicized writing quickly engulfed Philippine literature as evidenced by the PAKSA-produced volume of stories *Sigwa* (Storm, 1972).

Under the slogan of "literature from the masses, to the masses," writers of poetry, short stories, and novels recommitted themselves to social concerns and examined their use of language in the process of communication. The result of this self-examination process was not simply the intentional use of the vernacular, but also a search for the most direct and simple words and story lines and a renewed interest in folk traditions and popular literature and storytelling. Among the leaders of this movement were Clarita Roja (*A Comrade Is as Precious as a Rice Seedling*, circa 1982), Rogelio Sicat, Ricardo Lee, and Lualhati Bautista. With the imposition of martial law in September 1972, the Marcos government sought to suppress such "committed" writing but could not. Some writers joined the resistance movement in "underground" activities that produced literary works such as *Magsasaka: Ang Bayaning Di Kilala* (*Farmer: The Unknown Hero*, circa 1970), an anthology of protest literature. Still other authors remained "above ground" and continued to test the regime's limits.[30]

Since the popular movement dubbed "People Power" and the revolt by government rebels that overthrew the Marcos regime in 1986, the nation's writers have not forgotten the lesson of their activist past. Pilipino has continued to become more and more important in the nation's literature, and there is continued social concern about basic social inequalities and the poor.

What is remarkable about this continued social interest is that the single focus of the Marcos regime that had united writers before 1986 no longer exists. So, while individual writers have moved on to pursue personal interests, especially the growth of a true feminist literature, as an intellectual group they continue to share a broad social concern. Supplementing the creative writing programs and workshops of the nation's premier universities has been the National Commission for Culture and the Arts, which was founded in 1992 and whose Committee on Literary Arts has funded numerous publications and activities designed to help in the creation of a national literature. The development of such a literature has been greatly promoted by a consortium of university presses, which have initiated a Panitikan series especially designed for courses in Philippine literature. As well, commercial presses such as Solidarity, New Day, and Anvil are publishing numerous titles of serious literature.[31]

New literary influences for Philippine literature written in English are evident in F. Sionil Jose's novel *Viajero* (1992), and the novels of Linda Ty-Casper, *A Small Party in a Garden* (1988), Michelle Skinner, *Mango Seasons* (1996), and Carlos Constes, *Longitude: A Novel* (1998). In the United States, two Filipina expatriates, Ninotchka Rosca (*State of War*, 1988) and Jessica Hagedorn (*Dogeaters*, 1990), are writing powerful surrealistic novels that critique Philippine society, and they are finding an appreciative international audience. Meanwhile, a number of new Philippine-based writers have produced masterful works that indicate that the use of English, while reduced, is not at an end.[32] At the same time, the continued influence of the former "underground" left is clear in novels from leftist writers groups such as the 1990 title *Sebyo* and Ruth Firmeza's *Gera* (1991). Finally, other writers of the left include Levy Balgos de la Cruz, whose 1989 collection of short fiction appeared as *Bukal ng Tubig at Apoy*, and Jason Montana, who produced *Clearing* (1987), a volume of poems in English.

Poetry continues to be enlivened by the work of a number of authors, most especially Virgilio Almario, who has been described as the voice of contemporary poetry in Tagalog. Some of his best works, including *Mga Retrato at Rekwerdo* (*Photographs and Souvenirs*, 1984) and the 1989 *Palipad-Hangin* (*Hints*), are firmly based in the poetic traditions of the Philippine past while thoroughly a part of the historical present. Also influential in the contemporary period is Jose F. Lacaba, whose poetry is written in the idiom of the common people, while retaining a sharp edge in its sparse style of expression, Cirilo Bautista, whose collection *The Archipelago* (1970) has few equals; and Alfrredo N. Salanga, whose works include *Commentaries, Meditations, Messages* (1985) and *Turtle Voices in Uncertain Weather* (1989).

Literary criticism has attempted to define a new direction for the nation's literature in the post-martial law age with the strongest contender being the Marxist activists from the Marcos era. Within this recent tradition are Gelacio Guillermo's *Ang Panitikan ng Pambansang Demokrasya* (1990), Alice Guillermo's *Images of Change* (1988), and Elmer Ordonez's *The Other View* (1989). Meanwhile, still other academic writers have put forward new alternatives for the study of Philippine literature that include post-structuralist and post-colonial approaches such as Cristina Pantoja Hidalgo's, *A Gentle Subversion: Essays on Philippine Fiction in English* (1998), and Priscelina Patajo-Legasto's *Philippine Post-Colonial Studies* (1993), Soledad Reyes's *Kritisismo* (1992), and Isagani Cruz's *Beyond Futility* (1984).

Since the restoration of a democratic form of government in 1986, women's writing has taken on a great importance. Central to this new development such writers as Joi Barrios, whose poetry in *Minatamis at Iba Pang Tula ng Pag-Ibig* (*Sweetened Fruit and Other Love Poems*, 1998) ranges from her revolutionary roots to occasionally satirical tongue-in-cheek collections of love poems. Meanwhile, University of Hawai'i Pilipino instructor Ruth Elynia S. Mabanglo has produced the stark *Kilalanin Ang Bayan Ko* (*Get to Know My Country*, 1986). This movement has progressed far enough so that there has also emerged a field of feminist literary criticism as represented by Sylvia Mendez Ventura's *Feminist Reading of Philippine Fiction* (1994). Also appearing in the recent democratic period is openly gay writing as anthologized by J. C. Neil Garcia and Danton Remoto in their *Ladlad: An Anthology of Philippine Gay Writing* (1994) and its sequel *Ladlad 2* (n.d.). Openly lesbian writings have not emerged as a separate literary movement, but individual works have been included in anthologies of women writers.[33]

THE *KOMIK*

Another form of Philippine literature is the ubiquitous *komiks* that cater to the reading tastes of many millions of Filipinos. Like their American counterparts, the Philippine *komiks* began as entertainment supplements in the vernacular magazines of the pre-World War II period. After the war, these became independent publications and by the 1980s had blossomed into approximately fifty titles that had a combined circulation of over two million with a huge diffusion rate as friends and neighbors passed and traded the *komiks* between themselves. Since the *komiks* are very inexpensive, this was a very affordable form of literature, and they are readily available at almost any magazine stall and even corner stores (sari-sari stores). The *komik* format is also used to mold opinion by a variety of agencies, such as government agriculture programs and private fertilizer companies seeking to disseminate the latest planting instructions to farmers.

By far the most frequent use of the *komiks* is for entertainment. The use of detailed graphics and simple dialogue in captions and dialogue balloons allows even those with a minimal reading ability to follow the stories of their heroes. Even when a part of other magazines, such as *Liwayway*, the *komiks* developed their own stable of stock characters and situations. Sometimes these were modeled on American models, but they also included the barrio doctor and the local Chinese merchant. These *komiks* were intended only for humor, but when the *komik* became an independent publication, they became a vehicle to present short stories and serialize novels. The original humorous function of the medium remained but was supplemented by soap opera-style romances, adventures, supernatural tales, and stories based in the Filipino folk tradition. It was through this development of the medium that the *komik* became linked to more "highbrow" Philippine literary developments, and writers such as Clodualdo del Mundo began to write for this literature along with his writing of standard prose for print journals.

Female characters are represented rather strongly in the *komiks*, but these women are often associated with the supernatural, such as Darna, the simple barrio girl who happens to possess supernatural powers (a Philippine-style Wonder Woman), and the lovely siren Dyesebel. The former became especially popular and was featured in a whole series of Tagalog movies in the 1960s. Male hero figures predictably right wrongs against seemingly insurmountable odds thanks to their incredible powers, and they always emerge triumphant whether the setting is urban or rural. Women are also the center of the extremely popular love story *komiks* as they rise above tyrannical lovers, unreasonable family demands, and exacting parents, including cruel mothers-in-law. These stories, especially, deliver powerful messages of esteemed social values and behavior that are not lost on the *komik*'s reading public. Beyond geographic setting and the cultural emphasis of various universal human themes that are present in the romance stories, the *komiks* also utilize Filipino folk sensibilities and myths. This utilization is especially evident in the retelling of epic stories and myths such that traditional stories and their characters, motifs, images, and perceptions are retold in the *komik* format. This Philippine folk tradition incorporates such elements as supernatural tales of monsters, vampires, talismans, and enchanted forests in its reinforcement of cultural beliefs and symbols.[34]

As is true of other aspects of Philippine culture, the Filipino people have incorporated various forms of foreign literature and the languages of Spanish and English while retaining elements of their own culture that are refracted through the use of these new mediums. Philippine reality, values, perceptions, traditions, and social-political concerns are evident in the nation's literary genres propagated in a variety of language and dialects. Philippine literature will continue to evolve such that the outsider will recognize its basic forms but will puzzle over the style and content, but these will make perfect sense to the Filipino literary consumer.

NOTES

1. This discussion relies heavily on David Baradas's pamphlet, *Sining Biswal: An Essay on Philippine Ethnic Visual Arts* (Manila: Cultural Center of the Philippines, 1992). Three years earlier, Alice G. Guillermo also wrote the pamphlet *Sining Biswal: An Essay on Philippine Visual Arts* (Manila: Cultural Center of the Philippines, 1989), and I have drawn materials from pages 4–8 of her work.

2. This discussion was aided by Regalado Trota Jose's pamphlet, *Sining Biswal: An Essay on the Spanish Influence on Philippine Visual Arts* (Manila: Cultural Center of the Philippines, 1992).

3. See Nick Joaquin and Luciano P. R. Santiago, *The World of Damian Domingo* (Manila: Metropolitan Museum of Manila, 1990).

4. See Alice G. Guillermo's pamphlet, *Sining Biswal: An Essay on the American Colonial and Contemporary Traditions in Philippine Visual Arts* (Manila: Cultural Center of the Philippines, 1994).

5. Rodolfo Paras-Perez, *Edades and the 13 Moderns* (Manila: Cultural Center of the Philippines, 1995).

6. Melbourne International Biennial, "Philippines: Gerardo Tan," in *Melbourne International Biennial Program* (Melbourne, Australia: Melbourne International Biennial 1999), 201–208.

7. Jose, 44–46.

8. Alice G. Guillermo, *Color in Philippine Life and Art* (Manila: Cultural Center of the Philippines, 1992), 15.

9. Alice G. Guillermo, "The Popular Arts," in *International Popular Culture* 1, no. 1 (1980): 53–59.

10. This discussion is based on Valerio Nofuente's wonderful article, "The Jeepney: Vehicle as Art," *International Popular Culture*, 1, no. 1 (1980): 38–47.

11. Florentino H. Hornedo, *Panitikan: An Essay on Philippine Ethnic Literature* (Manila: Cultural Center of the Philippines, 1992), 1–21, 29–39, and Bienvenido Lumbera, *Revaluation, 1997: Essays on Philippine Literature, Cinema and Popular Culture* (Manila: University of Santo Tomas Publishing House, 1997), 5–6.

12. Jaime Biron Polo, *Panitikan: An Essay on the Spanish Influence on Philippine Literature* (Manila: Cultural Center of the Philippines, 1992), 4–10.

13. Ibid., 10–14, and Lumbera, 8–9.

14. Reynaldo C. Ileto, *Pasyon and Revolution: Popular Movements in the Philippines, 1840–1910* (Quezon City: Ateneo de Manila University Press, 1979).

15. Doreen G. Fernandez, *Panitikan: An Essay on Philippine Literature* (Manila: Cultural Center of the Philippines, 1989), 15.

16. Lumbera, 9–12.

17. Polo, 29–33.

18. Jose Rizal, *Noli Me Tangere*, trans. Ma. Soledad Lacson-Locsin (Honolulu: University of Hawai'i Press, 1997) and *El Filibusterismo*, trans. Ma. Soledad Lacson-Locsin (Makati, Metro Manila: Bookmark, Inc.).

19. See Rodney J. Sullivan, *Exemplar of Americanism: The Philippine Career of Dean C. Worcester* (Ann Arbor: Center for South and Southeast Asian Studies, University of Michigan, 1991) for a biography of the man who brought the case, and Daniel B. Schirmer and Stephen R. Shalom, *The Philippine Reader: A History of Colonialism, Neocolonialism, Dictatorship, and Resistance* (Boston: South End Press, 1987), 49–51, for a document "Taft's Terms of Probation, El Renacimiento," criticizing the American government's heavy-handed approach to the case.

20. For a quick biography, see Quijano de Manila, "Viva Villa!" in *The National Artists of the Philippines* (Manila: Cultural Center of the Philippines, 1998), 347–372.

21. Salvador P. Lopez, *Literature and Society: Essays on Life and Letters* (Manila: Philippine Book Guild, 1940).

22. See N.V.M. Gonzalez, *The Bread of Salt and Other Stories* (Seattle: University of Washington Press, 1993), and two titles by Carlos Bulosan, *America Is in the Heart* (Seattle: University of Washington Press, 2000) and *On Becoming Filipino: Selected Writings of Carlos Bulosan*, ed. E. San Juan, Jr. (Philadelphia, PA: Temple University Press, 1995).

23. Luis H. Francia, ed., *Brown River, White Ocean: An Anthology of Twentieth-Century Philippine Literature in English* (New Brunswick, NJ: Rutgers University Press, 1993).

24. Resil B. Mojares, *Panitikan: An Essay on the American Colonial and Contemporary Traditions in Philippine Literature* (Manila: Cultural Center of the Philippines, 1994), 9–11, 16–17, 19, 34–36.

25. Ibid., 39–41.

26. Ibid., 30–31, 35.

27. Andres Cristobal Cruz, "Filipino Literature and Commitment," in Cultural Center of the Philippines, *The National Artists of the Philippines* (Manila: Cultural Center of the Philippines, 1998), 189–93.

28. Mojares, 12–13.

29. Jose's five Rosales saga novels have been published in the United States by the Modern Library of New York. They include *Po-on* published as *Dusk* (1998), a double volume titled *Don Vicente* (1999) that combined *Tree* and *My Brother My Executioner*, and another double volume *The Samsons* (2000) that finished the five-part series by combining *The Pretenders* and *Mass*.

30. Mojares, 20, 29. For examples of the socially committed literature during the martial law period, see Alfrredo Navarro Salanga, in *Writings in Protest, 1972–1985* (1993) and, with co-editor Esther M. Pacheco, *Versus, Philippine Protest Poetry, 1983–1986* (1986), both published by the Ateneo de Manila University Press.

31. Bienvenido Lumbera, "A Report on Philippine Writing Since 1986," in Japan Foundation, *Contemporary Philippine Culture: Selected Papers on Arts and Education* (Manila: 1998), 83–85.

32. Ninotchka Rosca, *State of War* (New York: Fireside Books, 1988) and Jessica Hagedorn, *Dogeaters* (New York: Penguin Books, 1991). Prominent among the new writers in English are Alfred Yuson, *Great Philippine Jungle Energy Cafe* (1996), Jose Y. Dalisay, Jr., *Killing Time in a Warm Place* (1992), and Eric Gamalinda, *The Empire of Memory* (1992).

33. Lumbera, "A Report on Philippine Writing, Since 1986," 86, and Joi Barrios, *Minatamis at Iba pang Tula ng Pag-Ibig* (Sweetened Fruit and Other Love Poems) (Pasig, Metro Manila: Anvil Publishing Co., 1998).

34. Clodualdo Del Mundo, Jr., "Komiks: An Industry, a Potent Medium, Our National 'Book,' and Pablum of Art Appreciation," in Clodualdo Del Mundo Jr.'s, ed., *Philippine Mass Media: A Book of Readings* (Manila: Communication Foundation of Asia, 1986), 179–185; Soledad S. Reyes, "The Philippine Komiks," *International Popular Culture* 1, no. 1 (1980): 14–23; Pio C. Estepa, SVD, "The Myth of Love in Filipino Komiks," in Leonardo N. Mercado, SVD, ed. *Filipino Thought on Man and Society* (Tacloban City, Philippines: Divine Word University Publications, 1980), 42–56; and John A. Lent, "Comic Art in the Philippines," *Philippine Studies* 46 (Second Quarter 1998): 236–248.

SUGGESTED READINGS

Carbo, Nick. *Returning a Borrowed Tongue: An Anthology of Filipino and Filipino American Poetry.* Minneapolis, MN: Coffee House Press, 1995.

Casal, Fr. Gabriel, et al. *The People and Art of the Philippines.* Los Angeles: University of California at Los Angeles, Museum of Cultural History, 1981.

Guillermo, Alice G. "The Evolution of Philippine Art," in *Southeast Asian Art Today.* ed. Joyce van Fenema. ed., Singapore: Roeder Publications, 1996, 118–163.

Ordonez, Elmer A. *Nationalist Literature: A Centennial Forum.* Quezon City: University of the Philippines Press, 1996.

Pacific Asia Museum. *100 Years of Philippine Painting.* Pasadena, CA: Pacific Asia Museum, 1984.

4

Architecture and Housing

A COUNTRY'S architecture tells much about its physical environment and climatic conditions, the role of the family, impact of religion on everyday life, general prosperity levels, and how individual families and the wider communities of town and nation fit together. Architecture in the Philippines also informs the perceptive observer about the country's history since there are functioning examples of architecture from each era in almost every town in the country. Much of the rural population still lives in a *bahay kubo* (*nipa* or palm house), which long preceded the Spandiards' arrival, they worship in a Spanish-style church located on the town plaza, and conduct public business in American-style municipal buildings. Meanwhile, the country's modern suburbs have business districts and shopping malls that are built in accordance with modern international architectural trends. This discussion of Philippine architecture starts with the family home and then discusses the wider community and the country's religious and public lives, while always noting the impact of various historical styles and influences.

HOUSING AND COMMUNITY

The current housing of the country's national minorities and that of many rural farm families across the country provide an excellent look into the types of housing that existed long before European contact. Other than the cave dwellings of some early peoples whose archeological remains have been discovered in the Tabon caves on the island of Palawan and the lean-tos of nomadic hunters and gatherers, Filipinos have long made sturdy houses that were well adapted to local conditions and needs. The primary characteristic of pre-Hispanic housing is the impact of the geographical and climatic environment on both the design of the housing stock and the materials used in construction.

The clearest example of the environment's impact is found on the northern island group of the Batanes, where the Ivatan people build strong fortresslike limestone houses that can withstand the fierce monsoons that annually ravage the northern Philippine coast. Other peoples have specialized housing needs, such as the seafaring Samal people of the southern Sulu archipelago who build their houses above the water on top of tall poles to which their boats are tied. In the same area, the Badjao people build and live in boathouses where they spend virtually their entire lives since they rarely venture onto land.

Among the many different minority peoples of the central Cordillera Mountains of Luzon Island, there are a number of stylistic variations in housing stock, but they all share the need to build houses that will offer protection from the cold mountain climate. There are, therefore, some common characteristics of house construction, including the use of wooden posts to raise the building off the cold and damp ground and wood planks for walls and floors to make the central one-room living compartment relatively airtight. As well, cooking is done inside the home, which gives added warmth, but with an absence of ventilation, the smoky interiors create significant health problems, especially for young children. Among many groups, the steep roof above the living area is made into an internal rice storage area with the addition of a plank ceiling. Frequently, too, a wooden ring is added to the wood house posts to prevents rats from getting into the house, and a ladder entrance to the door of the dwelling is pulled in every night, giving the occupants protection against intruders. Among the people of the Cordillera, the common practice is to assemble their houses close to each other in groupings of ten to forty for mutual protection and as near to their fields as possible. Some groups pool their resources and build separate communal sleeping buildings for the older children and single adults of the village, leaving husbands and wives in private with the smaller children.[1]

In stark contrast to the homes of the mountain peoples is the *bahay kubo* that was traditionally used by lowland Filipinos and can still be found throughout the country. For most people in the Philippines, it is the heat of the tropics rather than the colder mountain air that poses a problem. Since there is less available wood in the lowlands than the mountains, the primary building material of the *bahay kubo* is bamboo as well as rattan and various grasses that are used for roofing. This housing structure is also raised above the ground on either wood or bamboo poles, which spares the inhabitants of some of the effects of humidity. Unlike the mountain province houses,

Native hut (*bahay kubo*) being constructed. Courtesy of the Ambeth Ocampo Collection.

the raised *bahay kubo* uses the open area beneath the house for air circulation because the flooring is made of bamboo slats that allow the air to come up into the house after being cooled underneath away from the direct heat of the sun. Still more air is allowed into the house through large open window areas that can be closed off with a framed woven mat of flattened bamboo.

The roof of the *bahay kubo* is steep like the roofs of the mountain dwellers, but the purpose in the lowlands is not to create a rice storage area above the living quarters, but to allow hot air to rise away from the inhabitants. It is also common to have a small porch area in the front of the house that serves as a foyer and assists in keeping the house cool as does the overhang from the sloped roof. Meanwhile, internal partitions are kept to a minimum to further allow the air to circulate freely. In most homes, there is a main area, or *sala*, where the children play and the family eats and sleeps. A separate area, usually in the rear of the house, is reserved for cooking and cleaning. Because the *bahay kubo* is so open, the cooking smoke found in the mountain houses is never a problem. During the rainy season, the raised house is immune from flooding, while water quickly slides off the sloped roof.

Religious beliefs have long been a part of house construction and went into determining the site, time to build, and position of the house. There were rituals that had to be conducted before work was started and many details that had to be followed, such as making sure that the number of steps in a staircase is not divisible by three, which is a bad luck number, and cutting bamboo only at certain times of the year to avoid misfortune. Sometimes a

Francia house in Magdalena, Laguna, was constructed of stone and wood in 1890, thus combining Spanish and native architecture. Courtesy of the Intramuros Administration Photo Collection.

valuable object such as a gold coin was placed beneath the principle house post, and hot peppers were spread on the ground under the house to keep evils spirits away. While the *bahay kubo* was usually not decorated for religious purposes, the homes of mountain people frequently incorporated the skulls of water buffalo and sometime of humans killed in battle. Muslims in the south also decorated the exterior of their homes, especially their large ancestral homes, with curved roofs and woodcarvings in religious motifs. Even today, it is not uncommon for Filipinos to invite the local parish priest to visit a new home and to give a blessing for the house and its occupants.

When the Spanish first arrived, they built multilevel homes and government buildings out of stone until the frequent earthquakes taught them the value of lowland Filipino architecture. The resulting buildings soon developed into a style called *mestizo* (mixed blood) architecture. These structures, the *bahay na bato* (house of stone), were only built two floors high and utilized house posts that interlocked with crossbeams and only used stone for the ground level, which closed off and allowed for the use of the space underneath the living area, while the second floor living area used wood for its walls. Later, nineteenth-century improvements in building methods and the economic rise of the *mestizo sangley* (Chinese and Filipino mixed blood) saw a return of two-story stone houses especially in some provincial towns such as Taal, Batangas, and Vigan, Ilocus Sur, where this entrepreneurial group lived in large numbers. Whichever structural style was adopted, the Spanish-influenced homes were conspicuous in their use of room partitioning, grand monumental staircases of up to two meters in width, and aesthetic additions such as iron grillwork, glass, or thinly sliced *capiz* shell sliding windows and the occasional tiled roof. The airiness of the Filipino home was retained by incorporating as many windows as possible and by the addition of a back porch area, both of which were on the second floor.[2]

The Iberian influence also had an impact on the physical development of the native Filipino communities in which the houses were located. One of Spain's principle objectives was to Christianize the native people. To do this, the permanent town settlement was introduced because the priests wanted as many of the natives as possible to live within the sound of the bells of the church. Beyond this general goal were detailed plans for the layout of the town. In each town, the focus of activity was the plaza, which was dominated by the church and the *convento* (priest's house) located at one of the four sides of the plaza, usually the one with the highest elevation. When a town hall was later constructed, it was most often placed directly opposite the church, with the town's market either adjacent to it or somewhere close by. The remaining two sides of the plaza were occupied either by permanent stores or the impressive homes of the town's principal citizens.

In coastal communities, the plaza was near the landing of the port, with the church clearly visible from the water. In this case, the church also served a defensive function as a fortress protecting the town from pirates and attacking *moros* (Muslim Filipinos, from the Spanish term for the Muslim Moors of Spain). The plaza was the location of almost all public affairs and of those religious activities not actually held in the church such as, perhaps, a religious play. Meanwhile, the town's streets branched off from the church dominated plaza and were laid out in a grid pattern that was imposed, in part, as an attempt to rationalize the town population. The municipal area surrounding the plaza was known as the *poblacion*, while the other parts of the town branching off from the town center became known as barrios. As a result of this physical structuring, the towns created during the Spanish colonial period soon fulfilled social, political, and economic roles in addition to the religious function that first led to their creation.

The American period did not see any major changes in the country's architecture with regard to housing other than the introduction of the small single-family chalet housing style for the growing middle class and new building materials such as reinforced concrete and galvanized metal roofing. Major housing changes did occur in the postwar period with the introduction of sprawling one story and split level homes of the wealthy in gated communities. Many of the earliest of these suburban developments served the rising middle class and offered a bit of an escape from the congestion of downtown areas. Somewhat later, more up-scale developments appeared with guard posts to keep out unwanted visitors and curved streets with speed bumps to prevent the introduction of public transportation. The wealthiest of these subdivisions have their own churches and community centers and are near to shopping areas and restaurants, so the residents do not have to go far from home for their basic necessities and conveniences.

Another development has been the appearance of prestigious apartments and condominiums located either in the suburbs of Makati or Mandaluyong and, to a lesser degree, along Manila Bay. The less well-to-do have access to a variety of apartment buildings, duplexes, and prefabricated homes, which at least offer a measure of privacy and a sense of having one's own space. Urban residents below the subsistence level, however, are forced to live as illegal squatters in horrific shanties made out of plywood, tin sheets, and other inferior materials. Shanty areas dot the urban landscape and are, in effect, independent towns within major metropolitan areas. Of metro Manila's current population of about ten million, perhaps more than one million are living in these squalid conditions.

CHURCHES AND MOSQUES

When Miguel Lopez de Legaspi arrived in Cebu in 1565, he had in his company a number of priests who were as much a part of the colonial effort as was Legaspi and his fellow conquistadors; in fact, a priest, Father Andres Urdaneta, even served as the navigator for the expedition. These facts are not a simple curiosity but highlight the close unity of church and state in sixteenth-century Spain. In a real sense, religion and the priests of missionary orders, the Franciscans, Dominicans, Augustinians, Jesuits, and Augustinian Recollects, played a crucial role in affairs of state, and their importance was mirrored in colonial architecture. Not only was the church the most impressive structure on every town's plaza, the cathedral was one of the first structures erected in Manila, and the first stone building in the capital was the residence of Bishop Domingo Salazar. Structures for the civilian government were important too, but they were secondary to the church.

The oldest surviving stone church is the Church of San Agustin in Manila, the construction of which was started in the mid-1580s. Since then the building has survived a number of earthquakes and the devastation from the recapture of the city by American forces in 1945. In addition, there are also a number of especially important churches in the country that are referred to as basilicas, including the churches for the Santo Nino in Cebu, Jesus Nazareno in the Quiapo district of Manila, and the Manila Cathedral. Other large religious buildings were the monasteries that each of the missionary

The San Agustin Church in the old walled city is the oldest
Christian church in Asia, completed in 1607. Photo by the
author.

orders built in Manila and other provincial cities to serve as regional headquarters and the residences of the diocesan bishops. The Archbishop in Manila also required a large residence and office for his administrative work.

As newly arrived Spanish priests began to fan out around the archipelago
to convert the native population, their churches were first made of wood,
bamboo, and thatch. These materials were readily available, and the local
population was skilled in building with them. Over time, however, these
early structures were replaced with more permanent ones made of stone or,
frequently, roughly hewn blocks of coral reef. The buildings were fashioned

in conformity with the reforms of the Council of Trent (1545–1563), which emphasized preaching's central role for reform and instruction, so the architectural emphasis was on the strategic and elevated placement of the altar and pulpit. The front entrance often had a very large main door that was only opened on special occasions, such as the town fiesta, while smaller doors on either side served for everyday use. Most of the building's decorative detail was placed in the front to maximize its impact when viewed from the plaza. The architectural style of an individual church seems to have been a function of what was in vogue when the building was constructed, with the earliest being in the baroque motif followed by neo-gothic and rococo (for exterior decoration) until the latter part of the nineteenth century when the eclectic revivalist style became fashionable. Whatever style was chosen, the walls of many churches were very thick, up to almost two meters in some cases, to secure them against the archipelago's frequent seismic activity. Buttresses of all shapes and sizes were also added to further improve the chances of surviving an earthquake.

An extremely important structure was the bell tower, which was usually a part of the church building but could be a separate structure as a precaution against collateral earthquake damage to the church should the tower collapse. In either case, the country's frequent earthquakes required that all bell towers be squat and thick walled, with each floor smaller than the one beneath it. In addition to calling the people to mass, the bells heralded special events such as marriages and funerals and were even used for a variety of secular purposes, including warning people of a fire or an enemy raid. At night along some coasts, flares would be lit in one belfry after another to warn the next town when *moro* raiders approached.

The priest's house, the *convento*, was a separate structure to the side of or behind the church, but the two could be connected by a bridge or covered walkway. The *convento* usually had a stone first floor and a wooden second story but could be entirely of stone. While its primary function was as a residence, the *convento* was often much more, and it was built large to accommodate the priest's many obligations and activities. For example, the priest was frequently called upon to host visiting officials so there had to be a number of bedrooms and a substantial cooking and dining area. As well, since church and state were a single enterprise in the Spanish world, the priest and his missionary activity was heavily subsidized by the Spanish crown. In exchange, priests were expected to oversee the civil affairs of their parish communities, and this made them *de facto* government representatives. The priest oversaw the town's school, finances, public works projects, collection of taxes, and the fulfillment of *corvee* (state required public works labor) obligations. As well, the priest took the lead role in organizing town defenses against bandits and *moros*, and some even became quite accomplished at the design and construction of military fortifications. The church and the *convento* were also used as refuges during enemy raids or severe tropical storms and as storehouses for food and munitions. Since the construction of municipal halls was not a great priority, they were usually made of bamboo, making them unfit for many governmental activities. It even would not be unheard of for the *convento* to be used as the town courthouse and jail.[3]

The architecture of church buildings did not change drastically until after the Second World War. While the Japanese victory in 1941–1942 caused relatively little property damage, the country's liberation saw fierce destruction throughout the country. The nation's churches were primary victims, since Japanese troops used churches as fortifications. For example, of the country's six diocesean cathedrals only the one in Vigan in Ilocos Sur province survived. Many lesser churches and *conventos* were also lost, and the main cathedral in Manila was severely damaged during the savage fighting that marked the capital's liberation.

In the rebuilding process, a new generation of American trained architects adopted new international styles for the country's new church buildings. One of the best examples of these new styles is the Church of the Holy Sacrifice on the University of the Philippines campus. Designed by Leandro V. Locsin, the church is in the shape of an inverted bowl that is open all around its perimeter. Across the street is the campus's Protestant chapel with its distinctive saddle-like structure that makes abundant use of windows. The redesign of the nation's churches was given impetus in the 1960s by Vatican II, which reversed the dictates of the Council of Trent with regard to the relationship between the priest and the congregation. Now the emphasis is on greater participation and visibility of the rites conducted at the altar. The dominating pulpit has disappeared, and the priest stands before the congregation with only a lectern in front of him. In some cases, such as in the Church of the Holy Sacrifice, the altar is placed in the middle of the circular church, and the priest must address the faithful in the manner of theater in the round.

While Protestantism entered the Philippines under the open religious policy of the American regime, it did not win the large numbers of converts that its missionaries sought. The principle Protestant structures are located in Manila and a few of the country's other larger cities and towns. In general, they follow the neo-Gothic style frequently associated with Protestant church buildings in the United States or are relatively nondescript in style. The University of the Philippines chapel, however, is one of a handful of exceptions.

Main cathedral of the indigenous Christian church Iglesia ni Cristo. Courtesy of the Cultural Center of the Philippines Library Collection.

The most interesting recent development in church architecture has come from the rapidly growing indigenous Christian church Iglesia ni Cristo (INC or Church of Christ), which was started by Felix Manalo in 1914. After the war and until today under Manalo's son Erano, who now heads the church, the INC has pioneered a truly stunning form of architecture thanks to the work of a number of talented architects such as Juan Nakpil, Carlos Santos-Viola, and Raul Villanueva. In 1971, the church even created its own construction firm to assure uniformity in the church's buildings from its cathedral and administrative center in Quezon City to much smaller structures all of which employ exterior neo-Gothic vertical support columns with tall narrow windows between, interlocking trapezoids, and rosette motifs, as well as towers and spires that seem to shoot into the sky, giving each building an imposing presence that its true size might not otherwise warrant. In the larger buildings, there are separate entrances for men and women, who sit on either side of the center aisle. Focus is directed toward a dais upon which the Bible is placed and from where sermons are delivered. In the rear, there is a stage for a choir, and the larger buildings even have baptistry pools for adult immersion.[4]

The Islamic peoples of the southern islands built their first mosques as early as the late fourteenth century, long before the arrival of the Spaniards. In the Filipino Muslim architectural tradition, the first mosques were three-tiered structures made of wood and bamboo, which resembled Hindu temples found on the Indonesian island of Bali or the pagodas typical of Japan or China. Over time and with direct influence from the Middle East, the style changed to the more easily identifiable Islamic design of the onion-shaped, domed building with towers or minarets at the four corners. As a local modification, the top of the dome is frequently decorated with a crescent and star ornament and sometimes carved designs representing mythic creatures. While easily identifiable as mosques, those in the Philippines vary somewhat from buildings in the Middle East. The elevated pulpit (*mimbar*) found in the traditional mosque is either absent, having been replaced by a raised platform or a chair, or it is noticeably lower in height. Because of the region's frequency of seismic activity, the minarets are lower, too, leaving the tower more decorative than functional.

Instead of using the minaret, the *bilal* (prayer reader) will call the faithful to prayer by standing inside the mosque while facing the *mihrab* (prayer niche) that is in the direction of Mecca and beating special drums to make the announcement. Since the advent of electrification, the *bilal* will also use a microphone and loudspeakers attached to the minarets. The typical mosque will have only a few windows and separate entrances for men and women. The men stay in the main prayer hall while the women are not allowed beyond a wooden screen in the back. In a manner similar to differences in Spanish churches, there are two types of mosques. The true mosque hosts Friday noon prayer sessions, sermons, and special ceremonies and is a large permanent structure built on a stone foundation and located near water. These buildings can accommodate at least forty people. Meanwhile, the lesser structures, which are referred to as either *ranggar* or *laggal* depending on the ethnic group, are on the level of a chapel. Afternoon prayer sessions can be held there for the convenience of the villagers, especially during the Ramadan fasting season, but these buildings are not used for major religious ceremonies.

Like Roman Catholic churches during the Spanish era, the mosque accomodates a number of activities and frequently has a school and library. The structure may have additional meeting rooms, and the prayer hall can be used for conferences and meetings. The mosque complex thereby has a significance that includes cultural, social, and political, as well as religious functions. Prominent mosques include the King Faisal Mosque on the Mindanao State University campus and the one built in Manila's Quiapo district in the 1970s that incorporates stained-glass panels by artist Antonio Dumlao. This latter structure is near the Catholic Quiapo Church that houses the important Christian image of the Black Nazarene. The juxtaposition of the two religious structures symbolically underscores the presence of these two world religions in the Philippines.[5] Another symbolically significant positioning is the large mosque in Zamboanga City, located within sight of the Spanish Fort Pilar (first built in 1635, abandoned in 1663 and rebuilt in 1719) that played a key role in gaining the submission of the southwestern Islamic islands to Iberian authority by the mid-nineteenth century.

Public Spaces and Public Buildings

The Spanish, built fortifications throughout the archipelago to protect their settlements from Dutch and British rivals as well as Chinese pirates from the north and *moro* slave raiders from the south. In the process of building these defenses, they introduced Filipinos to stone and mortar construction methods. The Muslims also had effective wall defenses or *kuta* made of palm trees with dirt filling between that were reinforced with light Dutch- and Portuguese-made artillery. When Spaniards transferred from Cebu to Manila, they raised wooden walls for their new settlement, which was built on top of the palisade of defeated native ruler Raja Soliman. Within two decades, this original structure was gradually replaced by stone walls laid out roughly in the shape of a pentagon and having platforms for cannon that faced out to Manila Bay and commanded the Pasig River alongside the fortress. On the landward eastern side and along some of the walls facing the sea, a series of moats were added for further protection.[6]

When completed, the large walled-in area became the center for Spanish temporal and religious power and was called the *Intramuros*, or "the area inside the walls," and its five square kilometers was reserved exclusively for government and religious buildings and the homes of Spaniards. Seven churches were located here, the most prominent being the San Agustin Church and the Manila Cathedral, as well as the residences of church officials and heads of the monastic orders plus their monasteries. Of the government buildings, one of the most important was the Ayuntamiento (city hall) that contained a number of administrative offices with powers and responsibilities that extended far beyond the actual city. Nearby was the Palacio Real (Royal Palace), the home of the governor, that was destroyed by an earthquake in 1863 at which point the governor moved into his summer house, the Malacanang, located up the Pasig River from the walled city. This large two-story *bahay na bato* house became the official Spanish governor's residence until 1898 when American governor-generals took up residence there followed by Philippine presidents beginning in 1935. In 1986, President Corazon Aquino decided that she could not bring herself to live in a house formerly occupied by Ferdinand and Imelda Marcos, so Malacanang has since been turned into a museum.

In addition to religious and governmental buildings, the *Intramuros* also contained a number of charitable institutions, including two orphanages and four hospitals. One hospital each was reserved for Spaniards, Chinese, and lepers, with the fourth, the San Juan de Dios Hospital, being a charitable institution open to the public. Also within the walls were a number of schools, the oldest of which was the Dominican institution the Universidad de Santo Tomas, founded in 1611. There were six other colleges in the *Intramuros*, but caution should be advised when reading the word *college*, since these institutions were not always what would today be considered colleges, but were boarding schools and seminaries until the nineteenth century, at which time Filipinos were also admitted. The two most prominent colleges that opened to Filipino students were the Jesuit school the Ateneo de Manila and the Universidad de Santo Tomas. In 1927, the latter school transferred to its present location in the Sampaloc area of Manila in a facility that was specially designed for the earthquake-prone city. Its imposing main building has twenty-four separate sections and incorporates soft materials between the beams, walls, and floors that give the structure elasticity to withstand even the strongest of quakes. By the mid-nineteenth century, therefore, the residents of the walled city and eventually a select number of Chinese and Filipinos beyond the walls had access to facilities that offered the era's standard of medical care and education.[7]

The area outside the walls, in effect the rest of the country, was called the *Extramuros*, and the homes of the natives surrounded the walls. It was from these Filipino neighborhoods that the various districts of the contemporary city of Manila, such as Paco, Tondo, Quiapo, and Ermita, would eventually be created. In addition, there was one section of the city reserved for the Chinese, who were essential to the galleon trade that linked Spanish Mexico with China and provided Manila's Spanish population with an abundant source of commercial income. Despite their prominent role as the link between Canton and Manila, the Chinese were rigorously confined in their *de facto* ghetto, called the *Parian*, and could not travel to or reside in other parts of the archipelago. The primary reason for this restrictive policy was a desire to keep the Chinese focused exclusively on the profitable trade, but there were also security concerns because the Spaniards did not want a large alien population spreading throughout the islands and jeopardizing their control. Over time, some Chinese merchants did gain footholds in major provincial cities, and in the nineteenth century, their *mestizo* descendants were allowed to live in the countryside, which greatly accelerated the colony's entry into the international market economy after the decline of the galleon trade. Meanwhile, in the *Parian*, the Chinese community built a substantial business district, and their main street, the Escolta, became the country's business center in the pre–World War II era.

By the latter years of Spanish rule, Manila's urban growth and activity had already extended beyond the walls of *Intramuros* as exemplified by the growth of the Chinese commercial district and the transfer of the governor's office and residence from the walled city to the Malacanang Palace. The advent of American rule hastened this trend and witnessed the introduction of a new official architectural style. As early as 1901, Governor William Howard Taft appointed Filipino architect Arcadio Arellano as a consultant to the new government, and he began to break from Spanish architectural traditions. Then, in 1904, Philippine commissioner William Cameron Forbes invited noted American architect and city planner Daniel H. Burnham to visit the Philippines to redesign Manila. Burnham was asked to use his recent experience in Washington, D.C., where he updated and enlarged L'Enfant's original schema for the nation's capital. Specifically, he was asked to apply that imperial and monumental style of architecture to the capital of this Asian outpost of the new American empire. Burnham prepared numerous detailed plans for a new government center, street system, parks, and waterways, and recommended William Parsons to carry the project through to its conclusion.

Parsons was hired and served as consulting architect from 1905 to 1914, during which time he used his education at the Ecole des Beaux-Arts in Paris to bring the neoclassical or Greek revival style with its massive columns and steep marble stairwells to the Philippines. His reinforced concrete works included the Manila Hotel, the Philippine General Hospital, the Normal College, and the Army-Navy Club. His influence continued long after his departure and can be seen in the Post Office (completed in 1930) as designed by Juan Arellano; the Legislative Building, upon which Arellano also had a significant influence; and the Manila City Hall, designed by Antonio Toledo. These and many similar structures were heavily damaged during the fight to recapture Manila in 1945, but they were restored and continue today to serve the Philippine government.[8]

Social change was slower in the provinces during the last years of Spanish rule because of the influence of the friars on political affairs and because the attention of the government was focused on events in the capital. As a result, many towns did not even have a *casa real* (town hall), since the parish priest oversaw local affairs and because scarce local funds were required for its construction. Where town halls were built, they were usually made of the lightweight materials used in the *bahay kubo*, which were insufficient for the needs of such a building. Nevertheless, change did begin to occur toward the end of the nineteenth century, especially in wealthier towns and provinces linked to the growing export markets for sugar, tobacco, and abaca. The town halls that emerged in these places were constructed of more substantial materials and fit within the *bahay na bato* style of construction.

Change accelerated in the rural Philippines after the transfer of colonial rule from Spain to the United States. The introduction of the doctrine of the separation of church and state, combined with the American desire to foster democracy in its new possession, shifted support from Catholic priests to new democratically elected municipal and provincial governments. In 1901, the American government in Manila created a national bureau that was charged with overseeing the construction of local government facilities. At the town level, the resulting new *munisipyo* (from the Spanish *municipio*) halls were two-story structures built in a neoclassical style with columns as well as porticoes and vestibules. These were sturdy facilities made of reinforced concrete and galvanized iron roofs, and they had offices for the mayor, a meeting chamber for the town council, offices for local government activities, and a court and jail.

Meanwhile, new provincial governments received executive office buildings, called *kapitolyo*, which mirrored the multiple uses made of the *munisipyos*, since they housed most of the offices needed to conduct provincial affairs. *Kapitolyos* were much larger than town halls and were occasionally three stories with the front entrance located at the top of a steep set of steps. Since the design of these buildings fell under the authority of William Parsons, they reflected the neoclassical style being introduced as part of the American imperial effort. Frequently, the *kapitolyos* had impressive Greek-style columns that stood almost the entire height of the building. Although a prominent provincial town was designated as the capital, the *kapitolyo* itself was usually set off from the town proper for majestic impact, either by being placed within a large park or on a boulevard away from the town center.[9]

Another American priority was the expansion of primary and secondary education, which had received very little attention during most of the Spanish colonial period. It was only in the closing decades of Iberian rule that there was a healthy push for school construction, but even then, most elementary schools in the provinces were small and shabbily constructed. By the close of Spain's rule, it was estimated that only 4,000 to 5,000 students attended school daily. The new American regime occupied these structures, sequestered many other buildings and rented out still others to begin a massive program of education even while thousands of schoolhouses were being built around the country. William Parsons designed fifteen basic floor plans for schools that ranged in size from one-room rural barrio schools, to elementary schools for municipalities, to large provincial capital high schools and technical schools.

The schools were generally called Gabaldon schoolhouses after assemblyman Isauro Gabaldon, who authored the spending bill that got the construction program underway. The elementary schools were single-story buildings while secondary and trade schools could be two stories. Most schools were raised about four feet off the ground to protect them from humidity and had high ceilings to allow hot air to rise and windows along the walls to ensure constant air circulation. Most schools were arranged longitudinally with a single row of rooms that opened on to a porch so there would be no hot and stuffy central corridor between the classrooms. Construction of the Gabaldon-type schools continued until supplanted by the inexpensive "Marcos-type" of pre-fabricated iron frame school houses in the mid-1960s, which incorporated walls of pre-stressed concrete, open door transoms, and wood jalousie windows to facilitate air circulation.[10] The Philippine program of education and school construction has been a resounding success. Schools are currently found in every town and many barrios, and the nation's basic literacy rate is in the ninetieth percentile.

Another change begun during the American period was the transition from traditional open markets with their makeshift stalls to the modern super-market. Although there were some permanent stores in the Chinese sections of Manila and Cebu, most markets were open and not designed well. In the interest of improved sanitation, the Burnham plan included public markets, and Parsons saw many of these through to completion, the first being in the Paco district of Manila. Others followed in Manila and also in other cities and towns as new sanitation laws were passed by local governments leading to the construction of permanent facilities and health inspections.[11] The appearance of the modern grocery store, meanwhile, is a relatively recent post-World War II phenomenon and has been linked with the growth of the country's department stores and malls, since they are usually combined under one roof.

In a sense, the mall is simply a modern air-conditioned version of the old market and the town plaza combined. In the past three decades, metro Ma-nila, especially, has witnessed a phenomenal growth in malls, with each one striving to outdo its predecessors. One early mall was the open shopping area in the suburb of Makati, which has now been replaced by the Galleria, an enclosed multilevel complex covering a couple of city blocks. Meanwhile, the Ali Mall in the Cubao section of Quezon City was eclipsed by the SM City Mall that has since been overshadowed by the SM Mega Mall and the Ortigas Shangri-la Mall. Some of these larger malls even have major art galleries, Catholic chapels, ice skating rinks, multiplex cinemas, fine restau-rants, and supermarkets, as well as the usual array of stores and fast food eateries normally found in any shopping mall.

Amidst these changes and alterations in the style and use of public space, one public institution has remained relatively constant, the cock fighting arena. The cockpit, or *sabungan*, is built in a variety of shapes and sizes but has a number of features that remain constant, such as the square center court with its dirt floor to absorb the blood of the losing rooster, the surrounding arena seating, open sides or wood louvers to allow for maximum ventilation, and a protective roof. Older cockpits are found within the town proper, while the newer *sabungan* are located outside of town. Due to its efficient seating arrangement, cockpits have also been used for political meetings and theatrical performances.[12]

BURIAL PRACTICES AND CEMETERIES

Early Filipinos, just as today's ethnic minorities, took care in the preparation of their dead, whom they sometimes mummified and always buried with care to insure a good existence in the afterlife. Oftentimes, burial practices involved the opening of the original grave for a second internment of the bones in a permanent grave or special burial jar. There was, thus, continuity in the Catholic church's concern for the deceased and the afterlife and in its practice of a second burial of the remaining bones of the deceased in a niche of the church walls or floor with a stone tablet to mark the spot. While the practice of the second burial within a church continued into the twentieth century, the nineteenth century witnessed the greater awareness of the value of sanitation and the creation of special burial grounds outside the town proper. Nowadays, municipalities, as well as religious institutions, own cemeteries that provide a range of services to the family of the deceased.

In more prosperous places, the new cemeteries became well-designed parks for the well-to-do. One such park is the Paco Cemetery built in Manila in 1823. This cemetery is circular in shape and has two concentric walls with niches for the dead and open spaces between for walkways and an elliptical chapel in the center. Similar cemeteries were created in a number of other prominent towns in Ilocos Sur, Laguna, Albay, and Iloilo provinces. In the closing years of Spanish rule, the large La Loma cemetery was build just north of Manila. During the American period, the Chinese and the North cemeteries were opened on adjacent land, while South Cemetery was built in present-day Makati. These burial grounds incorporated a number of architectural styles for their walls and mausoleums, including Chinese, neo-classic, Gothic, modern, and art deco. After World War II, the American Cemetery, built for the Pacific War's fallen, was laid out in a modern memorial park pattern as was its Filipino counterpart the *Libingan ng mga Bayani* (National Heros Cemetery).[13] More recently, the funeral and memorial park industry has become big business, and each park has its own chapel, burial vaults, and mausoleums on acres of green grass and trees with modern sculptures to comfort the bereaved.

CONTEMPORARY PHILIPPINE ARCHITECTS AND THEIR WORKS

The recent development of Philippine architecture has been greatly enhanced by Filipino architects who studied in the United States or Europe and subsequently introduced new styling. During the American colonial period, these new architects worked for the emerging commercial elite of the era, and they were particularly taken with the art deco styling of the Paris Ecole des Beaux-Arts. This stylistic influence can be seen in the 1928 six-story Perez-Samanillo office building on Escolta Street designed by Andres Luna de San Pedro and Juan F. Nakpil, who gave the building a light and airy appearance because of the large windows they employed. Nakpil continued this style in his designs for the Administration Building and the Main Library of the University of the Philippines at its new campus in the Diliman area of Quezon City. Experimentation with new styles continued after 1945 and included the sun-breaks of the international style as seen in Carlos Arguelles's horizontal aluminum baffles that shield the windows of the Phil-Am Life Building. Many of the new architects also took advantage of the strength of reinforced concrete to stretch the limits of cantilevered canopies and balconies. An example of this innovation is Angel E. Nakpil's design of the triangular-shaped Lopez Museum, with its extensive use of cantilevered floors.[14]

Just when Philippine architects appeared to become a part of the international mainstream of architectural currents, a particularly innovative man with only domestic training, Leandro V. Locsin, emerged and made his mark. Locsin used the latest materials but applied them to evoke indigenous building concepts and to give the appearance of floating volume. These characteristics are seen very clearly in his design of the massive Cultural Center of the Philippines inaugurated in 1969. In a bit of acoustic daring, Locsin used concrete walls instead of wood for the center's Main Theater, and throughout the interior, he made copious use of native designs and decorative materials, the most striking being large *capiz* shell chandeliers in the lobby. His other notable works combine mass with grace and include some of the most notable buildings in contemporary metro Manila's financial center of suburban Makati from its Stock Exchange to the Ayala, Tuason, Sarmiento, L. V. L. and First National City Bank buildings. Meanwhile, many of his residential designs make use of traditional Filipino architectural elements such as steep roofs with protective eaves that are combined with the clean lines and geometric abstraction of contemporary design.[15]

Locsin's joining of international and indigenous architectural traditions and designs is also prominent in the work of Gabriel Formoso, whose design for the Asian Institute of Management building includes stone walls and

Headquarters of the San Miguel Corporation designed with a tier effect that mimics rice terraces. Courtesy of the Cultural Center of the Philippines Library Collection.

wooden panels reminiscent of the *bahay na bato*. Another example of the indigenous adoption of Philippine architecture is the San Miguel Corporation's office, designed by the Manosa brothers, Manuel, Jose, and Francisco. The design of the building was inspired by the rice terraces of the central Cordillera and so has tiered balconies edged by flower boxes filled with green shrubbery.[16] This wedding of Filipino romanticism's yearning for indigenous roots while using the latest in construction materials has yielded some buildings of legitimate beauty despite the metropolitan area's headlong rush into a high-rise future.

As the prestigious areas of Manila and the country's other larger cities become developed with new high-rise office towers and condominiums, more middle-class housing developments spread further into the countryside. Like their American counterparts, the inner cities in the Philippines struggle to hold off urban blight so that Manila's current mayor must even renovate the Lacson underpass in Quiapo that is only thirty years old. Meanwhile in Manila and the historically important provinces of Pampanga, Ilocos Sur, and Negros Occidental, many of the *bahay na bato* homes of the nineteenth century are being adopted by private foundations or declared national treasures to preserve their legacy. One of the more innovative efforts is being undertaken in Silay, Negros Occidental, where local civic leader Lyn Gamboa reports that the historic Don Victor Gaston house will serve as a stop on a tour itinerary.[17] Whether modern urban center or provincial town, the Filipino continues to incorporate a variety of foreign architectural styles and new materials to transcend environmental limitations and serve the needs of an ever-evolving society, even as the past is preserved for a new generation.

NOTES

1. See Maria Corazon C. Hila, *Arkitektura: An Essay on Philippine Ethnic Architecture* (Manila: Cultural Center of the Philippines, 1992).

2. A detailed description of the *bahay kubo* and Spanish innovations is given by Regalado Trota Jose, *Arkitektura: An Essay on the Spanish Influence on Philippine Architecture* (Manila: Cultural Center of the Philippines, 1992), 7–8, 31–38, while Norma Ipac-Alarcon discusses the role of superstition in residence construction in *Philippine Architecture during the Pre-Spanish and Spanish Periods* (Manila: Santo Tomas University Press, 1991), 6–19.

3. Information on the Spanish-era church complex is found in Rene B. Javellana, S.J., and Fernando N. Zialcita, "Simbahan," in *CCP Encyclopedia of Philippine Art*, vol. 3, *Philippine Architecture* (Manila: Cultural Center of the Philippines, 1994), 164–175, and Ipac-Alarcon, 84–101.

4. Javellana and Zialcita, 176–177.

5. See Maria Corazon C. Hila, "Masjid," in *CCP Encyclopedia of Philippine Art*, vol. 3, *Philippine Architecture* (Manila: Cultural Center of the Philippines, 1994), 150–151.

6. Jose, 12–15 and the entries by Corazon Hila and Rene Javellana, "Kuta," pp. 146–148, Rene Javellana, "Fort Santiago," pp. 230–231 in *CCP Encyclopedia of Philippine Art*, vol. 3, *Philippine Architecture* (Manila: Cultural Center of the Philippines, 1994).

7. Jose, 38–44, Rodrigo D. Perez, "Malacanang," *CCP Encyclopedia of Philippine Art*, vol. 3, *Philippine Architecture* (Manila: Cultural Center of the Philippines, 1994), 246–247; and Rodrigo D. Perez, *Arkitektura: An Essay on the American Colonial and Contemporary Traditions in Philippine Architecture* (Manila: Cultural Center of the Philippines, 1994), 10.

8. Thomas S. Hines, "The Imperial Facade: Daniel H. Burnham and American Architectural Planning in the Philippines," *Pacific Historical Review* 41, no. 1 (February 1972): 33–53, and Perez, *Arkitektura*, 5–6.

9. Rene Javellana, "Casa Real," p. 136, "Munisipyo," pp. 152–153, and Rodrigo D. Perez, "Kapitolyo," p. 145, in *CCP Encyclopedia of Philippine Art*, vol. 3, *Philippine Architecture* (Manila: Cultural Center of the Philippines, 1994).

10. Rene Javellana, "Eskwelahan," in *CCP Encyclopedia of Philippine Art*, vol. 3, *Philippine Architecture* (Manila: Cultural Center of the Philippines, 1994), 138–141.

11. Rene Javellana, "Palengke," in *CCP Encyclopedia of Philippine Art*, vol. 3, *Philippine Architecture* (Manila: Cultural Center of the Philippines, 1994), 153–155.

12. Rodrigo D. Perez, "Sabungan," in *CCP Encyclopedia of Philippine Art*, vol. 3, *Philippine Architecture* (Manila: Cultural Center of the Philippines, 1994), 160.

13. Rene Javellana, "Sementeryo," in *CCP Encyclopedia of Philippine Art*, vol. 3, *Philippine Architecture* (Manila: Cultural Center of the Philippines, 1994), 161–163.

14. Perez, *Arkitektura*, 9–10, 19–21.

15. Cultural Center of the Philippines, *Artista ng Bayan, Leandro V. Locsin* (Manila: Cultural Center of the Philippines, 1990), 60–71.

16. Perez, *Arkitektura*, 20–22.

17. The following two stories appeared in the *Philippine Daily Inquirer*: James P. Ong, "Reinventing Silay for 21st Century," July 13, 1998, and Alex Y. Vergara, "Seedy Walkway in Quiapo Undergoes Face Lift," July 26, 1999. See also the March 8 and the July 27 and 28, 1998, editions of the paper for other stories of historic preservation efforts.

SUGGESTED READINGS

Jose, Regalado Trota. *Simbahan: Church Art and Architecture in Colonial Philippines, 1565–1898*. Makati, Philippines: Ayala Foundation, 1991.

Polites, Nicholas. *The Architecture of Leandro V. Locsin*. New York: Weatherhill, 1977.

Zialcita, Fernando N., and Martin I. Tinio, Jr. *Philippine Ancestral Homes (1810–1930)*. Quezon City: GCF Books, 1980.

5

Cuisine and Fashion

THE PHILIPPINES' long colonial history under two Western nations, as well as frequent contact with many Asian neighbors, has made this island nation a unique case study of cultural adoption. Most properly said, Philippine culture is syncretic in that it adopts external influences and reshapes them to fit local conditions and preferences. This syncretic process is most clearly seen in the nation's widely varied cuisine that combines influences from many other cultures and creates new dishes and tastes that are truly Filipino. The same is less true for fashion, since Filipinos are very conscious of contemporary international fashion trends that many emulate. But even here, the choices of clothing styles are still culturally molded, and some traditional dress has been maintained, at least for special occasions, out of a sense of cultural pride and assertion.

ENVIRONMENTAL FOUNDATIONS OF PHILIPPINE CUISINE

What is indigenous about Philippine cuisine? This basic question is addressed first so the process of integrating later foreign cuisines can be appreciated. Of all the factors enabling or limiting a culture's cuisine, the most basic is the physical environment. The Philippine's location in tropical Southeast Asia ensures warm year-round temperatures and abundant rainfall, resulting in a near continuous growing season. While some areas of the country receive more rainfall than others, the monsoon rains of summer support an extensive rice culture; rice, then, is the foundation of the country's cuisine.

Rice is the most important part of every meal and serves as the bed upon which all other foods lie. In the Filipino diet, rice fulfills the role of the necessary cereal of substance for the country's farmers and manual laborers who demand lots of the grain at every meal and who equate cereal intake with good nutrition. Rural and urban workers know about the nutritional value of other foods, but the lack of meat, vegetables, and fruit does not leave them feeling hungry nor would it limit their ability to work as does the absence of rice. Therefore, to the average Filipino, rice is the primary building block of nutritional health.[1]

Rice is also made into other foods such as porridge (*goto*) or a gruel that serves as a base for recipes like *arroz caldo* that contains chicken and is flavored with ginger. Rice is also ground into flour and made into the popular *bihon* noodle or baked into a wide variety of cakes, such as *puto* and many others, that are consumed at midday breaks and ceremonial occasions. As well, sticky, or glutinous, varieties of rice are the basis of a number of desserts, including *suman*, which is wrapped in a tightly bound coconut leaf. Young rice is pounded into flat flakes to become *pinipig* and used as a dessert with coconut milk or as a topping to chocolate.[2] Rice can also be made into wine, but except for the mountain people of the central Cordillera, the culture of rice wine is not as strong in the Philippines as other Asian nations.

Rice is not just the basic food of lunch and dinner but is an important part of breakfast. At daybreak, leftover rice from the evening meal is moistened, crumpled up, and heated in a skillet with cooking oil and two or three cloves of garlic plus salt and pepper. Sometimes onions, and vegetables, such as peppers, or shreds of fried egg are added if available. Whether supplemented with extras or not, the fried rice accompanies a fried egg, sausage, salted anchovies, dried beef stick, or leftovers from the night before. Another clear indication of the essential nature of rice comes from the culture's linguistic base. The word for cooked rice is *kanin* and is the root of the whole nomenclature of eating: *kain* is to eat; *pagkain* is food; *kumain* is to take a meal; *nagpapakain* is to feed people; *nakakain* means that something is fit to consume; *pang-kain* is money set aside for food. In contrast, the word *ulam*, which is a generic term for victuals of meat, fish, or vegetables, has only that one application, and the word *papak* is to eat without rice, meaning between meals.

A second prominent geographic feature shaping the Philippine's cuisine is the proximity to water. Composed of over 7,000 islands, much of the country's population lives near saltwater oceans and seas. In addition, most islands are dissected by numerous rivers, and there are a few large lakes on Luzon and Mindanao islands that provide still more freshwater resources. Even the rice paddies are water reserves that have a dietary impact beyond the production of the rice grain. This relationship between people and water accounts for the primacy of fish in the diet of many Filipinos. The widest variety of fish come from saltwater and are caught by commercial fishermen going out into the relatively shallow inter-island waters in groups of small boats to cast their nets. Most fishing is done at night with kerosene lanterns to attract fish to the surface. Because the country's interior waters are relatively shallow, there are numerous coral reefs that support a large fish population. Filipinos, therefore, enjoy a wide variety of fish and shellfish. People on the island of Samar catch small and medium-size sharks to be eaten as *pulutan* (finger food consumed while drinking) or for a meal's main course, although most Filipinos find shark a little too exotic for their taste.

In some saltwater areas, where the water is particularly shallow and calm, and in freshwater, corrals are used to trap the fish. In rivers and streams, handheld bamboo traps are used to catch extra protein for the family's evening meal. Rivers, lakes, and rice paddies contain frogs, crayfish, eels, snails, and clams. Fish and shrimp are also preserved as fish sauce (*patis*) and as fish or shrimp paste (*bagoong*) and used in many recipes and as a flavoring condiment that appears on many Filipino tables. Sometimes *bagoong* is mixed directly into rice for a poor man's viand. Both *patis* and *bagoong* are also found in the cuisines of neighboring states of Southeast Asia under a variety of local names.[3]

Filipinos make extensive use of their land's bounty to supplement their diet with a variety of root crops, including sweet potatoes, taro roots, and yams, such as the purple-colored *ube* root. There are also a number of vegetables, tendrils, leaves, some flowers, and even common weeds, such as *saluyot* and the swamp growth *kangkong*, that makes for a robust greenery to add flavor and considerable nutritional value to a meal. The Philippine climate produces an abundance of fruits that are eaten directly or, in the case of some sour fruits, used as a souring agent in dishes.

The most versatile fruit may be the coconut, the sap of which is fermented into an alcoholic drink, the water inside the nut is drunk, while the flesh of the young coconut is eaten directly or cooked with meats. Meanwhile, the white meat of older coconuts is added directly to recipes, mixed with water and squeezed for coconut milk, or grated and used as a topping on cakes and desserts. As well, there are a variety of local spices and a range of chilis and peppers.[4] Finally, one cannot ignore the animals that are a part of the Filipino diet. The pig and chicken, especially losing fighting cocks, have long been staples just as have the water buffalo (*carabao*), ducks, deer, and wild boar. Though Westerners might be off-put, since Filipinos live close to their environment, they make use of virtually any and all animals that might be edible, including field rats, dogs, insects such as beetles and locusts, bats, snakes, woodworms, and even ant eggs.

COOKING STYLES AND REGIONAL VARIATIONS

Methods of preparing Filipino cuisine are relatively simple and direct, and freshness is prized. Foods are either roasted, fried, steamed, or boiled/stewed soon after being obtained, since traditionally, there was no refrigeration, and food had to be prepared before spoilage in the tropical heat set in. As well, cooking methods had to act as a preservative in case the food could not be consumed immediately or if there was more than could be eaten in a single meal. This is accomplished by salting meat and fish or marinating food in vinegar and spices to be eaten raw.

Two well-known Filipino dishes, *adobo* and *sinigang*, are prepared by stewing. Since the name of the former is similar to a dish in Mexico and a relish in Spain, some people assume this dish was imported. In fact, the first Spaniards noticed how similar this local dish was to their own and called it the *adobo de los naturales*, the *adobo* of the native peoples.[5] The meat, which is usually either chicken or pork or a combination of the two, is stewed in vinegar and spices such as garlic and peppercorns. In the Philippines, there are a number of regional variations for *adobo*, for example, in Manila soy sauce is added, while the cooks of neighboring Cavite add mashed pork liver. Cooks of Laguna have a yellowish tinge to their *adobo* thanks to the addition of turmeric. In the far south of Muslim Zambonga, the local *adobo* is made especially rich and delicious with the addition of coconut cream to the sauce.[6]

As well known as *adobo* is to many foreign visitors and as widespread are its regional recipes, it is *sinigang* that is, perhaps, more representative of Philippine cuisine. *Sinigang* has been referred to as the "pride" of native cuisine and a genuine Filipino concoction. This dish is as elastic as the local environment, since there is no one or two specific ingredients that must be present, virtually whatever is on hand will do. *Sinigang* may include any meat or fish and just about any local vegetables. What makes the recipe is its sour taste, which comes from the inclusion of acidic fruits such as tamarind, green mango, guava, or tomatoes.[7] Because a sour broth has the effect of cooling the body, this dish is especially welcome in tropical climates and the flexibility of ingredients make it a natural choice for busy housewives.

Although a quick cooking method, roasting can be difficult since meat or fish becomes dry if over done, so Philippine roasting methods attempt to retain natural juices as long as possible. This is certainly true for *lechon* (pig roasted on a spit), which is well timed so the frequently basted skin becomes a hard crunchy shell keeping the meat inside soft and juicy.[8] Foods that are more difficult to monitor, such as fish, are first marinated to increase their chances for emerging succulent from the roasting process. Banana leaves are a frequently used cooking tool for steam cooking, since they can wrap and protect delicate foods so they will retain their full flavor and juices. *Pinais*, for example, is the term for fish or shrimp wrapped in banana leaves and steamed with onions, tomatoes, and young coconut.

Fish that cannot be consumed immediately is salted to prevent spoilage. The lowly anchovy is salted and appears as a crunchy breakfast food that is consumed in a manner similar to bacon. Larger fish are split down the back, salted, and then sun dried. The flesh of water buffalo, beef, pork, and other meats is also cut into strips, salted, and sun dried to become *tapa* and eaten with rice at any meal. Fish and meats, such as goat, are also marinated in vinegar and lime juice, the acids of which "cook" the raw foods without the use of fire. Sometimes, too, chili peppers and salt and pepper are added for additional spice. This method, known as *kinilaw*, also makes use of the abundant seafood of the country and adds variety to the Filipinos' taste choices. Fish and meat prepared in this manner are an especially popular finger food, or *pulutan*, and are consumed with beer, gin, and a variety of alcoholic drinks made from the fermented juices of palms (*tuba*), sugar (*basi*), and coconut (*lambanog*).

Philippine cuisine also has a practice of using sauces (*sawsawan*) that increases taste variety and allows the diner to adjust the flavor. In addition to *patis* and *bagoong*, use is made of almost any food, spice, or liquid that can enhance flavor. Filipinos have a wide array of sauce combinations that are either spread on food or used as a dip. A sauce can be as simple as vinegar and garlic or a more complex medley of lime (*kalamansi*) juice, soy sauce, *patis*, and garlic. The possibilities are extensive, and their use is actually encouraged by the Filipino cook who, in effect, invites the diner to participate in the food preparation process. This openly communal attitude toward the preparation and consumption of food is very Filipino and is part of the general culture. In this sense, the culture of Philippine cuisine is quite different from others, where tampering with a dish would be interpreted as a high insult.[9]

Various regions also put their distinctive stamp on the cuisine's diversity. The poor soil and harsh climate along the northwestern coast of Luzon has made the Ilocanos a hardy and frugal people. Their environment has also affected their local cuisine, which is low in meat and high in vegetables and rice. Their best known dish, *pinakbet*, is a stewed combination of vegetables flavored with *bagoong* and a bitter melon called *ampalaya*. Consumed directly, the ampalaya has a strong bitter taste but, when used in *pinakbet*, produces a pleasant taste despite its strength. Their meat dishes in this area tend toward rather high cholesterol uses of pork liver, sausages, and deep-frying. Meanwhile, the Bicol region of Luzon is well noted for the use of hot chilies, coconut milk, and *pili* nuts. Especially popular is their *pinangat*, a spicy dish of taro leaves stuffed with meat and hot chilies.

The central Visayan Islands are known for raising *kinilaw* to an art by the use of marinades of palm-wine vinegar, lime juice, chilies, and coconut milk. The regional cuisine of Mindanao and its smaller neighboring islands shows the frequency of contact with Malaysia and Indonesia in its abundant use of coconut milk, chilies, pimento, lemongrass, and, especially, curry. Among the Maranaws living around Lake Lanao along the northern part of Mindanao, chili is pounded with garlic, ginger, and onions to create a hot relish that spices up any dish. A number of the country's more exotic fruits are found in Mindanao, such as the extremely pungent smelling *durian*, plus the milder sweet fruits *mangosteen, rambutan, marang*, and *lanzones*.

Manila and the immediately surrounding provinces have a high level of sophistication in their food preparation and a marked variety of food ingredients. Freshwater foods are found in Laguna and Batangas provinces, which have major lakes, as well as Pampanga and Bulacan, which have extensive river systems and commercial fishponds. Meanwhile, saltwater products are never far away. In addition, Pampanga produces a remarkable number of desserts thanks to its extensive sugar plantations, while the coffee and beef industries of Batangas strongly influence its variations on the national menu.[10] Because it is the nation's political and business capital and a magnet for people looking to improve their lot in life, Manila's cuisine also includes the full array of regional dishes. Manila has also served as the principle conduit through which foreign influences were introduced and where they first began their process of indigenization. In this process, the foreign dish is adopted to local conditions and tastes to such a degree that it is transformed into something new and becomes an integral part of the national cuisine.

FOREIGN INFLUENCES AND THEIR INDIGENIZATION

Among the early foreign influences on Philippine cuisine were the merchants of China's southern coast, who traded with the Philippines for many hundreds of years. These merchants undoubtedly brought some food with them for the trip and when in the Philippines they probably had occasion to share a meal with their Filipino trading partners. These contacts took place over an extended period, but it is likely that the process of adopting elements of Chinese cuisine moved slowly until the establishment of the Spanish colonial presence in Manila. Previously, Filipino centers of power and commerce were numerous, small, and spread over an extensive geographic area so Chinese traders had no reason to linger in any one place. However, the concentration of mercantile activity in Manila, where Chinese traders were allowed to establish a residential area, plus the promulgation of laws limiting travel around the country greatly facilitated the integration of the two cuisines. The process was further accelerated as Chinese merchants began to marry local women and make a permanent life in the Spanish colony.

This process of cultural adoption and indigenization is clearly seen in the noodle dish *pancit*, which like the other noodles in Philippine cuisine, including the rice noodle *bihon*, plus *miki, miswa*, and *sotanghon*, all came from China. Once the noodle dish came to the Philippines, it was subject to the process of local adoption. So, for example, in coastal communities, fish, shrimp, and even squid were added, while in intensive rice-growing areas, crumbled rice cakes were included, and in still other areas, local vegetables or sausages appeared in the recipe. Additionally, each cook felt free to adapt the dish, and everyone felt free to change the dish even further by a liberal dose of whatever sauce they felt was most appropriate. Furthermore, like the indigenous *sinigang, pancit* is modified whether the meal is ordinary or a special occasion when other toppings are included.

Other Chinese foods were adopted, including noodles cooked in a broth (*mami*), vegetables wrapped in thin rice crepes (*lumpia*), meat encased in rice dough (*siopao*), and dumplings (*soimai*). Even the lowly soy sauce, miso, and bean curd are used in some *sawsawan* recipes. Whatever the dish, a common characteristic of Chinese foods is that they have permeated deep into Philippine society and are so much a part of the average person's daily diet that their foreign origin is hardly noticed. It has been suggested that this complete indigenization came about because the Chinese arrived in the Philippines as lowly merchants and eventually blended in with the local population. Their foods were the inexpensive dishes of commoners in China and fit into the cuisine of the same social-economic class in the new country. Additionally, these dishes could be adopted easily because climatic and soil conditions in southern China were not that different from those in the Philippines, so the basic ingredients or acceptable substitutes were at hand and affordable.[11]

Spanish recipes entered the local cuisine, too, but not to the same degree as Chinese dishes, since many of their ingredients, such as olives, cannot be grown in the Philippines and because of the greater use of meat, especially beef. As well, Spanish food was that of the elite colonizer, and it assumed a status greater than lowly Chinese food. Dishes such as stuffed capons (*relleno*), meat, and sausage stews (*cocido*), and rich desserts (*brazo de Mercedes, tortas* and others) were far beyond the daily household budget of all but a handful of Filipinos. Instead, Spanish dishes became status food reserved for the fiesta table or for other special occasions. Still, some dishes of Spanish commoners were transformed and indigenized in a manner similar to Chinese recipes. A good example is *paella*, originally a dish of rice and meat favored by Spanish peasants that became the Filipino dish *bringhe*, made with coconut milk instead of olive oil and saffron. Other Iberian dishes that have entered the Filipino diet include meat balls, the sausage *longaniza*, the breakfast roll *pan de sal* (bread of salt), the popular dessert made of egg and condensed milk, *leche flan*, and the rich egg yoke candy *yemas*. Yet even these foods, while not reserved exclusively for upscale restaurants and fiestas, are, nevertheless, on the tables of upper- and middle-class Filipinos and are rarely seen in the homes of the country's lower classes and peasants as are foods that originated in China.[12]

Mexico had an impact on the Philippines that is not often recognized. When journeying to their distant Asian outpost, Spaniards traveled by way of Mexico, taking the annual galleon that linked Spain with China. In the process, a number of fruits such as guavas, pineapples, papayas, and avocados, and vegetables, spices, and tubers, including corn, tomatoes, sweet potato (*camote*), and peanuts, were successfully introduced into the Philippine agricultural culture. There were fewer introductions of Mexican dishes, but the dish *menudo* and *mole* sauce can be found in the Philippines along with local *tamales* that are considered a snack food rather than a real meal. Most Mexican foods are used as flavoring supplements to pre-existing recipes or, in the case of the fruits, simply added to the Filipino table and have been completely incorporated into the cuisine. Still, *tamales* are another case in point, illustrating how a foreign dish becomes indigenized. Now *tamales* are no longer wrapped in cornhusks but in banana leaves and its spicy flavor has become so sweet that in some areas of the country it is a dessert.[13]

When it came to food, the American turn-of-the-century imperial thrust took on the reform ethic of the Progressive era and sought to change Filipino ways of doing things. The new conquerors were appalled when they saw the "dirty" Filipino kitchens, and through their new educational system, they sought to uplift the island's cuisine. In the Philippine Normal School, new courses in "domestic science" taught dish washing, care of kitchen utensils; nutrition; ways of cooking new recipes, such as cakes, fricassee, and sandwiches; menu planning; and food costs. The graduates were then sent out to transform society. These efforts were supported by articles in magazines such as the *Ladies' Home Journal* and *Good Housekeeping*, showing elite Philippine households what was "modern" and sophisticated. The buzz words of the day were *scientific* and *sanitary*. Over time, some technological changes began to make over the Filipino kitchen, as gas and electric stoves, refrigerators, various food processing machines, and, more recently, microwave ovens and rice cookers have streamlined the task of food preparation. But very often the "dirty" wood and coal burning kitchens are used to cook the most authentic dishes, and during fiestas, the backyard becomes an open cooking ground.[14]

Where American food culture has made an impact on Filipino cuisine is in the realm of the modern fast-food industry. But even here, there is strong evidence that the juggernaut of corporate America is being indigenized by stubborn Filipino taste buds. In today's greater metro Manila area right beside every new McDonald's restaurant is a branch of the Filipino hamburger chain Jollibee. This local fast-food outlet makes no attempt to copy its American competitor but stuffs its hamburgers with minced onion in a manner similar to the Filipino *bistek* (beefsteak), and *pancit* is on the menu, too. International soft drink giant Coca-Cola has adapted itself to the local habit of Leyte Island, where Coke is never drunk by itself "on the rocks," but is always mixed into the alcoholic fermented beverage *tuba*. In a brilliant marketing maneuver, a Leyte-based Filipino employee of the Atlanta corporation suggested the advertising slogan "Tuba Coke," which is now on all of their billboards and promotional glasses and pitchers. As a result of this deliberate self-indigenization, Coca-Cola has outstripped Pepsi and domestic soft drink producers for dominance of Leyte's market.[15]

CELEBRATIONS AND THE SIGNIFICANCE OF FOOD

It is during the annual fiesta that the Filipino pulls out all the stops. This is the occasion when hospitality is extended to everyone and where prosperity and generosity are judged. In the wealthiest homes, the fiesta table takes on a decidedly elite Spanish flavor, where vegetables are almost completely absent, since the consumption of quality expensive meat is the best indication of one's prosperity and elevated social status. The actual food preparation begins days in advance and involves the voluntary labor of a host of relatives and household helpers who bring generations of skill and recipes to the collective task. The backyard is filled with preparation tables and cooking fires over which large vats of food are cooked and animals roasted.

The centerpiece of a proper fiesta table is a roasted pig (*lechon*) surrounded by such Spanish dishes as the meat rolls *embutido* and *marcon* and *rellenong manok*, a deboned and rolled chicken stuffed with pork sausage and egg. Also on the table are richly enhanced versions of the Chinese foods *pancit* and *lumpia* and perhaps one or two indigenous dishes such as *adobo* and *kari-kari*, a beef dish using a rich sauce thickened by ground peanuts and rice. Beside the main table is another for the desserts, which shows an even greater Spanish influence, since desserts do not play a significant role in either Chinese or indigenous Philippine cuisine.

The day begins with a large breakfast for the helpers and host family, since they will be so busy preparing for and entertaining guests that they will only eat in furtive spurts for the remainder of the day. After the fiesta's morning mass, the house is open to visitors, and there will be many seatings and changes in the menu as the day progresses through dinner. Guests are treated to levels of hospitality and positioning at the table depending on social rank with priests and government officials given priority and then other people of status and family rank. The host must repeatedly urge guests to eat, since it is seen as bad manners to appear to accept the invitation too readily. The host cannot spend a great deal of time with each guest but usually devotes most of his attention to guests of greatest status. At the end of a visit, the departing guest is given a small package of food, a *pabaon*, to take home as a reminder of the feast or as a gift to someone unable to attend the fiesta meal.[16]

The fiesta table and hospitality of less prosperous town residents mirrors that of the wealthy host with some significant adjustments. Some of the ingredients in the *pancit* may be more ordinary than special, there may be more *adobo*, and the table is more likely to include *bringhe* rather than *paella*. *Lechon* will be served, but chopped up on a small platter, since the pig and the expense of buying it may have been shared with some of the neighbors. Desserts offered by less prosperous hosts tend to be local rather than Spanish, and include fresh fruits, the sweet root *ube*, and the sweet coconut meat *makapuno*.[17] Despite these differences in the foods, the hospitality in every home is warm and genuine and centered around food.

While the fiesta is a social event, a very private family occasion is the *Noche Buena*, or night of goodness, which refers to Christmas Eve. The meal is eaten after midnight mass (absolutely never before), and it is a time when Filipinos are only with those close to them. Generally, a meat or fish dish is eaten with rice, but the predominant tendency of this meal is toward lighter foods, such as *pancit*, roasted chicken, and rice cakes such as *puto*. As well, there may be delicacies like ham slices, cheeses, American-style sandwiches, and sweet desserts made of glutinous or sticky rice. The social significance of this meal is its communion of close family loved ones through the sharing of food immediately after attending the special midnight mass celebrating the birth of Jesus Christ.

SOCIAL-ECONOMIC CHANGE AND CUISINE

One change that has directly affected contemporary Philippine cuisine is the development of hybrid rice strains by the International Rice Research Institute in Los Banos, Laguna. These high-yield varieties have doubled harvests and have thereby improved the supply of this important staple, helped maintain nutritional standards, and lessened the extent to which valuable foreign exchange is spent on imported rice. On the other hand, the increased use of fertilizers and insecticides necessary to get the seed's full potential has killed off many fish, frogs, and other edible creatures that lived in the rice paddies. The farmer has, therefore, lost a free source of protein. As well, since modern agricultural chemicals are costly, the price of rice has risen sharply. Finally, with the downturn of the Philippine economy as part of the 1997 Asian economic crisis, food costs have become an even greater part of the average family's budget. As a result of these developments, many families are making greater use of food extenders such as *patis, bagoong*, chilies, and soy sauce. There has also been a noticeable decline in the kinds of foods eaten, with the incorporation of what was formerly scrap, for example, chicken intestines, into the diet of the poor.

Another important development is the increased and accelerated process of urbanization throughout the country. Greater metro Manila's current population is over 11 million, and a number of the nation's smaller cities are well above the one million mark. In fact, it is estimated that early in the new millennium over half of the population will be urban based, a significant milestone in a long-term demographic trend. Already, Manila has extended far beyond what urban planners had predicted only a few short decades ago, as rural communities and agricultural land disappear at an alarming rate. Along with the sheer growth of the urban Philippines is the creation of a new urban lifestyle. It is no longer unusual for couples to commute great distances through heavy traffic to get to work. As well, the number of these working couples, blue collar and professional alike, has increased markedly as more opportunities open for women with advanced educational degrees and as the growing disparity between wages and inflation drives middle-class women to seek work outside the home. These changes in population size, urban concentration, urban sprawl, and gender employment patterns have directly affected an increasingly important aspect of the country's cuisine; the growth of the restaurant industry, both fast-food and regular dining places, and the incorporation of greater amounts of "street food" into the daily diet.

The culture of the street vendor walking through a town's streets hawking rice cakes, ice cream, fruits, breakfast breads, and fertilized duck eggs (*balut*) has a long tradition going back well into the Spanish period. These marketers serve residential areas and have daily fixed routes and regular customers. Meanwhile, sidewalk food stalls also have a long lineage and are equipped to sell hot noodles, boiled corn, barbecue, syrup-coated sweet potatoes, and bananas, *halo-halo* (a mixed fruit and bean iced dessert), and any of a number of other dishes. Sidewalk vendors concentrate on everything from public markets and schools to construction sites and office buildings or set up their operations outside of churches on Sundays and special occasions. Similar are short term and permanent operations near bus terminals and at highway rest stops that service either bus passengers and truckers or the motoring public and offer distinctly different levels of cuisine and amenities.[18]

The primary reason for street food popularity is economic, since food sold from a vendor's cart is always cheaper than restaurant fare. For many urban poor, squeezed by a money economy over which they have no control, street food is an increasingly important part of the daily diet. A recent study noted that an estimated 80 percent of metro Manila's poor have become dependent on street food.[19] As well, street food is usually quite good, the servings are substantial, and the service is fast, which makes the vendors popular lunch and snack venues for time pressed students, office workers, and travelers. Considering the rushed nature of modern urban life, many a husband or housewife has been known to purchase a "to go" package for the family's evening meal. Finally, because the overhead expense of setting up a business is minimal, many a budding entrepreneur can easily get started so there is no lack of eager low-cost vendors waiting to please the public.

The country's restaurant industry has increased particularly in Manila but in other major urban centers as well. Manila always had some quality restaurants, but these were usually located in the formerly upper-class district of Ermita along the bay shore. With names such as the Swiss Inn and the Taza de Oro, they served European, Spanish, and American foods. As well, there were a number of Chinese restaurants in the city's Chinatown, and there was always the uninspired but safe Kowloon House chain for Chinese food. Filipino food was generally not available except for the Barrio Fiesta and a few places that hid their cuisine behind such foreign borrowed names as the Aristocrat, Grove, and Selecta.

The restaurant business began to change in the 1960s as dining out became less of an elite habit and as American fast-food chains such as A&W Root Beer began to develop a market. Now Filipinos have a wide range of dining options from which to choose. There are Filipino fast-food chains with names such as Jollibee and Goldielocks and a number of American outlets, including McDonalds, Shakee's Pizza, and Burger King. As important as the growth of fast-food places, is the amazing growth of all-Filipino restaurants with names to match. These establishments are now found throughout the metro Manila area and proudly display their Filipino names, which often indicate the specific nature of the house specialty. Examples include *Ang Luto ni Lola* (Grandmother's cooking), *Pancit ng taga Malabon* (Pancit a la the town of Malabon), and *Bakahan at Manukan* (Place to eat beef and chicken).

Clearly, Manila's booming restaurant business is the result of a number of factors. As the nation's urban areas grew and the pace of life increased so too did the need for restaurants where one could go for a business meeting. The hectic lifestyle of professional couples also made the restaurant alternative increasingly attractive. There is also the nostalgia factor that works on busy urbanites longing for the simple life of the province. What else could explain the phenomenal growth of restaurants where diners eat food with their hands served off of banana leaves and where diners are not given silverware even if they ask. There are also regional restaurants offering a true taste of the home province. Most of these represent provinces adjacent to Manila, but more distant regional restaurants have opened for the curious to sample. Even some five-star international hotels now offer Filipino dishes on their menu; the first to do so was the prestigious Manila Hotel. Finally there are some restaurants in the international business suburb of Makati that offer Filipino food in nouvelle cuisine style.[20]

SOCIAL DRINKING AND EATING

With a tropical climate and a large variety of fruits and trees, Christian Filipinos have a wide variety of sources for alcoholic beverages in their cuisine. A few drinks define the Philippine drinking tradition. The basic fermented drink is *tuba*, which is obtained from the nipa palm and the coconut. The juices from these sources can be drunk fresh but are often allowed to ferment. *Tuba* is itself a popular drink, but it is also the basis for stronger drinks. In coconut-growing regions, tuba is distilled through a boiling process, and the steam's condensation is collected and becomes *lambanog*, which eventually has a potency of 80 proof and easily ignites when touched by a match. A similar distillation process for nipa tuba produces a drink called *laksoy*, which is then aged and tempered by the addition of fruits. Ilocano speakers are known for the sugar cane alcohol drink *basi*, which is made by boiling the cane juice and fermenting it in a jar after adding yeast, leaves, and bark. A good *basi* is thus aged anywhere from two to ten years, depending on the quality desired and the patience of the brewer.[21]

In addition to homemade brews, the Philippines is also home of San Miguel beer, which is well known throughout Asia. There are other smaller beer manufacturers, but the original nineteenth century German beer manufacturing process has kept the Filipino loyal to the San Miguel brand name. San Miguel has shown keen market savvy in offering different sized bottles at a range of prices for tight pocketbooks, new lite and dark beers and new brands such as Red Horse that appeal to the whims of a demanding clientele. San Miguel also makes gin that, along with rum, are the drinks of the urban poor, who do not have access to provincial home brews and who cannot afford beer.

As with food, there is a culture surrounding the act of drinking. Filipinos are extremely social, and this characteristic extends to sharing drink and *pulutan* (finger food). The purpose of drinking is to socialize. While there is always plenty of drinking, Filipinos do not respect the drunkard, since that person has lost control of him or herself. The objective of drinking is to consume alcohol to feel good and enjoy each other's company. Simply getting drunk is considered boorish and indicative of a flawed character. Further-more, there are communal customs that must be adhered to when drinking. So, for example, when drinking *lambanog*, the host customarily throws the first shot on the ground and drinks the next. He then refills the shot glass for the next drinker. Only one glass is used, and each person must empty the glass before the next person can drink. In many areas, there is no dis-crimination against women who drink especially with other women, although mixed company drinking is not considered unusual. It is always an insult to refuse a drink, although one is not obliged to remain with a drinking group for a long period if there are competing demands.

In most drinking sessions, *pulutan* is consumed and may consist of any-thing from peanuts and eggs to meat and fish but usually not fruit or vege-tables. As well, many exotic foods such as iguana, frogs, squid, and dog meat become *pulutan*. The latter food is especially popular among Ilocanos and a few other groups, including the people of Pampanga province. Within the past few decades, consumption of dog meat has entered Tagalog areas, but it is still stigmatized as an underground tradition. Meanwhile, people in the rest of the country do not share this culinary interest. Much more common is goat meat, and raising these animals for eventual *pulutan* consumption is a profitable business in many parts of the country.[22]

CLOTHING AND FASHION

Long ago, Filipinos welcomed Western fashion into their daily lives such that by the early nineteenth century, only vestiges of pre-colonial clothing styles remained. In the twentieth century, this trend continued and the in-fluence of modern international fashion has greatly affected the traditional formal Philippine woman's dress, called the *terno*. In something of a contrast, the *barong tagalog*, a loose-fitting shirt of sheer cloth that is frequently adorned with varying amounts of embroidery, continues to enjoy popularity and has kept a place for itself in the man's wardrobe thanks to the creative adaptation of the shirt's style to contemporary lifestyle demands. In other respects, however, most lowland Filipinos dress very much like people in the

United States. Only a few of the minority mountain peoples and some of the Muslims in the southern islands have kept to their indigenous fashions for more than special ceremonial occasions.

The *Terno*

The present-day *terno* dress is elegant in its ankle length and form-fitting cut and defines the idealized attire of the Filipina. The cloth is often decorated with intricate embroidery but can also be adorned with hand-painted flowers or other embellishments that include pearls, teardrops, beads, sequins, and rhinestones. Most characteristic of all, is the *terno*'s dramatic "butterfly" sleeves that clearly differentiate it from Western evening wear. Though unique to the Philippines, the present dress is markedly different from its much more elaborate predecessors.

The contemporary *terno* evolved from a much older union of the European-style skirt, the *saya*, that was combined with a pre-Hispanic sarong-style dress, the *tapis*, which was used as an overlapping attachment similar to an apron. It should be noted that upper-class *mestizo* women of Spanish and Filipino parentage would often shun the *tapis* because of its visual association with a work apron. Meanwhile, the upper body was covered by a blouse (*camisa* or *baro*) that was topped with an embroidered kerchieflike drape (the *panuelo*) that was worn around the bodice to preserve a woman's modesty. This Spanish-era fashion development culminated with the Maria Clara dress, named after the hapless heroine of Jose Rizal's novel, *Noli Me Tangere* (1887). This dress combined the *camisa* and *panuelo* with a unique *saya* of numerous vertical panels of heavy satin in contrasting colors.

The gown of the *mestiza* quickly evolved into the *terno* during the American period, as the *camisa* and the *saya* became matched in material and color, and the *tapis* was replaced by a smaller, sheer embroidered wraparound piece called the *sobrefalda*. It was also during the American period that the butterfly sleeves first made their appearance as additions to the *camisa*. At the same time, the American colonial administration put greater emphasis on the use of domestic cloth as part of its program of colonial economic self-sufficiency. Prominent among the local fabrics was *pina*, a fiber made from the pineapple plant, and *jusi*, a blend of banana fiber (*abaca*) and silk from China. The biggest advance in the evolution of the Filipina's dress was the union of the blouse and skirt, creating the elegant one-piece *terno*. This innovation appeared in the 1940s and was quickly embraced by active post-World War II women professionals who could not be bothered by the cumbersome multi-faceted apparel of the past. Other developments at about the same time

The Maria Clara dress ensemble, which by the 1880s included all portions of the well-dressed Filipina's attire, the embroidered baro, the silk panuelo, a saya and a tapis. Courtesy of the Ambeth Ocampo Collection.

were the abandonment of first the *sobrefalda* and then of the *panuelo*, which finally disappeared by the late 1960s.[23]

As the pace of modern life accelerated, the *terno* became increasingly relegated to the role of clothing worn only on special occassions. During her lengthy term as first lady, Imelda Marcos championed the *terno* and supported the work of many designers and craftsmen. Because of her efforts, the *terno* gained an international stature, but it also became so closely associated with the first lady that a reaction against the dress set in immediately after the Marcos couple fled the country in 1986. Only gradually has the dress regained its stature as harsh feelings against the Marcos regime have moderated.

The *Barong Tagalog*

Just as women quickly adopted Western dress styles, Filipino men switched from loincloths to loose-fitting trousers. The Muslim men of the southern islands adopted tight-fitting breeches and open jackets with tight fitting sleeves and integrated them into their customary fashion along with a kerchief. By the mid-eighteenth century, Christian Filipinos had taken to trousers that reached slightly below the knee and wore loose shirts of short sleeves called the *baro*, which over time became decorated with embroidery. Other than the native hat, the *salakot*, there were very few other clothing items, and male clothing styles did not change markedly for a long period. By the early nineteenth century, however, upper-class Filipinos began a wholesale adoption of the Spanish style of dress, which even included walking canes, as a way of integrating themselves into the colonial power structure. In the face of this native imitation, a regulation was passed in the 1830s requiring natives to wear their shirts outside of their trousers—the practice of tucking in one's shirt was a privileged manner of dress reserved for Spaniards.

This discriminatory dress code soon made the lowly *baro* a symbol of nationalism. Faced with colonial snobbery and derision, the nationalist sought to embrace what his oppressor rejected. It was not long before the *baro* became today's *barong tagalog*, the physical embodiment of things Filipino and of national pride. In its process of transformation, the *baro* gained a collar and was made in long and short-sleeve versions. The formerly plain shirt also became colorful with differently dyed cloth, design patterns, and elaborate embroidery. No matter what the color, decoration, or peculiar cut of the individual shirt, the *baro* was always made of a sheer native cloth, which made them especially well adapted to the country's tropical climate— certainly more so than the heavy layering of thick fabric required of dressing in a European fashion.[24]

Quite ironically, the *barong tagalog* virtually disappeared during the revolt against Spain and during the entire American colonial era. It could only be imagined that the stigma of inferiority attached to the *barong* was so strong that the shirt was shed immediately as young revolutionaries sought to establish an independent nation, and during the relatively benign American period there was a desire to emulate the "modern" ways that the coat and tie represented. Only for a brief period, when Philippine Commonwealth President Manuel L. Quezon wore a specially designed *barong* with embroidered American and Philippine flags, did the shirt enjoy a brief flicker of popularity.

It was not until the post–World War II era that the *barong tagalog* truly came into its own, thanks in no small part to the movie industry that sought to contribute to the development of values fitting the newly independent nation. The *barong tagalog* was chosen as the visual representation of humility and integrity. The hero always appeared in a *barong*, while the city-slicker villains were impeccably dressed in Western cloths. The popular 1950s movie star Leopoldo Salcedo, pioneered a Valentino-style of *barong tagalog*, and soon the shirt became fashionable again. The reputation and status of the shirt was affirmed as all Philippine presidents wore the shirt on state occasions and as designers for Pierre Cardin and Christian Dior used the *barong* and redesigned it for high culture fashions.[25] With the addition of pockets at waist level and short sleeves, the *polo barong* became an acceptable work shirt for office workers and managers thus assuring its inclusion in a typical male wardrobe even as the women's *terno* became limited to formal occasions only. In fact, elements of the *barong's* cut and its typical embroidery patterns have appeared on more casual women's dresses.

Minority peoples had their own traditional woven cloths for men and women. These cloths ranged in quality and artistic sophistication from hill dwelling Aetas, who remained clad in little more than loincloths until recent times, to the Mandaya and other ethnic groups on Mindanao island, whose dress is colorful and elaborate. Even these latter folks have, for the most part, adopted Western clothes for everyday use and only retain their traditional costumes for ceremonial occasions. Most lowland Christian Filipinos wear Western clothes for most daily activities and for casual wear as they have since the American period when all the latest fashions for both men and women made their appearance in the country. Nevertheless, there are preferences for Western clothes that allow for the greatest comfort in tropical climates as witnessed by the popularity of the men's "shirtjak," a short-sleeve shirt cut square at the midriff, which popular in the 1960s and 1970s because it was not tucked into the pants, and its loose fit allowed for maximum air circulation.

That Philippine culture has indigenized a variety of foreign culinary influences on the one hand but largely incorporated Western clothing styles is a provocative study in contrasts. The explanation may lie in the environmental and climatic basis for Philippine cuisine which lends resilience to adapting foods to native taste. However, specific clothing styles are not as fundamental to daily existence as is food nor were pre-Hispanic forms of dress as fit for the needs of the modern world as were the clothes introduced by Westerners.

Only the *barong tagalog* has made the transition to contemporary use thanks to selective adoption, bolstered by pride in the shirt as a national costume.

NOTES

1. Esther Manuel Cabotaje, *Food and Philippine Culture: A Study in Culture and Education* (Manila: Centro Escolar University, 1976), 153.

2. Doreen G. Fernandez, and Edilberto N. Alegre, *Sarap: Essays on Philippine Food* (Metro Manila: Mr. & Ms. Publishing Co., 1988), 3–4 and 12.

3. Ibid., 10–11.

4. Ibid., 11–12.

5. This phrase was used by dictionary writer Pedro de San Buenaventura in 1613. See Doreen G. Fernandez, *Tikim: Essays on Philippine Food and Culture* (Pasig, Metro Manila: Anvil Publishing, 1994), 196.

6. See Corazon S. Alvina's discussion of variations for *adobo* and other dishes in "Regional Dishes," in Reynaldo G. Alejandro, *The Food of the Philippines* (Boston: Periplus Editions, 1998), 11.

7. Fernandez and Alegre, 2–6, 45.

8. For a discussion of the culture of *lechon*, see Gilda Cordero-Fernando, *Philippine Food and Life* (Manila: Anvil Publishers, 1992), 42.

9. Fernandez and Alegre, 14–15, 41–42.

10. Alvina, 10–13, and Fernandez, 118–120.

11. Fernandez and Alegre, 17–18, and Fernandez, 40–43.

12. Fernandez and Alegre, 148–152.

13. Fernandez, 183–200.

14. Ibid., 109–111.

15. See Michael Tan's report " 'Tuba,' Coke and Edu," in the *Philippine Daily Inquirer*, April 30, 1998.

16. See, Ruth V. Estupigan, "Dining at the Filipino Table," *Manila Bulletin, Philippine Centennial Issue*, June 12, 1998, 85–86, and Fernandez, 107–108, 160 162.

17. Gilda Cordero-Fernando's essay "The Festive Board of Landlord and Peasant," in Gilda Cordero-Fernando, ed. *Philippine Food and Life* (Pasig, Metro Manila: Anvil Publishers, 1992), 74–76, is not specifically about the town fiesta, but reflects the social-economic differences found in various homes during those festivities.

18. Fernandez, 3–13, and Cordero-Fernando, *Philippine Food and Life*, 89, 130–131.

19. See Grace P. Perdigon, "Street Foods and the Filipino Family: A Historical Account," in Celia A. Florencio and Flor C. F. Galvez, ed. *Studies on Filipino Families* (Quezon City: College of Home Economics, University of the Philippines, 1995), 139–152.

20. Fernandez and Alegre, 198–208, and Millie Reyes, "Eating Out, Filipino Style," in Reynaldo G. Alejandro, ed., *Food of the Philippines* (Boston: Periplus Editions, 1998), 19–21.

21. Cordero-Fernando, *Philippine Food and Life*, 32–33, 151.

22. Fernandez and Alegre, 177–188.

23. See the discussion of the *terno*'s evolution in Eric V. Cruz, *The Terno: Its Development and Identity as the Filipino Woman's National Costume* (Quezon City: University of the Philippines, 1982), 1–12.

24. See Sahlie P. Lacson, "The Evolution of the Filipino Dress: Then, Now and Beyond," *Manila Bulletin, Philippine Centennial Issue*, June 12, 1998, pp. 60, 62–63, 71 for an overview of Philippine fashion and its development during the Spanish era.

25. The ideological and nationalistic role of the *barong tagalog* is fully developed by Eric V. Cruz, *The Barong Tagalog: Its Development and Identity as the Filipino Men's National Costume* (Quezon City: University of the Philippines, 1992), 8–11.

SUGGESTED READINGS

Alegre, Edilberto N. *Inumang Pinoy* (Filipino Drinking). Pasig, Metro Manila: Anvil Publishing, 1992. Despite its title, this book is almost completely in English.

Montinola, Lourdes R. *Pina*. Metro Manila: Amon Foundation, 1991.

Noriega, Violeta A. *Philippine Recipes Made Easy*. Kirkland, WA: Paper Works, 1993.

6

Marriage, Family, and Gender

THE FILIPINO FAMILY plays a more central role in the lives of its members, and in the nation's greater social and political life, than do families in many other cultures. To a significant degree the Filipino gains his or her sense of identity and self-worth from family membership despite the social impact of contemporary urban culture, which places increasing emphasis on the individual, and even in the face of sometimes competing friendships and associations outside the family circle. A basic reality of Philippine society is that one's family is as intimately linked with an individual's social status as is material wealth, while social, economic, and political success, especially in small towns and villages, is in large part contingent on the size and strength of one's family.

THE FILIPINO BILATERAL FAMILY

The importance of the family in Philippine society is especially noteworthy when one considers that the Filipino family is structurally similar to families in other cultures, such as the United States, where there is an emphasis on the individual rather than the family. Like its American counterpart, the basic Filipino family unit is composed of the husband, wife, and their children biological and/or adopted. In addition, the Filipino kinship structure is "bilateral," meaning that one's relatives are calculated to include individuals from both the father's and the mother's families. In the bilateral family structure one's relatives and descendants from both sides of the family are respected and treated equally.[1] One's affinity to a relative is more a matter of variables, such as proximity and frequency of contact, affinity, and calculated mutual benefits, such as favoring your rich uncle, than of socially defined relationship. The basic egalitarian nature of Filipino kinship is readily seen in the nongender specific nature of kin terms in which there is only one word for spouse (*asawa*), son or daughter (*anak*), sibling (*kapatid*), cousin (*pinsan*), parent-in-law (*biyenan*), and so forth. If the individual's gender needs to be indicated, the extra words for male (*na lalaki*) or female (*na babae*) must be added.

As well, the process of choosing a marriage partner is relatively informal and not restricted by family lineage rules so that choices are frequently left to the marriageable son or daughter. For their part, while parents may let their son or daughter know who they consider to be an excellent prospect, a primary concern is that a daughter's future husband can support her and their children, while a son's future wife should have sufficient domestic skills and good maternal capabilities. Philippine parents do not dictate marriage choices nor are they actively involved in the selection process by hiring matchmakers or otherwise interfering. In societies characterized by bilateral kinship structures, not only is marriage and descent calculated along both lines but inheritance can go to daughters, especially unmarried ones, as well as sons. Furthermore, in the bilateral kinship system, a young couple has the option of choosing to live with or in close proximity with either the groom or the bride's family. Frequently in the Philippine context, the new couple elect to reside in the same house or in the family housing compound as one of the parents until they become economically established and can afford to build their own house. Additionally, women have the potential to play an active role in the family decision-making process and might even become involved in activities outside of the home. Visitors have long noted the Filipina's dynamism and how she is frequently treated more as a partner to her husband than as a subservient appendage doing his bidding.

In many respects, then, the bilateral Philippine family contrasts sharply with some other Asian kinship structures that calculate their membership only along a single bloodline, either through the father (patrilineal) or the mother (matrilineal). In a patrilineal society, best exemplified by China's traditional family structure, the new bride makes a near total break from her family and enters into that of her new husband, virtually losing her identity in the process. Marriage choices are also strictly controlled so that couples with similar family names (i.e., the same family lineage) may not marry, and the parents choose their child's partner, frequently with the help of a professional matchmaker. In the patrilineal family descent, inheritance and power are all located in the male line, while female family members are in a distinctly inferior position. The wife may control the daily life of the household, and she is responsible for child-raising, but she has no claim to the family's wealth and is subservient to her husband in all matters and decisions.[2] In wealthy patrilineal families, there may even be multiple wives and concubines who service the male head of the household. In this situation, it is only the senior wife who has even a modicum of power and influence in family affairs.

THE EXTENDED FAMILY

What the Filipino family lacks in terms of the strength of the Chinese patrilineal style of kinship descent, it makes up for with its extensive network of actual and fictive relatives. The broad Filipino network of actual relatives is called the "extended family." In its ideal form, the extended family includes all of the nuclear family's siblings and their children extending outward. Practically speaking, however, the typical extended family usually consists of the immediate brothers and sisters who remain united while their parents are still alive or who continue the relationship due to mutual interest and benefit. In an everyday sense, the extended family includes the nuclear family plus the elder parents who often live with one of their children and, perhaps, a few other blood relations, such as a sibling's family. Beyond the family group residing in the same house, Filipino families will locate their residences in close proximity to each other. Well-to-do extended families will even cohabit a single compound in which all their houses are built.

In most cases, however, common residence is simply not possible, especially in the modern urban reality of Manila and other large cities. Employment opportunities also pulls at the extended family, taking siblings and their families to different parts of the country and, increasingly, to various parts of the world. Nonetheless, the Filipino family retains its vitality as an extended entity, since visits are made as often as possible. As noted in the chapter "Festivals and Entertainment," a primary function of festivals and religious holidays is to reinforce family bonds. Returning to the hometown for the annual fiesta and Christmas mass, especially when *lolo* (grandfather) and *lola* (grandmother) are still alive, is an important vehicle to maintain and renew the extended family's ties.

Beyond ties of affinity, the traditional Filipino family was a source of economic security for its members. This economic function was certainly true in the culture's rural and agrarian origins where landownership was the key to survival. Land was usually passed from father to son and sometimes to a daughter and her husband. Families worked the soil together sharing the tasks and the rewards. Local power could be increased by a fortunate marriage of one's son or daughter to another landowning family, which would benefit both parties. Wealthy families were especially aware of the close connection between consanguineal relations and landed wealth and occasionally practiced first-cousin marriage to maintain the family's ownership of haciendas especially those devoted to the profitable export crop of cane sugar.[3]

Supplementing the biological extended family is a category of "fictive kin" who are incorporated through ritual relations. The phenomenon is known in the social science literature as *compadrazgo*, or ritual co-parenthood, and refers to *compadre* relations established when these extra familial individuals act as sponsors at marriages and, especially, baptisms.[4] Between the two ritual events, the marriage sponsor is probably the singularly most important, but since there are far many more baptisms than there are marriages, it is the baptismal relationship that has the greater social importance. Besides, marriage sponsors are usually limited to two sponsors while there is no limit to the number of sponsors that an individual can have at a baptism. In any case, the baptismal *compadre* is always carefully chosen, since the act of standing as the child's sponsor means much more than a willingness to take on a religious obligation. The sponsor also accepts some responsibility for the child's general development and welfare and may legitimately be asked to help with things such as education and later employment. The sponsor must, therefore, possess the means to supplement the family resources and already be close enough to the family to be willing to accept a more intensive relationship with them. One mistaken model of the relationship has the poor rice land tenant seeking to have his landlord become a sponsor at his child's baptism. In practice most sponsors are at approximately the same social economic level since the families are creating close long-term bonds. A *compadre* relationship between a tenant and his landlord is usually impractical.

The one who is sponsored takes on the role of a son or daughter to the sponsor, and they, in turn, show the sponsor the same respect they give their biological parents. As well, the sponsored child enjoys a pseudo-sibling relationship with the sponsor's children and a grandparent-grandchild relationship with the parents of the sponsor.[5] Additionally, a sponsorship obligation is reciprocal and the parents/marriage partners are obligated to their *kumpadre* and *kumadre*. As a *compadre* relationship develops, the interaction between the parties can become quite close and may actually approach levels of intensity found among biological siblings. In many instances, close *compadre* relationships develop such that it is not uncommon to find them as business partners and political coalition allies. In fact, the basis of the Philippine political alliance system has provincial roots reaching up to the national level that combine regular biological families plus their allies, who include their *kumpadres*.[6] While there are indications that *compadrazgo* is declining as a social institution, the practice still remains an important aspect of the greater extended Filipino family and still exerts a tremendous social pressure.[7]

GENDER SOCIALIZATION AND DATING

While the Filipino family structure appears similar to that found in the United States, it is in adolescence when the real differences between Philippine and American family and social practices become dramatically clear. The major distinction between the two cultures is the Filipino practice of a "double standard" between what men and women can do. American women might also feel restricted by standards set for them compared with those that apply to American men, but whatever differences exist in American culture is magnified many times over in the Philippine context.

During adolescence even as the body changes and develops in new ways, the sex roles of boys and girls are more defined, with boys being allowed to indulge in more "adult" practices, such as drinking and even visiting girls, although in the company of other boys. Mixed company is allowed, but serious courtship is not permitted by the young adolescent male. The basic premise is that boys and young men do not fit in the house and take their recreation and form their identity from activities that take place outside the home in the world of men. Thus, the men perform the heavier tasks on the farm and take on additional jobs in local towns. In urban areas, the men always find employment that takes them outside of the house, and with some exceptions, such as teachers, the gender divisions of employment are as sharply drawn in the urban environment as they are in the rural areas. The guiding premise that men do not work in the house accounts for the young Filipino male's extreme reluctance to become involved in household matters and especially to perform common housekeeping tasks of any sort. Later in life, the husband will surrender virtually all control of household affairs to his wife who manages the family budget, raises the children, and plays a strong role in creating social linkages with neighboring households. Instead, the male gains status from his ability as a provider and from his public image in the community.

It is also expected that boys will form extra-familial bonds with other boys in friendship groups known as *barkadas*. The Philippine *barkada* can sometimes be mistaken for American adolescent "gangs," but there is no antisocial or criminal behavior in these groups as is often the case in the American context. Rather, the *barkada* relationship between young men forms a bond that is extremely strong and long lasting and closely regulates the behavior of its members. Within the *barkada*, the young male learns to sacrifice his goals for the greater good of the group, and personal loyalties reach intense levels. Frequently, a man's youthful gang-mates remain lifelong friends who can always be counted on in any situation and without questions being asked.[8] The lessons that a young male learns as a member of a *barkada* have a lasting impact on the young man's development and follow him through his life, even as he forms similar bonds with other males in other situations, such as work or politics.[9]

This pattern of male bonding is first developed in the *barkadas* of one's youth and affect how men later relate to each other in a wide variety of situations. In college, the fraternity often plays the role of the *barkada* and at the nation's primier institution, the University of the Philippines, "rumbles" between rival fraternity groups are not uncommon and sometimes lead to deadly shoot outs. The fraternity linkage later forms the basis of many partnerships in business and, especially, political life in the same way that regional ethno-linguistic ties do. Former Philippine president Ferdinand Marcos was known to select some of his closest advisers and confidants based on their membership in the same University of the Philippines fraternity. This same fraternal bonding is even present in the Philippine military's officer corps where classes of cadets from the Philippine Military Academy (PMA) remain tightly bound and identified throughout their careers in the armed forces. An excellent example of this continued linkage was seen during the 1986 overthrow of the Marcos regime when many of the reform officers who joined the head of the armed forces, Fidel V. Ramos, and the secretary of national defense, Juan Ponce Enrile, were members of the same PMA class.[10]

Even as young men are being socialized in activities and groups outside of the home, socially constructed gender specific roles for girls are also intensified during adolescence, as domestic feminine tasks are passed on from mother to daughter in a more rigorous way than in the games of little girls. Instruction in food preparation and household maintenance take on serious overtones, since it is believed that a girl's ability to attract a good future husband is dependent, at least in part, on her domestic skills. Older female children frequently take on the role and authority of a surrogate mother in managing the house and younger siblings. On the farm, young women can participate in work activities outside the home, but these are closely regulated by gender divisions so that a girl will feed the smaller farm animals such as chickens and pigs and will join in planting and harvesting, but she will not plow a field or tend the family's water buffalo.

Even as girls consciously fashion themselves into stereotypic housewife roles, their freedom of movement with regard to boys becomes sharply limited. Especially in rural communities and among traditional families in urban areas, interaction with boys must only take place in public and in closely regulated circumstances. Spending inordinate attention on a boy or young man is not permitted and being alone with him for any length of time is avoided at all cost. The safe assumption that parents make is that every boy will try his luck and that sexual experimentation may happen. If the girl loses her virginity, her marriage possibilities will decline dramatically; a girl of suspect morals is only sought after for sexual favors and not potential marriage. Worse, the girl not only shames herself but she also ruins the family name at the same time. For this reason, chaperones are still used in many rural and traditional families, especially in the evening hours, as adolescents make their first tentative steps toward adult sexuality.

An excellent example of the tentative nature of adolescent sexuality can be seen at public dances held in conjunction with barrio and town fiestas and at school functions. Initial contact is made by the boy as he asks a girl to dance. When he does, the girl is not expected to accept too readily. Instead, she will avoid eye contact and look to her friends, or perhaps a chaperone, to gain approval before taking the boy's hand. During a slow dance, the couple will stand quite a ways apart from each other with the boy's hand only just reaching the girl's waist. She, in turn, stands very stiff as if she is not enjoying the experience. The couple may talk to each other but rarely smile or otherwise indicate that they might be enjoying each other's company. If the music is fast, the girl will be as demure as possible even while wiggling around on the dance floor. At the conclusion of the music, the girl will utter a short word of thanks, perhaps offer a coy smile, and return to her seat. In sharp contrast, if the girl dances with a sibling or other relative or with one of her own female gang mates, she can be much more relaxed, can move in tempo with the rhythm, and can obviously enjoy herself.[11]

To be fair, this traditional outlook with regard to sexuality by adolescent girls and young women and their interaction with young men is changing rapidly as the family loses its traditional dominance and ability to control its young people. One factor that must be mentioned is the broad availability of public education that began during the American colonial period and has accelerated in the post-World War II era. Coeducation has increased informal contacts between boys and girls to such a degree that gender separation seems increasingly quaint and anachronistic. As well, the *barkada*'s alternative to family control means that different values and expectations will be brought to bear on young men and women. Most important, though, is the availability of nonagricultural employment that frees both sexes from the economic clout that underlies the strength of traditional familial bonds. Aided by improved transportation systems, the nation's young men and women can migrate to the nation's urban areas and find a hitherto unknown level of individual autonomy. Though hardly the dominant norm, the impact of modern urban society has increasingly allowed women to play an initiator role, such as asking young men to go see a movie or sending notes and small gifts. In the urban social environment, little thought is given to young men and women "hanging out" together informally in groups with little or no parental supervision and even American-style dating by single couples.[12]

As a result of these changes, even the traditional emphasis on virginity is becoming less important for young men when selecting a mate. Still, young women even in the most open-minded sectors of the country must be careful to maintain a proper image. Dating is still practiced in group situations until a couple has developed a relationship, and even then open sexuality is not common. For example, the American practice of a young couple living together before marriage is practically unheard of except among a relatively small number of Manila's young people. Thus, the Filipino female's social world remains relatively limited in comparison to that of her male counterpart, who can enhance his reputation by being known as a ladies' man. The contrast between tradition and modernity becomes more obvious when casual dating escalates into a serious relationship, which then leads to formal courtship.

COURTSHIP AND MARRIAGE

In comparison to the American and Chinese social alternatives, the process by which increasingly modern and urban Filipinos enter into dating and serious courtship seems to align very strongly with the American model. That perception may owe a great deal to the Filipino penchant for unabashed expressions of romantic love and its role in their lives. If one were simply to listen uncritically to popular music, view run-of-the-mill Filipino movies, and read the popular short-story pulp fiction of many magazines and *komiks*, one's impression would be that the Filipino is a very passionate person whose romantic life and marriage choices are affected only by affairs of the heart. In fact, romantic love plays an increasingly important role in courtship and marriage, but not to the degree that a first impression would suggest. A number of traditional considerations, including the active influence of the family, still plays an important role in the choice of marriage partners.

Serious courtship can begin during adolescence, especially in the country's rural areas, but family and economic pressures are delaying marriage more now than ever before. This tendency to delay marriage is becoming especially strong as the need for advanced education to increase the possibility of upward social and economic mobility is increasingly recognized. Not only are young couples marrying later than before, but many traditional courtship practices have disappeared since the 1950s. At that time, a number of courting practices were still common that have since receded to only a few relatively isolated rural areas. These practices included, for example, charming evening serenades of the young woman by the suitor and his friends. The young woman would be notified in advance of her admirer's plan, so she could assemble in anticipation with her friends. After the opening musical numbers, the couple would frequently engage in a musical contest to see who knew the most songs and could use them to advantage in good-natured teasing. In pre-World War II days, it was also not uncommon for a suitor to have a friend who was more eloquent than he approach the young woman to express the suitor's feelings and to let her know his intentions. As well, it was expected that a young man seriously interested in a woman would perform free labor around the family farm to demonstrate his ability as a provider and his personal character. When the match looked favorable even to the young man's *barkada*, the two families would formally meet, gifts would be offered to the girl's parents, and arrangements would be made for the future nuptials.[13]

While these quaint bucolic days of courting are largely passed, some traditional aspects of courtship and marriage remain firmly in place. Despite the increased freedom that young people enjoy in the contemporary Philippine modern urban environment, parental control is far from absent. Parents are still known to actively encourage couplings they believe would work particularly well, especially with the offspring of close friends and economic or political allies. As well, parents will not hesitate to actively discourage what they see as a bad match and will deliberately embarrass the suitor in an attempt to drive him away. In extreme situations, parents have even been known to send a daughter away on an extended holiday, usually with relatives in another province, to end a budding relationship. For their part, the young couple want to earn their parents' blessing, since the bonds between children and parents, especially the mother, are extraordinarily strong.[14]

The tension between youthful autonomy and parental control is seen everywhere in contemporary Philippine social life and was most clearly represented by the tension between former President Corazon Aquino and her favorite daughter Kris. The attractive young woman sought a career in the entertainment industry and had moderate success in movies and hosting a daytime television talk show. She met and fell in love with Phillip Salvador, a talented older actor who had children by a former partner with whom he was then estranged. The former president and first mother was so aghast at the relationship, which violated her sense of Christian morality, that she forbade her daughter to see the actor. The rebellious youth defied her mother, moved in with Salvador and had a child by him. In retaliation, Aquino broke off all contact with her daughter. The tensions between mother and daughter served to bring to light the fact that the public was divided on a whole range of modern personal issues. Eventually, Philippine tradition and the strength of a mother's hold over her children won out. Kris reconciled with her mother and Salvador disappeared into the background.

Any discussion of courtship would not be complete without noting a series of additional factors that further pattern behavior and limit choices. While these additional factors are also breaking down with increased urbanization, they still retain significant social relevance. Even though Filipinos are very open to foreign visitors and to the latest international styles of clothing and music, they are not always receptive to marriage links with others who are thought to be outside of their own group. It could be said that Filipinos have strong endogamous (within the group) marriage preference. Preferences include the desire that one's children marry someone from the same town or from the surrounding area. Since marriage links formerly independent families, the best linkage will be with another family with whom fortunes can be combined to increase one's collective standing in the community. Similarly, there is a strong tendency to select suitable marriage partners from one's own social economic class; stories of the rich boy marrying the chaste and beautiful but poor girl are extremely rare in the Philippine context.

There are also strong ethno-linguistic and racial lines beyond which, until recently, few Filipinos were willing to cross, unless for some clear social or economic advantage. For example, marriages between ethnic Chinese men and Filipinas were usually only attractive to poorer women. Meanwhile, until recently it was also rare that Filipinos from one language group would consider marriage with someone from another region of the country. When this did occur, it was most likely that the couple came from very wealthy families whose social-economic interests were more than locally based. A final factor pushing courtship and mate selection in an endogamous direction is religion. While Philippine culture is extremely tolerant of competing religions, that toleration stops at the marriage bed. Both the Roman Catholic church and the domestic Iglesia ni Cristo are opposed to marriage with outsiders and a non-Muslim cannot marry a Muslim without first converting. Since religion and social identification is closely linked, the individual contemplating a religious mixed marriage is certain to encounter strong opposition from family and friends alike.[15] So, while earlier traditional strictures on courtship and mate selection are loosening up under the combined influences of modern industrialization and urbanization, there are still a number of constraints that apply to young people who are testing the dating waters.

One interesting social fact is that women in the Philippines are not necessarily more interested in getting married than are Filipino men. Being a spinster in the Philippines is not shameful and is sometimes a lifestyle that some women take on for a variety of reasons, including everything from

being rejected by her true love, to fear of childbirth, to obligations to take
care of younger brothers and sisters and so forth. Especially in the provinces,
an educated and successful woman who is, say, a local teacher may not find
a suitable marriage partner. On the other hand, becoming an elderly bachelor
is open to ridicule for not being a man.[16] For example, one of the ways that
the traditional Filipino male gains self-esteem is by the number of children
he is responsible for bringing into the world. This basic social value, augmented by the clout of the Roman Catholic church, has meant that introducing modern birth control into the country has been an uphill battle; the
Philippines still has one of the highest birth rates in the world.

Eventually, the courting couple will decide to marry and become engaged.
It is at this point that the traditional family system returns in full force
because marriage is the glue that holds the family together. The actual engagement period will vary depending on other family obligations, the desire
to prepare properly for the wedding, and if the bride is already pregnant. For
Filipinos, the only valid marriage ceremony is a religious one since a civil
ceremony does not have strong enough connotations. Because marriage and,
perhaps more importantly, its stability is essential to the maintenance and
strength of the Filipino family, it is believed that there must be the sanction
of God behind the vows and that anything less is of little consequence. This
commonly accepted belief takes on legal weight in the Philippines where the
influence of the Roman Catholic church is so great that divorce is not a legal
option. The familial expectations of the married couple, supported by the
legal system, thereby gives the Philippine marriage a level of permanence that
adds a greater seriousness to the commitment made by the young Philippine
couple than might be experienced by bridal partners in other cultures, where
divorce is a relatively accessible option out of a marriage vow.

In the Philippines, wedding expenses are assumed by the parents and relatives of the bridegroom, not the bride. In the provinces, the reception is
often held in the home of the bride, while in urban areas, the wedding party
and guests hold their festivities in a restaurant or hotel as newlyweds do in
the United States. Especially among the urbanized, the honeymoon is very
much in vogue, but even many provincial couples look forward to their
wedding trip to a distant resort where they can finally be alone for a while
before beginning their new life as the creators of yet another Filipino nuclear
family and branch of an extended bilateral system. Once they return from
the honeymoon, the newlyweds will often spend their first year with the
bride's family before striking out on their own, unless overriding circumstances such as employment make this arrangement impossible.

For the country's poor, however, the happy picture of an engagement, the
marriage ceremony, a honeymoon, and the beginning of married life under

auspicious circumstances is not a reality. Marriages are expensive propositions that they cannot afford. Instead, many poor couples simply live in common-law marriage relationships or, at most, seek a civil ceremony at the town hall. These marriages are often just as stable as religiously sanctified bonds, but the partners cannot meet the societal obligation of an expensive church wedding and reception. Since the Philippines has a grossly imbalanced economy, the number of poor is significant. Chapter Four "Architecture and Housing," noted that at a conservative estimate at least one million of metro Manila's near eleven million people were squatters who made their homes out of any available materials. These people, and many more in the rural areas of the country, cannot afford to participate in properly sanctified religious ceremonies.

Another aspect of marriage that also served as a marker of the country's depressed economic circumstance was a phenomenon of "mail-order brides" from the Philippines who made themselves available to an international market of potential husbands. The practice was made illegal in 1990, but until that time, thousands of Filipinas contacted marriage agencies that placed ads in foreign newspapers and even distributed videotaped interviews of the women so prospective foreign clients could view the women as they answered standard questions about themselves and what they were looking for in a marriage partner. The phenomenon was a desperate response by some women to the social-economic conditions that impacted their lives. As the economy worsened, otherwise eligible men were unable to assume the provider role necessary for a husband. The participating women were frequently well-educated professionals who saw no possibilities for themselves in their native land. Many hoped that by marrying a foreigner their own lives would improve. Once a citizen in a new country, they could possibly petition to bring over their aged parents and siblings. Eventually, escalating reports of abusive foreign husbands and unscrupulous syndicates that used some agencies as fronts for international prostitution rings, as well as nationalistic pride and outrage at the idea that Filipinas were offering themselves as marriage partners to foreigners, was enough to halt the practice.[17]

FAMILY RELATIONSHIPS

The arrival of a child firmly establishes the new family as a productive unit in Philippine society and is heralded with much fanfare. Until a child is born the partners are still only a couple rather than a family. While a son is preferred, gender is not as important in Filipino society as it is in patrilineal societies such as the Chinese. The important thing is that a true family is created because of the birth of an offspring. Additionally, new social roles are created as the married couple become parents and their parents, in turn, become grandparents; everyone gains additional respect and honor in the community. In rural farm families, children continue to be valued as future helpers in the family's daily economic life. As well, among the urban poor it is expected that children will supplement the family's meager income by doing odd jobs. In any case, all families, rich or poor, welcome children with the expectation that they will provide for their parents in old age.

Children also give the parents added meaning to their lives and a reason to achieve. The material needs of starting a family demand that more money be earned for the child's support and education. Parents will sacrifice as much as they can to ensure the child's success in life. In addition, children are important because they reaffirm God's blessing on the marital union and further cement the bond between the two partners. When otherwise serious conflicts occur between the married couple, these differences are patched over for the sake of the children. Finally, just as male masculinity is calculated by the number of children he sires, so too is the wife's womanhood established by giving birth. All of these expectations adversely affect a couple that cannot have their own children and must adopt.

Since public institutions are relatively less developed in the Philippines than in Western societies, it is the family that provides the principle vehicle for socialization, which the parents usually take very seriously. Since the Filipino male's orientation is that of provider whose activities take him outside of the home, the task of child raising falls primarily to the mother, at least in the early stages of growth. Her burden is eased somewhat in the case of a male child, who may later accompany his father outside the home. Because of the mother's intense involvement with her children, male and female alike, she takes on a status in the effective authority of the working of the family that the male cannot equal.

Because of the mother's importance, most Filipino families are *matrifocal,* that is to say that they are organized around the mother and, perhaps, some of her relatives and friends. Mothers not only give birth, they also nurture, feed, teach, encourage, punish, and, above all, expend any amount of completely unconditional love. Compared to the distant father figure, the mother is always present in the child's life and is the source of all that is good. More importantly, the debt that the typical Filipino child feels toward his or her mother goes far beyond the gift of life—to the child, mother is everything. Since the child can never fully repay his or her mother, the relationship between them is always unequal and requires that complete loyalty will always be given to her. The father may earn the child's respect but being psychically distant, and frequently absent from the household, he is difficult to approach and is somewhat forbidding.

What is the effective consequence of the mother's role in her children's development? Some critics contend that the freedom of the child to develop in her or his own way is greatly limited and this stifles personality growth and circumscribes individual initiative. As a consequence, the child's ego is subordinated to the family and not allowed to grow to its fullest potential. The family, then, can become authoritative despite its loving and caring bonds. Extrapolating further, since the family, with the mother at its core, is the focus of every Filipino's worldview, wider concerns about and feelings of responsibility for the greater Filipino community and nation are neglected. In public life, the Filipino society's family focus is responsible for much government nepotism and corruption, since public office is not an abstract trust but is a gain for the sake of the family and its allies.[18] The counter-argument states that the warm and loving familial womb protects the individual and provides a comfortable base from which the child may launch him or herself into the world. In point of fact, both of these interpretations are correct even if seemingly incompatible because the close and loving family can be either supporting or limiting depending on the degree to which either tendency is taken. While the Philippines offers numerous examples of each tendency, most observers agree that the country's familial matrifocal bonds are often a limiting factor, complicating personal lives and public participation.

Since the father is provider and distant authority figure who gains respect for his ability to operate in the wider world beyond the family circle, much of his potential authority is delegated to his wife. Instead of a role in the family's home life, many men spend a great deal of their free time associating with their *barkada* friends and work mates. Frequently, these activities are constructive and even necessary for his enhanced role in business and community affairs, but this comes at great cost to the development of his affective bonds with his wife and children. Over time, distance can grow between a married couple, especially as the husband is increasingly a stranger and guest in his own house. Eventually, the husband may be tempted to seek comfort in extramarital affairs, since divorce is not an option to escape from an unsatisfactory marital relationship. As well, having sex outside marriage has the attraction of confirming the husband's manhood, especially if a child is born to the girlfriend. Meanwhile, the same activity by the wife is strictly forbidden, and social sanctions for any sexual transgressions she may commit would be immediate and severe.[19]

Though few men can afford the luxury, the *querida*, or mistress, is a long established practice with roots that go back at least to the Spanish colonial period. In Philippine society, extramarital relations by men are expected and may even be encouraged by their *barkada* mates. A Filipino male's extramarital relations are not just tolerated but are admired. This can be seen in the example of Philippine President Joseph Estrada, who never made a secret of his numerous relationships. While the estimates of the number of his "girlfriends" varies slightly, he acknowledged a dozen, some of whom are close enough in his affection that he put them up in large mansions in elite neighborhoods of Manila during his presidency. Estrada's predecessor, President Fidel V. Ramos was much more modest, and he never commented on an alleged linkage with a prominent society lady who was his active political supporter. Clearly, it is in the realm of extramarital relations that the culture's double standard is most sharply revealed.

How does the wife react to the double standard and her husband's extra-marital activity? In most instances, the man's infidelity only confirms the woman's role as the long-suffering upholder of virtue that, in turn, strengthens her bond with her children and further decreases the husband's role in the family. In most cases, the girlfriend and wife never meet, since the husband is usually careful to select a partner outside of his own community. One problem that can arise is when the girlfriend becomes pregnant. Since the child is the husband's, the legal wife cannot completely disown the child, and in instances where the birth mother is unwilling or unable to care for the child, it may be brought into the primary home where it is accepted and given love, despite the child's birth circumstances.

Despite the sexual proclivities of the husband, the Philippine family is an extremely resilient institution, and there is considerable pressure put on the wife to forgive extramarital affairs. Usually, unless the man's transgressions are truly extreme, the husband is re-incorporated into the fold, since that is the only way the family can survive. In the idealized traditional world, as the couple age the conflicts of the past will recede in importance, and the pair grows more accustomed to each other until their children grow up to spin off from the household and further extend the family line. At this point, the parents are now the sage and respectable elders their parents once were.

THE FILIPINO FAMILY IN THE NEW MILLENNIUM

As indicated throughout this chapter, family life in the Philippines has undergone significant changes since the end of the Second World War. It is especially among the country's growing middle class that changes in the family seem to be taking place most rapidly. In the home the husband may still be reluctant to shoulder household chores, but he is more available to his children than fathers were in the past and he is more overtly affectionate and is willing to spend time with his young. In metro Manila shopping malls,

Young Manila professional couple with one child standing in front of their modern ranch-style home in a gated community. Photo by the author.

husbands can often be seen with and caring for their children in ways that would have seem unmanly only a decade or so ago.

To a significant degree, these changes in middle class male social behavior seem to be the result of greater economic and social forces. For example, with increased opportunities for women in the workforce, many more professional women have demanding jobs, which give them more compensation than ever and higher degrees of self-confidence but also require increased commitments of time and energy. Since many young professional women are making significant contributions to the family income, there is a need for their husbands to help in the care and nurturing of the children. It is no longer sufficient to leave the children in the care of a household helper.

Supporting these economic changes is a growing sensitivity to the inequalities of the traditional family and the double standard. Though not frequent, there are more stories in the national press about spousal abuse and a greater tendency to condemn the errant husband. Symptomatic of these changes in social attitudes and helping to push them along has been the rise of an organized feminist movement, Gabriela, since the 1980s. While few women are members of Gabriela, their ideas about themselves and their role in Philippine society are being studied and reshaped by new women's studies centers at schools such as St. Scholastica's College and the University of the Philippines. This movement has the active support of liberal members of the country's Roman Catholic clergy, which means that women's issues are now included in any review of the nation's human rights conditions.[20] Traditional attitudes that subordinated women or treated them in a paternalistic manner are becoming increasingly anachronistic. In fact, President Estrada's cavalier attitude toward his numerous affairs and his occasional degrading references about women have backfired with a significant portion of the informed electorate and may have helped pave the way for the storm of criticism that greeted revelations in October 2000 of his central role in a huge bribery and corruption scandal.

Within the last decade, the availability of contraceptives has increased, along with the respectability of birth control, both of which have implications for the future of the Filipino family. Though the Philippines still has one of the highest birth rates in the world, more and more young married couples are limiting their family size in response to the high costs of child rearing in the modern economy. Meanwhile, despite the fact that divorce is still not possible, annulments are gaining in popularity, thereby sidestepping violation of the formal marriage vow. So far only a tiny fraction of the country's population are in a position to take advantage of this option, but there is increased recognition that something should be done about dysfunctional marriages.

For the near future, however, the tightly knit Filipino family remains strong and provides a warm and loving environment to its members, despite its problems and weakness. That it is undergoing changes is not at all surprising and neither is its strength. The bilateral family has served the Filipino people well and has the capacity to modify itself to the new environment. While more Filipinas will demand a greater degree of equality in the family and in society in general, and while youth will strive for greater freedom in dating and mate selection, the bonds that hold family members together will remain strong.

NOTES

1. Belen T. G. Medina, *The Filipino Family: A Text with Selected Readings* (Quezon City: University of the Philippines Press, 1991), 19–25.

2. See another book in this series, Gary Marvin Davidson and Barbara E. Reed, *Culture and Customs of Taiwan* (Westport, CT: Greenwood Press, 1998), 167–189, for a discussion of the Chinese family as it exists in that island nation.

3. The author's research in the Philippine sugar economy of Negros province has certainly found this marriage pattern to have been practiced until the post-World War II era.

4. See Donn V. Hart, *Compadrinazgo: Ritual Kinship in the Philippines* (DeKalb: Northern Illinois University Press, 1977).

5. Medina, 28.

6. See Alfred W. McCoy, ed., *An Anarchy of Families: State and Family in the Philippines* (Madison: Center for Southeast Asian Studies, University of Wisconsin, 1993), for an extensive discussion of the relationship of family networks and entrenched political dynasties. A number of the articles in this volume stress the role of fictive as well as actual kin in the construction of political alliances.

7. F. Landa Jocano, *Filipino Social Organization: Traditional Kinship and Family Organization* (Metro Manila: Punlad Research House, 1998), 46.

8. Isabel S. Panopio, Felicidad C. Cordero-MacDonald, and Adelisa A. Raymundo, *General Sociology: Focus on the Philippines*, 3rd ed. (Quezon City: Ken, Inc., 1994), 93–94.

9. I learned the importance of the *barkada* while a graduate student in the Philippines and working part-time at a Manila radio station. On the surface, this was a "job" similar to any other with co-workers, shift schedules, authority levels, and seniority, but that was only the surface reality of the work environment. All decisions including when, and even if, one worked were socially determined, and formal hierarchy had little practical meaning. What really mattered was the cohesiveness within the group. So, no announcer could simply do his airtime every day and leave promptly at the conclusion of his shift until the next workday. It was expected that announcers would stay and "hang out" with the other guys who worked at the station. Even after work, station personnel constantly socialized with each other such that old friends became distant memories. Announcers who tried to buck this social reality usually did not last long.

10. See Alfred W. McCoy, ed., *Closer Than Brothers: Manhood at the Philippine Military Academy* (New Haven, CT: Yale University Press, 1999).

11. Jocano, 129–130.

12. Medina, 66–68.

13. Ibid., 65–66, and Jocano, 134.

14. Medina, 81–82.

15. Ibid., 80, 84–85, 87–89

16. Ibid., 70, and Jocano, 132–133.

17. Elena L. Samonte, and Annadaisy J. Carlota, "The Mail-Order Marriage Business: A Reconsideration of the Filipina Image," in Amaryllis T. Torres, ed., *The Filipino Woman in Focus* (Bangkok: UNESCO, 1989).

18. This argument is made strongly by the Dutch anthropologist Niels Mulder in his book *Inside Philippine Society: Interpretations of Everyday Life* (Quezon City: New Day Publishers, 1997), see especially pp. 37–44. Though Mulder is an outsider and subject to the possibility of misinterpreting an unfamiliar cultural milieu, many of his criticisms are echoed by Filipino social scientists, most of them women.

19. Medina, 106–108.

20. See, for example, the Church-sponsored report, authored by the Philippine Human Rights Information Center, *Growth 2000: Selective Prosperity, Human Rights on the Fourth Year of the Ramos Administration* (Manila: Philippine Human Rights Information Center, 1997).

7

Festivals, Theater, Film, Media, and Other Entertainment

THIS CHAPTER looks at a broad range of Philippine cultural productions beginning with a survey of its numerous festivals. These festive occasions are enjoyed by all Filipinos and have inherent social dimensions in addition to their celebration of the country's religious life. Next, the origins and development of Philippine theater is explored, including its indigenous forms and the foreign influences that have deepened this medium to become a vibrant expression of Filipino values and a mirror of the social changes and political concerns of the modern nation. Moving on to a more technologically developed cultural product, the Philippine film industry, one of the most productive in the world, is examined. Despite the ubiquitous presence of Hollywood films and inroads made by VCRs, the local movie industry remains extremely popular and reflects cultural values and social concerns as few other aspects of Philippine culture can. Closely connected with the film industry, the nation's newspaper, radio, and television industries perform many of the same functions. How these industries grew and their present state will be looked at briefly before turning to sport and games. Here, the Filipino's fascination with basketball and cockfighting is highlighted, since they, as well as a number of children's games, illustrate the passions of the common folk for competition and social celebration.

THE PHILIPPINE FESTIVAL COMPLEX

As a warm, gregarious, and open people, the image of the fiesta aptly suits the Filipino. Indeed, the fiesta is a trademark of the country, but Philippine festivals are not simply parties, no matter how much Filipinos enjoy them—

selves. The celebration of holidays usually has significance at deeper levels that includes agricultural life, religious devotion, societal values, and familial bonds. As well, the country's festivals gave birth to significant forms of the Philippine's theatrical tradition, some of its music, and even aspects of its literature and art. The first-time visitor to the Philippines is immediately aware that most of the country's celebrations are religious or are at least heavily infused with religious meaning and symbolism that reflects the sincere religiosity of the people. Clearly, the dominance of Roman Catholicism is not limited simply to its having the largest number of adherents. Its cultural impact is deep and long-lasting and is apparent during celebrations. The social importance of these festivals is, perhaps, less noticeable but it is just as important as the religious aspect. Festivals serve as opportunities for the wealthy to display themselves and for the reaffirmation of commonly held societal values and the central importance of the family. Festivals are also central to the lives of the country's non-Christian ethnic minorities, such as the people in the Central Cordillera Mountains of the main island of Luzon and the Islamic peoples of the far southern islands. As well, celebrations associated with the Philippine's national existence serve to instill pride in the country and in the united Filipino people. All of these festivals and holidays play a role in forming a Philippine cultural identity.

The Town Fiesta

The festival combining the most cultural and religious elements is the annual fiesta honoring a town's patron saint. The fiesta is directly linked with the Roman Catholic church, but the fiesta's relationship with the municipality is a secular dimension to the celebration that is less obvious but also important and rooted in the nation's history. During the Spanish colonial period, the creation of an independent parish for a specific community was an important step in the process of its becoming an autonomous municipality. Since the colonial government in Manila wanted each town to be under the administration of a priest, only those communities would rise to full municipal status. Communities that only rated a visiting priest were virtually doomed to remain dependent barrios under the sway of an established municipal government. Thus, the celebration of the feast day of the patron saint is also the celebration of the town's existence and identity. Today, long after the presence of a parish priest has been dropped as a requirement for the creation of new municipal governments, the importance of the fiesta remains for all towns.

Just as the fiesta is a merger of the religious and the secular, the actual celebration is also the product of a combined effort. The parish priest organizes the true fiesta honoring the patron saint, including the processions, a novena (a nine day prayer devotion) and at least one mass. Meanwhile, a committee of prominent individuals is in charge of all the nonreligious festivities, which include a dance, a beauty contest to select the Queen and King of the fiesta, sporting contests (basketball tournaments and cockfights, *pintakasi*), raffles, dramas, speeches, commercial activities, and, perhaps, a carnival. Membership on these committees and one's position in the organizational hierarchy is a clear indication of social status and, more practically, how much money one is contributing to the event. The annual fiesta is unique, since the religious and secular halves in the planning must closely coordinate, which is not always the case in other celebrations. During celebrations that are strictly religious, such as Holy Week, there are no additional secular festivities and, conversely, secular events such as Independence Day do not have a religious component.

Since the fiesta has a strong link to the community, towns compete with each other as a matter of pride to see who can put on the best fiesta, and some towns are locally famous for the quality of their celebration, so there is a tremendous pressure on all of the town's citizens to participate and contribute, even non-Christians and individuals not known for their religiosity. The fiesta is also a time when social alliances between neighbors and friends from neighboring towns can be reinforced. Virtually anyone can visit anyone else and everyone is always invited to have something to eat from the specially prepared fiesta foods laid out for guests (see Chapter Five, "Cuisine and Fashion"). In fact, care must be taken to visit friends and social and political allies during the fiesta and to have at least a little something to eat as not to give offense by appearing to snub a friend.

Yet, the Philippine fiesta's most important and basic social function is an opportunity for families to reunite and maintain their tight bonds, this sometimes includes distant relatives as well as members of the nuclear family. Filipinos will make extraordinary efforts to return to their hometown for fiesta. This behavior is true even for Filipinos who may have migrated to a far distant city many years or even decades ago and whose lives now have little connection to their extended family's rural past. Even though it might be more convenient to visit the old ancestral home on other occasions, the pull of the town fiesta is usually overwhelming.[1]

Major Christian Religious Festivals

As a historically Christian country, the Philippine's religious holidays are similar to those celebrated in many other countries. There are, however, some interesting variations on the actual celebration of common Christian holidays and some particular holidays are emphasized more in the Philippines than other places. These variations and emphases are frequently related to the Filipino family and its involvement in ceremonial life. They are also related to the country's agricultural life and sometimes show lingering pre-Christian elements, which give Philippine Christianity its folk dimension.

Christmas is certainly a central feature of religious devotion and is celebrated in the Philippines as elsewhere with Santa Claus, caroling, manger scenes, the Christmas tree, and gift giving. In addition, many Filipinos have a star-shaped lantern, or *parol*, made of bamboo sticks and colored paper hanging in their window symbolizing the star that guided the Magi to the Christ child. San Fernando, the capital of Pampanga province, is even noted for its Christmas lantern festival. All churches hold early morning (about 4 A.M.) masses, the *misas de gallo*, for nine days before Christmas to build anticipation. In some communities, the celebrations extend until January 6 with the Feast of the Three Kings, during which special pageants and plays are held.

Another extremely important holiday is the extended period of Lent that is celebrated as elsewhere, but with some markedly different variations. For example, on Palm Sunday, artistically wrought palms are brought to the church for the priest to bless after mass. They are then taken home and hung over doorways and windows in the belief that they will protect the occupants from evil spirits. As well, it is often customary during the holiday for town residents to gather nightly for a *pabasa*, where they sing and recite the story of Christ's passion. Many towns additionally stage religious plays, *sinakulo*, where various incidents in the Passion are acted out. Of especial note are the Good Friday flagellants who beat themselves on the back with ropes containing embedded pieces of glass or sharp pieces of bamboo attached at the end of the twine. The beating continues until their backs are pieces of bleeding raw flesh and then vinegar is rubbed into the wounds. Some of the more fanatical believers will actually have themselves nailed to wooden crosses that are then raised for a short time with the faithful flagellant hanging in imitation of Christ. In some towns, Easter Sunday services are also combined with a ceremony called the *salubong*, or encounter, in which two entourages, one being the image of the risen Christ and other that of the mourning Virgin Mother, are taken on separate routes from the church until they encounter each other at a specially constructed platform in the town plaza.

One especially artistic Lenten festival variation is the *Morion*, or mask, festival held on the island of Marinduque. This festival is based on the legend of Longinus the Roman centurion, who was blind in his left eye and who pierced Christ's side with a spear. As Longinus drew the blade out, a drop of blood landed in his eye, restoring his sight. The centurion immediately converted to Christianity but was put to death by his fellow Romans as a result. The men of the island's towns make their own large and colorful masks of paper-mâché and vie for the honor of playing the part of Longinus in the annual festivity that is acted out before large and appreciative crowds.[2]

Another religious holiday that holds especial meaning for the Filipino family is All Saints Day held on the first of November. This is a holiday to honor the memory of the dead, especially deceased family members. Graves are cleaned, late night vigils held, prayers said, and flowers and food left for the spirits of the dead, who are said to visit the earth on this day. Since this celebration is so intimately wrapped up with the family, linking as it does the living with the deceased, it is an important time for family reunions. Unlike the playful American Halloween, All Saints Day is a serious national holiday during which public transportation is in extremely short supply as entire cities seem to leave for the provinces, and highways are jammed with vehicles.

Other Religious Festivals

Filipinos celebrate a number of other religious holidays, some of which are within the Roman Catholic tradition while others combine pre-Christian elements with Catholicism. Among the more traditional are the numerous Marian festivals honoring the Virgin Mary. For example, there is one Marian festival held in thanksgiving for the defeat of attacking Dutch ships by the Spanish navy in the mid-seventeenth century (the *La Naval de Manila*), a celebration that continues to the present day. Numerous, other Marian festivals in parishes around the country originated because of a miraculous event or apparition associated with a carved image of Mary. There are also a number of festivals associated with the worship of the Holy Child. Principle among these is the veneration of the image of the Christ child, the *Santo Nino*, originally brought to the island of Cebu by Ferdinand Magellan. The image was found almost fifty years later by a soldier in Don Miguel Lopez de Legazpi's expedition, when the Spaniards returned to establish a colony, and is today the centerpiece of a massive festival in Cebu City. Similar celebrations of the *Santo Nino* are held in various sections of Manila and other towns in the country. A distant variation of this worship is held in Kalibo, the capital of Aklan province of Panay Island, where worship of the *Santo Nino* is mixed with a fiesta celebrating the mythical arrival of ten Malay *datus* (title given a local leader) and their friendly relationship with the original dark-skinned natives, the Atis. In the contemporary *Ati-Atihan* festival, celebrants blacken their skin with soot, paint their faces in a profusion of

Flores de Mayo celebration. Courtesy of the Cultural Center of the Philippines Library Collection.

designs, garb themselves with all variety of wild costumes, and celebrate mardi gras style for almost a week.[3]

There are still other religious festivities that seek to ensure immediate benefits for their celebrants, such as festivals related to agriculture, travel, and fertility. Agricultural celebrations are often held in May, a slack agricultural period when farmers are not as consumed with plowing, harrowing, and planting as they will be in June and July when the plentiful rains arrive to start the next rice season. One of these is the May 15 feast day of *San Isidro* that honors the water buffalo, the symbol of subsistence agriculture upon which much of the population still depends despite recent advances in the mechanization and commercialization of agriculture. Another particularly striking celebration of *San Isidro* is the *pahiyas* festival of Lucban and Sariaya towns in Tayabas province. Houses are decorated to unimaginable degrees with various agricultural products, including gourds, peppers, leaves, coconut husks and rice straw, but mostly with *kiping*, brightly colored rice paste shaped into large leaves and then hardened. The exterior of houses is covered with these products in unique folk art designs and are sometimes augmented by dressed-up straw dummies.[4]

Every May, tens of thousands of Filipinos make a pilgrimage to the image of the *Virgin of Antipolo* in Rizal province who is credited with miraculous events and served for hundreds of years as the protector of the galleon trade between Mexico and the Philippines. In the days of perilous sea travel when so many ships were lost to storms and pirates and when disease took even more lives, many people would visit the *Virgin* to ask her protection before starting on their journey.

The idea of travel by water and the importance of rivers in Philippine life is accented by a number of special fluvial celebrations that have pre-Christian origins. Many of these river festivals are centered in the provinces surrounding Manila, but the largest is the *Penafrancia* festival in Naga City in the Bicol region of Luzon. This festival is held on the third Saturday of November following a nine-day novena and a week of festivities. On that Saturday, the saint's image is taken from its church and brought to the diocesan cathedral and then returned by a river route. One writer has speculated that the long river route is chosen for the return trip because the journey represents pre-Christian ceremonies that exorcised the river of evil spirits.[5]

Non-Christian Festivities

The residents of the Central Cordillera Mountains in the northern reaches of Luzon worship their gods according to need and do not have specific annual festivals such as the Christmas, Lenten, and *Penafrancia* festivals. Rather, ceremonial activities relate to the agricultural cycle or major human events, such as birth, marriage and death. Among these ceremonies is the *manerwap*, which is a prayer for rain; the *ap-pey*, a three-day festivity held after rice seedlings have been transplanted and in which supernatural forces controlling the ultimate success of the crop are propitiated; the *lesles*, a thanksgiving festival held after the harvest; and the multipurpose *iyag* festival, during which the gods are called upon for any of a number of reasons.

Houses in Lucban, Tayabas province decorated for the *Pahiyas* harvest festival with gourds, peppers, rice stalks, and, especially, the brightly colored rice wafers, *kiping*, that are used to make chandeliers. Courtesy of the Bernie Cervantes Collection.

Accompanying these ceremonies are sacrifices of animals, specific dances for the occasion and a *canao*, or feast, given by the wealthiest man in the community.

In contrast to the northern mountain people, the Muslim population of the southern islands has a more complex series of festival occasions centered on their religious devotion. The principle holiday is the *hari-raya poasa*, a festival marking the end of the thirty-day fasting period of Ramadan. This festival has been compared to Christmas because of its religious significance, along with its feasting on specially prepared foods, the giving of gifts to children, and the holding of sporting events. Other important ceremonial days are *hari-raya hadji* held on the tenth day of the twelfth month of the Islamic calendar. On this day, Muslims who have made the *hadj*, the pilgrimage to Mecca to visit the tomb of the Prophet Mohammed, pray at their local mosques and serve visitors a variety of delicacies. Meanwhile, the *maolod en nabi*, held on the twelfth day of the third month of the calendar, commemorates the birth of the Prophet Mohammed while his ascension is celebrated on the twenty-seventh day of the seventh month. Both of these occasions are considered solemn, but feasts are offered for the poor. Finally, ceremonies with pre-Islamic cultural influences include the honoring of the dead on the eighth month when, like their Christian counterparts on All Saints Day, Muslims clean the graves of their deceased family members and offer them incense and flowers; and the *panulak bala* (easing misfortune) festival where a Muslim *imam* (mosque prayer leader) splashes the celebrants with water to cleanse them after which celebrants take a small stone and cast it into the sea or river as a symbolic act of throwing out their spiritual impurities.[6]

National and Secular Holidays

Even though the United States formally granted the Philippines independence on July 4, 1946, the national Independence Day is celebrated on June 12 to commemorate General Emilio Aguinaldo's declaration of independence from Spain. Though the Filipino republic created in 1898 was only in existence for a few months before being besieged by the U.S. army, the reason why Aguinaldo's declaration is celebrated as the country's true independence day is crucial. Independence given as a gift by a colonial power is not as genuine as that declared and fought for by a people, even if that government was vanquished by a stronger military force. Not being ungrateful, however, Filipinos also celebrate July 4th, but as Philippine-American Friendship Day, though it should be noted that the holiday no longer is as important as it once was. Filipinos also have two holidays to mark the sacrifices that their soldiers and American forces made defending the country against the Japanese onslaught in World War II. Bataan Day is commemorated on April 9 with a re-enactment of the gruesome forced death march made by the surrendered Philippine and American soldiers, and on May 6, the fall of the Bataan Peninsula's offshore island bastion is acknowledged in ceremonies for the Battle of Corregidor.

Like the official Independence Day, a number of other holidays celebrate the nation's heroes and the revolt against Spanish colonialism. Rizal Day is celebrated on December 30 with civic parades and events marking the national hero's martyrdom. A month earlier the birthday of Andres Bonifacio, founder of the revolutionary *Katipunan* society, is celebrated throughout the country with the center of events based at the hero's monument in the city of Caloocan immediately north of Manila. The Cry of Pugadlawin that called the people to arms against Spain is commemorated on August 26. The country also celebrates a number of secular holidays that are familiar to people of other countries. Labor Day celebrations are held on May 1 and a number of more commercial holidays, including Mother's Day and Father's Day, now appear on Filipino calendars. Of the latter two holidays, the first is far more important because of the role of the mother in the Filipino family.

THE DEVELOPMENT OF PHILIPPINE THEATER

Theater in the Philippines enjoyed its audience peak in the pre-electronic era of the late Spanish and early American colonial periods. In the nation's capital and numerous provincial towns, the population was entertained by a variety of productions ranging from the religious *sinakulo* to the comedic romantic farces of the *sarsuela*. During the unsuccessful fight for independence in the early years of this century, the theater also fulfilled the important function of spreading the nationalist message, often under the very noses of the American enemy. Later, while many theatrical troupes folded and theaters either closed or switched to show the new "moving pictures," Philippine theater remained alive simply because it fulfilled the human needs for self-expression and artistic creation. Foreign influences continued to enter during the American regime and in the modern era so that today's Philippine theater can truly be said to have a sophisticated international connection rare for an Asian nation. In addition, the social and political edge originally seen in the anti-American "seditious plays" of the turn-of-the-century continued to reverberate in socially conscious theater during the years of Ferdinand Marcos, and this spirit still enlivens contemporary theatrical productions.

Origins and Spanish Influences

Before Spain's arrival, indigenous Filipinos did not have a traditional theater with scripted dialogue and productions set in specially designed spaces. Rather, the function of theater, the telling of stories and the passing on of community values, was carried out by the rituals of native priests and priestesses and set to the accompaniment of indigenous music and dance as described in Chapter Eight. These ceremonies were proto-dramas, conducted to ensure a bountiful harvest, a successful hunt, prowess in battle, or the transition to the afterlife. These dramas were also used for the relief of sickness and on the occasions of birth, circumcision, courtship, marriage, and death. Frequently, too, there were mimetic aspects in which the performers' dances imitated animals such as monkeys and birds or acts such as planting rice and tubers or making war. All groups also had proto-dramas depicting courtship, which occasionally included the abduction of the woman. Beyond entertainment, this early form of dramatic representation served to bond the community, since members of the audience could also become players, and group values were transmitted and experiences shared.[7]

The religious orders were especially aware of the potential of theater to assist their efforts to convert the indigenous population. During the Spanish era, various forms of plays, both religious and secular, were introduced and became part of the culture. Most of these plays celebrated holidays such as Christmas, Lent, or Easter and they are still staged in towns across the archipelago. A popular form of play is the *komedya*, also known as the *moro-moro* plays, that invariably feature battles between Christian and Muslim adversaries in medieval Europe. The *moro-moro* frequently includes narrations about the lives of patron saints and has magical events that come to the rescue of besieged Christians. These plays conclude with the mass conversion of the defeated Muslim enemies thus ensuring a warm and appreciative reception by the audience.[8]

The most frequently staged religious play is the *sinakulo*, also known as the *pasyon*, which begins with creation but focuses its attention on the life and death of Jesus Christ. The *pasyon* is performed during Lent and for eight nights during Holy Week. The quality of productions range from relatively simple recitations to elaborately staged affairs supported by prominent members of local communities as an aspect of their devotional duties. In this particular gift-giving activity, the donors do not expect any immediate social return, but their generosity does underscore their social-economic position in the community. The importance of the *pasyon* cannot be overemphasized because it is still popular among the faithful across the country and because it is within the context of the annual performance through which religious and community values are transmitted and reaffirmed. Scripts for the *pasyon* were also an early form of Philippine literature with the first written in 1703 by Gaspar de Belen. The story was later adapted to the country's numerous regional dialects. Since the *pasyon* is so pervasive, its message has had an impact that extends far beyond the strict confines of religion. While the Spanish friars sought to use this vehicle for their own purposes, moral teachings, like ideas, cannot easily be controlled. Philippine historian Reynaldo Ileto has convincingly argued that the moral lessons of the *pasyon* as staged annually in community after community became the ethical framework that guided commoner Filipinos during the revolution against Spain and the resistance to American domination.[9]

In addition to the *komedya* and the *sinakulo*, there are a number of other religious plays performed during specific holidays and events, such as the *Tatlong Hari* (Three Kings) seen during Christmas and a large number of productions for other important religious days, especially Easter. One of the more colorful of these latter plays has become a festival event in and of itself. The *Moriones* (helmets) of Marinduque Island is a religious play that tells the story of a Roman soldier who witnesses Christ's resurrection and converts to Christianity.

In the late nineteenth century, secular theater entered the colony as Spain liberalized due to the influence of the Enlightenment. One of the earliest forms of the new theater to reach the Philippines was the *zarzuela* (or *sarsuela* in Pilipino) that features common people, love stories, contemporary themes, songs, and dances. While the first *sarsuelas* were staged for appreciative Spanish audiences in Manila, they were immediately adopted by Filipinos and spread like wildfire around the country. Soon troupes were formed in every province wealthy enough to support a company, and scores of actors, actresses, playwrights, directors, and musicians emerged to the delight of provincial audiences starved for something other than religious entertainment. The most prominent proponent of the new theater was Severino Reyes, who actively promoted it and used the *sarsuela*'s flexibility to present social commentary and either criticized social evils or satirized cultural foibles, as well as entertaining his audiences with love stories, song, and dance. At the same time that the *sarsuela* entered the colony so too did formal dramatic plays that did not feature musical numbers and dances. The dramas usually attracted a more sophisticated audience in Manila and the nation's provincial capitals, and their themes were often more serious. These, too, developed a significant following, though not as large as their lighter competitor.

The development of formal secular theater came at an important time in the Philippine's national development, since the country's emerging *mestizo* and native elites could adopt the new art form as yet another means to

Cast of the 1970s theatrical revival of the turn-of-the-century play *Walang Sugat* (*Not Wounded*), an anti-American nationalist *sarsuela.* Courtesy of the Cultural Center of the Philippines Library Collection.

embrace the secular enlightenment and loosen the tight bonds of ecclesiastical influence. This social-political edge to theater intensified during the nationalist struggle to overturn Spanish rule and resist the United States. *Sarsuelas* and drama were both used to carry the patriotic message, even after the defeat of most Filipino armies on the battlefield. Among many such plays was Severino Reyes's 1902 *Walang Sugat* (*Not Wounded*), which contrasted friar cruelty with the heroism of *Katipunan* soldiers, while the play's love interest, Julia, serves as an allegorical representation of the Philippines. Since there was an easy interpretative transition from Spanish friar to American colonial officer, the U.S. military attempted to curtail the seditious plays and frequently raided theaters. For example, in 1902, Juan Abad was arrested during a performance of his drama *Tanikalang Guinto* (*Golden Chain*), which had the character representing the United States tying the Filipina love-interest to a tree with his gift of a golden chain so she cannot leave him.[10]

The Twentieth-Century Decline and Rebirth of Philippine Theater

In the first decades of the twentieth century, the theater, especially the *sarsuela,* enjoyed a popularity that was not destined to last. In part, their dominance was undercut by the introduction of American vaudeville (or *bodabil* in Pilipino) with its combination of short dramatic skits, comedy sketches, chorus girls, and songs. Since most of the entertainment in *bodabil* shows was based on what was current in America, the increased popularity of stage shows limited the development of Philippine theater. It was first in *bodabil* that Filipino musicians and singers adopted and imitated popular American performers and thoroughly implanted the notion of the "American Dream" in the popular psyche. Even more devastating for Philippine theater was the introduction of the motion picture, which captivated Filipino audiences. Many *sarsuela* plots and actors and actresses made the transition to the new Philippine film industry, but only at the expense of the theater that had given them their training. By the late 1930s, only a few *sarsuela* troupes continued to exist. Only in the Ilokano-speaking provinces of northern Luzon Island did the local tradition continue, and even there, it did so at a much reduced level.

Even as the introduction of *bodabil* and motion pictures dealt heavy blows to the Hispanic-influenced theater, the new American colonial regime laid the basis for a new Filipino theater. The instrument for a new theater came through the teaching of English in the new American system of universal public education. Across the country, hundreds of new elementary schools were created, and English was taught, in part, through the vehicle of school plays. Soon theatrical groups and academic departments were started in the nation's colleges, where a new generation was trained in the mastery of English and its theatrical presentation. The first play in English was *A Modern Filipina* (1915), by Jesusa Araullo and J. Lino Castillejo of the Philippine Normal College, and other scripts and performances soon followed as did the notion of the need to develop a legitimate theater beyond the touring *sarsuela* companies. Important, too, were the staging of plays by British and European authors, which opened further vistas to the new generation. The new university-trained writers and performers eventually formed companies that went to major provincial cities to introduce formal theater to their countrymen and women.

Significantly, the scripts that emerged from the universities began to address domestic issues rather than simply copying the forms of American and European plays. By the post–World War II period, a core of talented writers, led by Wilfrido Ma. Guerrero, Alberto Florentino, and Severino Montano, led the way toward a more realistic portrayal of Philippine society as they began to address previously unasked questions about the country's poor and downtrodden. Special mention should also be made of Nick Joaquin's superior play *Portrait of the Artist as Filipino* (1954), which strongly condemned what the author saw as the post-war period's loss of moral bearings. Nevertheless, since the scripts of these writers were in English, the nuances of which only a minority of the population could fully appreciate, their impact was limited to a small urban intelligentsia. The big break came in the 1960s as the growing nationalist movement began to offer a coherent critique of the relevance of a culture that depended upon English for its language of cultural conceptualization and communication and the American model for its ideal form.

Contemporary Philippine Theater

Contemporary theater in the Philippines owes its existence to the synthesis of the use of the national language, the influence of new forms of socially relevant theater, and the rebirth of the Hispanic theatrical forms that had almost died out. This revival of theater in terms of its social importance was paralleled in the increased size of its audience. Although attendance figures for live theater cannot begin to compare with the huge crowds jamming the nation's movie theaters on a daily basis, interest in theater has been encouraging as different levels of society have come out to support new performances.

Fundamental to the rebirth of Philippine theater was its shift away from English, which allowed larger audiences to fully appreciate the play's dialogue and message. The leader in the movement to adapt Pilipino to modern theater and make it more accessible was Rolando Tinio of Atcneo de Manila University, who began by translating the works of Western playwrights such as Shakespeare and Chekhov. Meanwhile, playwrights, such as Alberto Florentino, who began their careers using English switched to the vernacular, and by the late 1960s, the shift was well underway. Supporting this movement was the formation of a number of new theater groups, such as the UP Repertory Company, Dulaang UP, Philippine Educational Theater Association (PETA), and the Ateneo Experimental Theater, that gave writers and directors forums to try new ventures. Not as well publicized as these groups was the Ateneo's *Dulaang Sibol* (Theater of Growth) nurtured by Onofre Pagsanjan, which recruited its members at the high school level. This small company nurtured its young members, and today some of the country's theatrical leaders received their start in *Sibol*.[11] In addition, theater professors and playwrights Amelia Lapena-Bonifacio and Bienvenido Lumbera, both of the University of the Philippines, began writing plays in Pilipino, which added further legitimacy to the movement. Even though some plays are still written in English and Broadway productions are showcased by Repertory Philippines, the change to Pilipino is virtually complete.

Rather than closing Philippine theater off from external influences, the switch to Pilipino and the reinvigoration of the art actually increased interest in new forms of theatrical expression. Realism and psychological themes, which had already made an impact on local stages, became even more prominent under the skilled pens of many new writers, including Rogelio Sicat, whose *Moses, Moses* (1969) was a devastating critique of the administration of justice in the country; Rolando Tinio, who wrote *A Life in the Slums* (1976) which brought a social reality of the country's poor to sophisticated theater patrons; while Tony Perez produced *Sa North Diversion Road* (*On the North Diversion Road*) in 1988 as a critique of the psychological tensions inherent in contemporary society. Other writers experimented with absurdist theater and elements of Bertolt Brecht's ideas that enhanced the portrayal of the oppressed of society. Meanwhile, Al Santos's *Mayo A-Beinte Uno* (*May 21*, 1977) portrayed the perspective of the peasant organization Lapiang Malaya in its 1962 confrontation with government troops that resulted in a horrifying massacre of its members. In the late 1960s and early 1970s, Filipinos even studied the performance art of the Chinese Cultural Revolution plays such as *Taking Tiger Mountain by Strategy* and *The Red Detachment of Women*.

Clearly there was a new urgency demanding that theater give expression to the aspirations of forgotten segments of the population, and this urgency had an obvious political basis. The political nature of the new theater was abundantly clear in the formation of community-based theater groups whose purpose was to use the stage for political ends. One of the earliest of these groups was Gintong Silahis whose *Barikada* (*Barricade*, 1971) sounded a clear call for artistic political commitment as it depicted the creation of the "UP Commune" of the pre-martial law period. Meanwhile, another group, Panday-Sining, staged Bonifacio Ilagan's *Welga, Welga* (*Strike, Strike*, 1972), the story of a union that has to struggle for its principles rather than simple economic gains. The call to political commitment continued to be heeded by many more new artists and theatrical groups such as the Adela Community Organization, which produced a bitter denunciation of the exploitation of migrant sugar workers in *Matamis Man Gali Ang Kalamay* (*Sugar Is Sweet After All*, 1991) and staged the play in Silay, Negros Occidental province, the heart of the sugar industry in the Visayan Islands.

The revival of Philippine theater also gave new life to the *komedya, sarsuela*, and *pasyon*. Even while experimenting with new forms of expression, there was a concurrent commitment to explore the past. The reasoning was that the *komedya*, for example, had been an effective tool to communicate and was fully integrated into Philippine culture after hundreds of years of Spanish contact. As well, the *sarsuela's* popularity, until its replacement by *bodabil* and movies, similarly indicated that it too could appeal to local audiences.

As early as 1962, Max Allanigue produced a *moro-moro* play, *Prinsipe Rodante* (*Prince Rodante*), that sought reconciliation between people of different faiths rather than featuring the religious conflict of the traditional play. Later in 1982, Nicanor Tiongson premiered his extremely successful *Pilipinas Circa 1907* that used the *sarsuela* form to examine the modern theme of economic exploitation of Third World nations by the United States. Al Santos presented a new *pasyon* play, the *Sinakulo ng Maralitang Taga-Lungsod* (*Passion Play of the Urban Poor*, 1988), whose crucified Christ characters were the homeless squatters who picked through garbage all day on Manila's "Smoky Mountain" in a desperate effort to find items that recycle merchants might be willing to buy.[12]

During the early years of Ferdinand Marcos's martial law regime, Filipino playwrights, directors, and actors had to temper their productions and use a language of indirection to deliver their message. But after the assassination of Begnino "Nonoy" Aquino in 1983, theater once again took a direct and open role in mobilizing public opinion against the government. So, for example, the group Peryante staged Chris Millado's play *Ilokula, Ang Ilokanong Drakula II* (*Ilocula, the Ilocano Dracula II*, 1983). President Marcos was an Ilocano from the province of Ilocos Norte, and in this play, he is depicted as a reincarnation of Dracula come to suck the life blood from the Filipino people. In the following year the performance of an innovative play by Bienviendo Lumbera was produced, which combined contemporary rock music with a modern opera about the Spanish-era national hero Jose Rizal. The play, *Bayani* (*The Brave*), used Rizal's life and martyrdom to question the current leadership by drawing parallels between the Spanish oppression that executed Rizal with the regime of Ferdinand Marcos. Coming so soon after the assassination of former Senator Aquino, the point of the play was not lost on the audience. Since the end of the Marcos regime, Philippine theater of protest and social realism has transformed itself to focus on systemic problems of poverty and injustice now that its primary and personal target no longer exists. Now, there are plays about the plight of Filipino overseas workers, such as Ricky Lee's *D.H.* (*Domestic Helper*, 1992), and women's issues in Joi Barrios's *Damas de Noche* (*Women of the Night*, 1991).[13]

In 1998, theatrical works played a prominent role in crystallizing the nationalistic patriotism of the country's centennial celebration. Since this was an historical celebration, the plays produced for it concentrated on the nation's independence struggle and the men who led it. Paul Dumol wrote a trilogy that was presented by the Cultural Center of the Philippine's Tanghalang Pilipino. The first two plays, *Cabesang Tales* and *El Filibusterismo*, were based on Jose Rizal's works, while the third play, *Ilustrado* (*The Young Educated Elite*) told the life of Rizal. In this work, playwright Paul Dumol and composer Ruben Cayabyab combined talents to "reinterpret and set to music for the Generation Y" the national hero's story so it would be relevant to today's youth. Other theatrical offerings included Lucien Letaba and Charley de la Pena's 1995 play *1896*, which was mounted by PETA and traveled beyond Manila thanks to translations into regional dialects such as Cebuano. The role played by the nation's theatrical community in making the centennial a resounding success clearly shows that Philippine theater is alive and well, even in this modern era of movies, VCRs, and the ubiquitous television set.[14] Fortunately, the Philippines has a wealth of dedicated artists such as Anton Juan and Tony Mabesa, who continue to write, produce, direct, and act as well as a number of institutions that support theater and audiences who appreciate an alternative to the movies and television.

FILM

Filipinos are probably among the world's most avid motion picture fans. In the past decade, television and videos have made a significant cut into theater attendance, but all of metro Manila's huge multistory shopping malls still boast multiscreen cineplexes. The interest in motion pictures is so great that the Philippines currently screens much of Hollywood's annual offerings as well as supporting one of the world's largest domestic film industries. This obsession with movies is not a recent development. Shortly before World War II, Manila's studios made almost sixty films per year, and in 1958, the one hundred films per year benchmark was topped. Despite declining theater revenues and profits, today's domestic film production is estimated at between 90 to slightly over 130 films annually, so there is no scarcity of cinematic variety for the Filipino audience to choose from.

But, Filipino films have often been noted for their formulaic sameness, overwrought acting, and general lack of quality. This state of the industry resulted from the traditional theatrical base from which Filipino films first developed; the dominance of American films in the Philippine market, which denied the domestic industry a critical and demanding audience; and the propensity of the industry to ape American genres and fads. Despite the odds, however, some Philippine films have always emerged from the pack to equal those produced anywhere else in the world. This was certainly true from the early 1970s through the late 1980s when a number of young directors, writers, and actors came on the film scene after the demise of a stultifying studio system. Many of this younger generation have since been lost to tragic deaths and early retirements, which have affected the industry. Still, some quality films are made every year, and Philippine films continue to entertain the fans and reflect contemporary reality on the big screen.

Shaky Start and Solid Growth

Motion pictures were first brought to Manila in the nineteenth century by enterprising foreigners who hoped to develop a profitable theater business by supplementing live acts with the new novelty. Later, when U.S. troops arrived in 1898, they brought along a cameraman to make a film record of the "glorious" expansion of the new American empire. Private American companies were also quick to enter the new colony; including the Biograph Company that sent Raymond Ackerman to make films from 1898 to 1902.[15] But, it was not until 1909 that the first short film was actually made in the Philippines and even then it was made by an American resident, Albert Yearsley. Three other Americans, the most prominent of whom was Edward Gross, also founded the first film company, Rizalina Photoplay Company, in 1912. Interestingly, all of the ex-patriots produced films that gave a sympathetic representation of the Philippine revolution, which occasionally caused them trouble with American military censors, who were anxious to dampen the fires of nationalism. For instance, in 1912, Yearsley's film version of *Walang Sugat*, the *sarsuela* by Severino Reyes, had to be withdrawn after eleven days of screening. Censors also demanded that scenes be cut from *Los Tres Martires* (*The Three Martyrs*), the story of the three Filipino priests executed by the Spanish colonial government in 1872.[16]

The pioneer of the domestic Philippine film industry was Jose Nepomuceno, who purchased the failing Rizalina Company's equipment in 1919 and made the first truly Filipino film, *Dalagang Bukid* (*Country Maid*) based on a *sarsuela* script. In the 1920s, a few young Filipinos were attracted to the glamorous world of Hollywood where they learned the techniques of the craft. One of these youths, Vicente Salumbides, returned home in 1926 to begin a directing career with his groundbreaking feature *Miracles of Love*. Soon, he and Nepomuceno churned out an ever-increasing number of silent films, and in 1932, they and other newcomers produced 23 feature films. Though impressive, this limited output was not able to satisfy the country's demand for motion pictures. In 1926, American companies controlled 95 percent of Philippine motion picture distribution, and this dominance of the industry was still 90 percent in 1937.[17] Just as the fledgling film industry was getting established, however, it was confronted with the need to adopt the new technology of sound motion pictures. Because Philippine filmmakers operated on very limited budgets, they were hard enough pressed to purchase the expensive new equipment and could hardly afford to make the additional investment of constructing a modern sound stage. So, after making some initial progress, it appeared likely that the nascent domestic industry might not be able to keep pace with modern innovations and would be swamped by the imported American "talkies" that were drawing the crowds away from the silent Filipino films.

American investors came to the rescue of a moribund Filipino film industry in the form of George Harris and Eddie Tait, who decided to invest in a production studio in Manila as part of their plan to make films for the budding Asian market. Their investment capital and equipment; the founding of their company, Filippine Films, in 1933; and a business alliance with Nepomuceno brought the needed technology to the Philippines to make motion pictures with sound. By 1935, there were only eleven films made in the Philippines, and they all came out of the Filippine studio. The success of the American company and the collapse of the original Filipino film industry pushed Philippine filmmakers to form studio companies of their own in cooperation with local moneyed investors. In a short while, the Philippines had a number of studios that slowly lifted the industry back to life. The first to form was the Parlatone Hispano-Filipino in 1936 followed a year later by Sampaguita Pictures under the able leadership of scenarist Luis Nolasco, director Carlos Vander Tolosa, and musician Mike Velarde, who combined to make the new studio the pre-World War II leader. The following year, the smaller studios X-Otic and Excelsior Pictures made their beginnings, and in 1939, the joint company, LVN, made an auspicious start with the film *Giliw Ko* (*My Love*).

Post-War Rebound and Development

The studios soon churned out more and more films every year until the Second World War temporarily saw a break in production because of the absence of negative film stock. While a few people worked for the occupation government making pro-Japanese propaganda films, most shifted to vaudeville or sought out the few engagements that were available on the legitimate stage. Unfortunately, the destruction of Manila during its recapture by American troops, as well as the habit of showing films until they were ruined, has resulted in the loss of all but four pre-war films.[18] Once the war was over, however, many pre-war studios rebounded and were joined by Premiere Pictures, founded in 1946.

While the studios were crucial to the growth and stability of the local film industry, they also retarded the development of film as an art, since they invariably opted for "formula" story plots. As well, Hollywood films attracted the country's intelligentsia, because English was the language of status. Since Filipinos had linguistic access to films made in the United States, the door was open to the idealized world of the American Dream. As the educated members of society were effectively lost to local companies they, in turn, had to cater to the less educated poor Filipinos who made fewer artistic demands. This demographic reality stigmatized the audience and reinforced genre trends in the films produced. It is said that the derogatory term *bakya* (Pilipino for the wooden clog slippers worn by the poor) for the patrons of Filipino films was coined in the 1950s by a movie director who was insulted that local audiences could not appreciate his artistry.[19]

Since its beginnings, the film industry has followed formats first developed in the country's theater, such as the *sarsuela* plots of *Walang Sugat* and *Dalagang Bukid*. In fact, the *sarsuela* provided plots for innumerable films, and while some were quality productions, most were easily forgotten. Also contributing to Filipino films was the *komedya* genre, though not usually in the *moro-moro* tradition that featured combat between Christians and Muslims, but as fantasy stories of princes and princesses in imaginary lands. Meanwhile, the influence of American vaudeville was seen in the popularity of musicals and slapstick comedies. A frequent theme in many films was the need for the hero and/or heroine to overcome odds dealt by an unjust society controlled by the rich. In both pre- and post-war Filipino melodramas, a common plot motif is the love triangle involving either young lovers or married couples, which is often complicated by class differences, family interference, and sometimes by contrasts between urban and rural lifestyles. In films a standard character is the long-suffering and faithful woman and/or mother, such as *Ang Luha ng Ina (A Mother's Tears)*, and occasionally the abused and suffering child such as *Roberta* (1951). In many cases, the influence of the *kontrabida* (the anti-hero), usually an actor who is well known for playing that particular role, is overcome after an extremely traumatic event and an extended tearful reconciliation involving all the parties.

Since all melodramas had a common format with simple variations, they clearly catered to their *bakya* audience. Occasionally, however, some of these films rose above the milieu, such as 1954's *Malvarosa*, staring Charito Solis as the long-suffering Rosa who sacrifices herself to the care of her five shiftless brothers and is almost raped by her scheming wealthy employer. Another example of a quality Filipino film in the standard format is the 1959 classic *Biyaya ng Lupa* (*Blessings of the Land*) staring Tony Santos and Rosa Rosal, which was recently shown in a Manila revival. However, in this case, one reviewer pointed out that the film's strength is due to its "restraint" and the absence of "long-winded dialogue" and "long weeping scenes or extended dying scenes" so typical of most local films.[20] One important criticism of the Filipino melodrama is that because they all seem to end on a hopeful note with even the most evil of oppressors and villains having a miraculous change of heart defying logic and reality, they effectively uphold the status quo by conditioning the poor to accept their status in life.

Philippine films also have a bevy of "stars" who enjoy the adulation of their fans. Some actors play clearly identified roles, such as the *kontrabida* (anti-hero) or the *bida* (hero) in the melodrama and action genres, and it remains a common practice to match up young stars in romantic duos intended to heighten the interest of their fans who see them in film after film. Even former Philippine president Joseph Estrada was a major movie star long before entering politics. In his films, he played the honest avenging policeman safeguarding the poor and downtrodden. It is little wonder that when he first became vice president, Estrada volunteered to lead a national war on crime, which continued his movie role persona and further increased his popularity with the electorate. One of Estrada's strongest supporters was Nora Aunor, who dominated Filipino film for years, first in her romantic coupling with Tirso Cruz, III, and later in her own right as a skillful actress. With his own background in film and politics and Aunor's support, Estrada breezed through the election with the largest electoral sweep in Philippine presidential politics, while her break from Estrada in January 2001 cut deeply into his base of support and hastened his fall from power.

Despite the weight of the standard genres, the late 1940s through the early 1960s witnessed two important and fundamental changes. The most immediate change was the appearance of some films in which disillusion over post-war Philippine political corruption and social conflict was clearly portrayed. One such film was *Backpay* (1947) where former anti-Japanese guerrillas openly talk of joining Communist rebels because of the government's failure to institute land reform and give them backpay for their wartime service. Another of these films was the powerful *Anak Dalita* (*The Ruins*, 1956), which featured Tony Santos and Rosa Rosal as a couple who have to live in the post-war ruins of the old Spanish section of the city. Adding to the pathos is the fact that Santos's character is a Korean War hero who must become a smuggler in order to live. The hard-edged realism of this film was rare for the period but it won praise for director Lamberto Avellana and the Golden Harvest Award for best picture at the 1956 Asian Film Festival. Another complex issue that some movies approached was that of collaboration with the enemy during the war. Some films merely presented the collaborator as stock character, such as the collaborator in *Manila Open City* (1968) who is finally killed by the loyal guerrillas. However, other offerings, such as Eddie Romero's *Apoy sa Langit* (*Fire in Heaven*, 1949), attempted to explore the topic with some sympathy and understanding showing what could happen when the lives of the movie's central family are at stake. While the 1976 film *Tatlong Taong Walang Diyos* (*Three Years Without God*) starred Nora Aunor as a Filipina who falls in love with a Japanese military commander.

The second major development of the era was the decline and eventual demise of the major studios. This situation was prompted by labor problems in the early 1960s, which led to a number of major stars leaving the studios. The decline was accelerated by the deaths of some major studio heads, and eventually the only remaining major studio was Sampaguita Pictures. The way was clear for smaller independent companies to capture a bigger portion of the market and for fresh talent to emerge. Some independent companies had been formed shortly after the war by major stars such as actor Fernando Poe, Sr., and director Manuel Conde, but the number of independents increased markedly. Of special note were Lea Productions and Tagalog Ilang-Ilang Productions, which soon rose to become major new film producers. At first, the rise of so many independents signaled very little in the way of changes, since many films were still using the standard formats. New "innovations" were nothing more than local versions of popular American mass market genres, such as the "James Bond" type, pseudo Italian westerns, martial arts extravaganzas, and "buddy" commando films. Still, in the more open atmosphere, directors were freer than ever before to explore modern themes, including the complexities of the breakdown of the traditional family and sexual permissiveness. One of the best of these films was Gerardo de Leon's *Huwag Mo Akong Limutin* (*Do Not Forget Me*, 1960), which had to be reworked to meet censor demands.

The True Golden Age

The 1970s and 1980s saw the rise of a new generation of directors who helped redefine Filipino film, making it an effective vehicle for social commentary and the artistic equal of any other national film industry. Their efforts were also in tune with the period's increased activism and nationalistic awakening, which led people to reconsider their prejudices against locally produced films as something only worthy of the *bakya* crowd. As well, various governments began to take active measures to support the local industry. As early as 1966, the city of Manila sponsored its first film festival, stipulating that for ten days only Filipino films could be shown in the city's theaters. Even the martial law regime of Ferdinand Marcos created the Experimental Cinema of the Philippines. Leading the way were a number of innovative new directors, such as Ishmael Bernal and, especially, Lino Brocka, who were joined by an equally talented group of screenwriters. In less than two decades, this new generation produced an amazing wealth of powerful cinema that attained the status of a legitimate art.

Especially noteworthy is that many of these films were made during the repressive era of Ferdinand Marcos's rule. In fact, many of the films, such as Bernal's first film *Pagdating sa Dulo* (*At the Top*, 1971), Brocka's *Maynila, sa mga Kuko ng Liwanag* (*Manila, In the Claws of Neon Lights*, 1975) and *Jaguar* (*Guard*, 1979), plus Mike de Leon's *Batch '81* (1981) contained harsh social criticisms of an exploitative and authoritarian society in which the sympathetic lead characters are crushed. These films did not project the image desired by the government, but Manila audiences supported them with their box office patronage despite the frequent tragic endings that offered no happy resolution. In addition, in the 1980s, issues of sexuality and the role of women in society were explored with a realism not seen before. Especially noteworthy is Marilou Diaz-Abaya's trilogy *Brutal* (1981), *Moral* (1982), and *Karnal* (1984). At their best, these new films explored sexuality in complex psychological plots, as in Laurice Guillen's multi-award winning *Salome* (1981) with script by Ricardo Lee. In this film, a woman is accused of murdering her lover, and the story is told from three different perspectives; the woman's, her husband's, and the victim's, with no clear answer presented for the audience. Meanwhile, Peque Gallaga explored the human spirit and the horror of war in *Oro, Plata, Mata* (*Gold, Silver, Death*, 1982), a film that won numerous awards and was described as operatic in its beauty and scope.

Other films were directly motivated by overt political concerns. Especially important was Eddie Romero's exploration of Filipino identity in *Ganito Kami Noon, Paano Kayo Ngayon* (*This Was How We Were, What Happens to You Now?* 1976), which looked at the country's past and forced the viewer to question the identity of the Filipino in the modern world, especially in his or her relationship to the United States. More topical was Bernal's *Sister Stella L.* (1984), a story based on the life of a nun whose concern for the poor and the atrocities she witnesses led to her political commitment and brought her into frequent conflict with the martial law government and military authorities. Meanwhile, Brocka's 1985 film *Bayan Ko: Kapit sa Patalim* (*My Country: Gripping the Knife's Edge*) told the story of a laborer who is crushed by his heartless employer. This film achieved far more notoriety than it may have otherwise warranted thanks to the reaction of the Marcos government that tried to ban it as subversive and inciting to rebellion. Only extended protests by the Concerned Artists of the Philippines got the ban removed, but the government then tried to have significant portions of the film cut because of its "lascivious" scenes. Brocka and his studio filed a case before the Philippine Supreme Court, which, in a landmark victory for free speech, issued a fundamental ruling sharply limiting the power of state boards. Brocka's political commitment continued after the Marcos regime was ousted from power. His 1989 offering *Orapronobis* (Latin for "pray for us") is a powerful political story about a human rights worker and a right-wing vigilante death squad that works in close cooperation with the military. This was an especially important film because it was made after Marcos's removal from power and the return to democracy under Corazon Aquino. Brocka was prominent among the anti-Marcos protesters, but this film clearly showed that he was not content merely with the overthrow of the dictatorship and would continue to use film as a means to critique continued government atrocities, even if under the leadership of a president he helped put into power.

Of all the new directors, Lino Brocka achieved the most international recognition and showed that Filipinos could make quality films that were also commercially viable. He was praised at the Cannes Film Festival in 1976, and until his tragic death in an auto accident in 1991, he produced over fifty films, most of which carried strong social messages. Under his guidance, a host of new method actors, such as Bembol Roco, Jay Ilagan, and Phillip Salvador, were introduced to the public while established actors, even including the former teen idol Nora Aunor, were able to expand their dramatic range. Despite his passing, Brocka remains a leading light, and his films were prominantly featured in a 1998 film festival at the Lincoln Center in New York.

The Contemporary Film Scene

The true golden age of Filipino films ended with the 1991 death of Lino Brocka and the passing shortly afterward of Ishmael Bernal. Other directorial talents arc not as active as before having gone into retirement or branching off to pursue other interests. Charo Santos Concio, a prominent TV and film producer with Regal Films, which produced a good number of the pictures made by the outstanding directors, has since lamented the resulting lack of passion in the industry.[21] The low point was reached in 1996, when two actors and their agent made a pathetically inept attempt to manipulate the winners in a nationally televised award ceremony. During the 1998 centennial celebrations, film enthusiasts had to content themselves with the retrospective showing of forty of the Philippine's best films.

In defiance of this discouraging trend, screenwriters Ricky Lee, Jose Lacaba, and others still produce first-rate scripts, and some directors, such as Marilou Diaz-Abaya, continue to make quality films, including *Milagros* (1997) and her 1998 offering *Sa Pugod ng Dagat* (*In the Navel of the Sea*), which was shown at the Berlin Film Festival and then went on an extended international tour before its opening in Manila. As well, new directors are beginning to make some quality films in preparation for a revival of Philippine cinema.[22] This revival may have been heralded in the summer of 2000,

Scene production shot of international award-winning director Lino Brocka's powerful 1989 movie *Orapronobis* (*Pray for Us*). Courtesy of the Cultural Center of the Philippines Library Collection.

with Carlitos Siguion-Reyna's powerful film *Azucena* (*The Dog Butcher*), which dealt honestly with tough issues of spouse abuse and child molestation. Other 2000 films showed a desire to tackle tough social issues, such as Laurice Guillen's directorial comeback release *Tanging Yaman* (*The Most Precious Treasure*), which won a Best Picture award for its portrayal of a dysfunctional family. There was also a sharp critique of the country's penal system in the film *Deathrow*, and a sympathetic presentation of homosexuality in *Markova, Comfort Gay*, the true story of a young gay man who was used as a sex toy by Japanese soldiers during World War II.

PHILIPPINE MASS MEDIA

Since the overthrow of the oppressive Marcos regime in 1986, the Philippines has regained its reputation for having the freest mass media in Asia. In fact, the Philippines has long been a regional leader in mass media with a tradition of regularly published newspapers stretching back into the early nineteenth century and the introduction of both radio and television well before many of its Asian neighbors. Again under free conditions, the country now has around 384 newspapers of which about one-fifth are dailies mostly located in the Manila area. Meanwhile, the nation's combined newspaper circulation is estimated at approximately nine million readers, and there are about fifty-two magazines published, though many of these are free supplements in Sunday newspapers. The electronic media is also very strong and in 1998, the nation had 454 radio and 116 television stations plus an inestimable number of cable stations, some of which operate outside government regulations. Of the nation's approximately 70 million people, it is estimated that 81 percent have access to radio transmissions, while 45 percent receive television signals. This is quite a feat for a nation that still does not have electric power in remote areas.[23]

The newspaper tradition was brought to the Philippines by Spain, but during its rule, the press in Manila was overwhelmingly in the hands of the colonizers. As a consequence, the young Filipino nationalists of the nineteenth century could not use the power of the press until they attended universities in Europe. There, they soon established the newspaper *La Solidaridad* that was smuggled back home, where it was considered subversive by authorities. During its brief existence, the independent Aguinaldo government established a series of newspapers, but these were suppressed by U.S. forces. Also in 1898, new papers were started by recently arrived Americans, while some Spanish newspapers remained in business for the newspaper reading elite, who were educated in the Castilian language. A few nationalistic Filipino papers appeared during the early American period, but they had to be very cautious with their editorial commentary, since the new government had a series of laws in place to limit dissent. By the 1920s and 1930s, however, the stability and prosperity of American rule had tempered the earlier nationalism, and most Filipinos who went into journalism were either businessmen or political leaders who wanted a favorable vehicle to promote their agendas. After the interregnum of World War II, many pre-war papers resumed operation, and some new ones appeared while the gradual transfer of newspaper ownership from American to Filipino hands, which had begun in the 1920s, continued until 1960, when the last foreign owner sold out to local interests.[24]

Radio was introduced in the 1920s but grew slowly, and as late as the outbreak of World War II, the nation only had five stations, four in Manila and one in Cebu. Radio began as an American enterprise. The first owners were Americans, as were many of its on-the-air personalities, and English was used exclusively. The daily format also resembled that of stations in the United States with live dance bands featuring torch singers, amateur hours, soap operas, quiz programs, spelling bees, variety shows, and periodic news reports to supplement the recorded music. Many of the radio personalities held the rank of "stars" in the Manila area and were often better known than movie stars, since the radio was on daily, and there were relatively few Filipino films in the pre-war period. The Filipinization of the radio industry began in the 1930s when sugar baron J. Amado Araneta bought two American stations. Under his ownership, new faces in the management appeared, and local content began to enter the airwaves, starting with advertising jingles in Tagalog. After the Second World War, radio went through a boom period as did the newspaper business, and by 1968, the country had 202 stations covering most of the country. This amazing growth was not without cost, since the growth was unregulated and lacked technical and professional standards. Still, most of the country was covered by radio, and with the invention of the transistor, national news could reach Filipinos out of range of national and regional newspapers.[25]

Television, meanwhile, first came to the Philippines as a gimmick in the failed 1953 re-election bid of President Elpidio Quirino. After that inauspicious introduction, the media began to grow, and by 1955, there were 6,000 television sets in Manila receiving canned American programs and a few local variety shows. The industry really took off in 1957 with the formation of the ABS-CBN network, the creation of other new independent stations shortly thereafter, and the introduction of color broadcasting in 1966. Despite this growth, a truly Filipino television medium did not emerge, since it remained cheaper to import American shows than to produce local alternatives other than a few talk shows and hastily produced soap operas.

When Ferdinand Marcos declared martial law in 1972, he immediately closed all newspapers except the *Philippines Daily Express*, which was owned by a political ally, and shut down the nation's radio and television stations. During his authoritarian rule, Manila's major daily newspapers were all owned by Marcos's friends and reporters. At the same time, religious and student newspapers, foreign correspondents, and National Press Club officers were harassed and sometimes detained by the military. Both the radio and television industries were also under strict control, although it must be said that in the case of radio the authoritarian regime did introduce some badly needed reforms as well as the positive requirement that original Filipino music be a regular part of each hour's airplay. However, with the August 21, 1983, assassination of Marcos's chief opponent, Senator Benigno Aquino, the media broke from its bonds and became a primary factor in the government's downfall. Small independent newspapers led the way by openly criticizing the regime and getting away with it. Then, when Marcos's secretary of defense and the head of the armed forces began a revolt that coincided with the election that pitted Aquino's widow, Corazon, against Marcos, it was the call of Manila's archbishop, as broadcast over the Roman Catholic church's radio station, Radio Veritas, that brought the city's residents to the defense of the coup. The response to this radio appeal was phenomenal, and hundreds of thousands of Filipinos camped out on the EDSA highway physically blocking government tanks sent to squash the rebellion.

With the restoration of democratically elected government and guarantees for free speech, a rejuvenated media soon surpassed its pre-martial law levels in terms of numbers of newspapers and radio and television stations. Manila dailies returned with their characteristic outspoken bombast, and in the past decade, there has been a noticeable growth of the vernacular press. Although English-language newspapers are still the preferred reading of the movers and shakers of society, more Filipinos than ever before are getting their news from Pilipino newspapers. A 1995 survey of twenty Manila dailies, ten each in English and Pilipino, revealed that the vernacular papers now have a substantially greater readership.[26] Since the end of the Marcos regime, there have also been many technical advances by the electronic media, especially television, which uses digital technology and satellite and microwave transmissions to create a national grid.

Despite its post-1986 resurgence, the Philippine broadcast media has not developed qualitatively, and some fundamental problems remain. Principle among its problems is the continued preponderance of American influence and the use of English. While Filipino musicians enjoy greater access to the airwaves, many radio stations still broadcast Top 40 hits straight from the United States and the use of English by announcers remains commonplace. In television, too, imported American programs still make up a substantial portion of the nightly viewing fare, and MTV now invades homes with teenage and pre-teen children. Still, there are an increasing number of locally produced shows for the ever-larger audience, and at least, the use of Taglish, an urban slang mixing Pilipino and English, is becoming acceptable. As television has entered more and more homes, local content has also increased. It should also be noted that Filipinos enjoy television as much as any other people, and theater and cinema attendance has fallen as a result, and this trend has also accelerated with the spread of videotape machines.

Common to both radio and television is the soap opera. After becoming a staple on radio, popular soap operas such as *Gulong ng Palad* (Wheel of Fortune), *Ilaw ng Tahanan* (The Light of the Home), and others transferred to television. These were eventually replaced by new soaps, such as *Flor de Luna* in the 1980s, as the soap format became entrenched in the new medium where it continues to captivate audiences. Common to all soaps is a centering on tragic women characters who are portrayed sympathetically as the repositories of all that is good and moral. The primary character is usually the Mother who is the basic strength of the family, and it is her good qualities that earn the eternal gratitude (*utang na loob*) of her children. It is the woman's fate (*tadhana*) to suffer, but her redemption is through perseverance (*pagtitiis*), which wins out in the end. In sharp contrast, the male character is often an unfeeling philanderer who neglects his duties to his children and spouse. While there are occasional female villains, even these, such as the mistress, are shown to be victims of the malevolent male. Though easily dismissed as escapist, the standard soap opera format reveals important mass perceptions of the mother figure and of gender relations and serves to promote a conjugal environment of sexual tension and exploitation and a tolerance of male irresponsibility.[27]

SPORTS AND GAMES

In addition to enjoying family-oriented festivals, theater, movies, and the mass media, Filipinos also enjoy sporting competition. Almost every activity, from solitary pursuits, such as jogging or biking to a wide variety of team sports that includes softball, are available for enthusiasts. It is in the country's urban areas, however, that the greatest variety of sporting activity is available. The metro Manila area, especially, is well endowed with a number of golf courses and activity centers that feature a range of sporting options. Even the dedicated figure skater can get a good workout on the rink at the ground level of the giant SM Mega Mall shopping center in the suburb of Mandaluyong. It must be acknowledged, however, that Philippine sports makes very little allowance for girls and young women, who are expected to center their attention completely on the home and, perhaps, a profession. Those few young women in Manila who do participate in sports are the exceptions who only prove the rule.

There are two sports that predominate and can be found anywhere from the largest urban center to the smallest town: cockfighting and basketball. Neither sport requires a heavy investment in equipment or coaching lessons and cockpits and basketball courts are readily available in just about any town. As in the rest of Southeast Asia, cockfighting in the Philippines is not only popular, but has deep pre-European roots. For his part, the successful *sabungero* (cockfighter) is held in high esteem by his male companions, and he spends a great deal of time every day tending, feeding, and caressing his prize cocks. The whole purpose of the special breeding and attention paid to the animals is, of course, to produce a fierce fighter who will vanquish any foe. The fights are usually held on Sunday afternoon in specially built cockpits, and there are often special three-day tournaments (*pintakasi*) held during fiestas. Each cock is armed with razor sharp blades affixed to the leg, and immediately before the match, each bird is allowed to peck at the other to inflame its fighting passion. Meanwhile, the assembled crowd wildly makes bets until the moment of combat. When the birds are released, they slash at each other in a fight that results either in death or ignoble withdrawal.[28] Although undoubtedly a blood sport, cockfighting is not simply about cruelty to animals. It has rules and referees, and its proponents attempt to cultivate a level of civility, which is not readily apparent to the first-time viewer.

But, if cockfighting is a traditional Philippine sport, why would the recently imported American game of basketball be so popular? The answer is that every town, and even many barrios, have a central public plaza with a cement surface for drying rice during harvest time and for playing basketball throughout the rest of the year. As well, the only real cost of the sport is for the ball, unless tournament participation also requires a uniform, and there is no great need for organization as a pick-up game can always be had readily. The only limiting factor is that Filipinos play very fast and loose so that only the young can keep pace. But it is as a spectator sport that basketball is in a class by itself, and town and school reputations are made by their basketball teams. This intense interest in the sport extends to the country's professional teams, which are sponsored by some of the country's biggest corporations. During the annual play-offs, basketball dominates the TV ratings more completely than the U.S. National Football League's Super Bowl Sunday. Successful professional basketball players have local star status, and some former players have gone on to make careers for themselves in national politics.

Philippine children, like their counterparts around the world, are keenly aware of every new Star Wars action toy and want the latest Furbie, beanie baby, Barney, or Teletubby, and Barbie dolls are readily available since they are manufactured in Quezon City. However, for many of the country's poor children, these toys remain a wish rather than a reality. Instead, most young Filipinos, especially those in the provinces, find amusement with games that are not too dissimilar to those that their parents and grandparents played when they were young. There are literally hundreds of Philippine children's toys and games that anthropologists have documented, but some of the more common ones are easily recognizable and include marbles, tops, yo-yos, slingshots, hide-and-seek, hopscotch, team tag, and jumping contests.

In addition, there are some games that are more peculiar to the Philippines, and these include *sungka*, which uses an oblong board with deep bowls cut into the ends and seven smaller bowls cut along each of the two sides. An equal number of shells, seeds, or pebbles are placed in the smaller bowls, and two opponents take turns scooping the shells from one small bowl and going around the board dropping a shell in each bowl along the way, including their "home" bowl. Eventually, one will have all of the shells in their 'home' bowl, and the game begins again. During fiestas, a greased pole is erected in the plaza with a prize attached to the top and young boys can try their luck in reaching the goal to the amusement of onlookers. Young boys will also capture beetles or spiders and attach them to thread tethers and match them in combat as their fathers might match up fighting cocks.[29]

NOTES

1. See Frank Lynch, S.J., "Town Fiesta: An Anthropologist's View," in *Philippine Society and the Individual: Selected Essays of Frank Lynch, 1949–1976*, ed. Aram A. Yengoyan and Perla Q. Makil (Ann Arbor: Michigan Papers on South and Southeast Asia, no. 24, University of Michigan, 1984), 209–223.

2. For a complete description of the Morion festival, see Alejandro R. Roces, *Fiesta* (Manila: Vera-Reyes, Inc., 1980), 171–185.

3. For an extended discussion of the various Marian festivals around the country, see Alfonso J. Aluit, *The Galleon Guide to Philippine Festivals* (Manila: Galleon Publications, 1969), 75–102.

4. Especially good description of the San Isidro celebrations are found in Roces, 133–153, and Doreen G. Fernandez, *Tikim: Essays on Philippine Food and Culture* (Pasig, Metro Manila: Anvil Publishing, 1994), 174–179.

5. Ibid., 168–169.

6. See ibid., 17–53, and Aluit, 103–128 for non-Christian festivities.

7. An excellent overview can be found in Nicanor G. Tiongson and Ramon M. Obusan, *Dulaan: An Essay on Philippine Ethnic Theater* (Manila: Cultural Center of the Philippines, 1992). Tiongson presented the notion of the 'proto-drama' in the 1989 edition of *Dulaan*, of which he was the sole author.

8. A comprehensive survey of this important theatrical form can be found in Felicidad M. Mendoza, *The Comedia (Moro-Moro) Re-Discovered* (Makati Philippines: Society of Saint Paul, n.d.).

9. For a detailed description of the *pasyon*, see Ricardo D. Trimillos, "Pasyon: Lenten Observance of the Philippines as Southeast Asian Theater," in Kathy Foley, ed. *Essays on Southeast Asian Performing Arts* (Berkeley: Centers for South and Southeast Asian Studies, University of California, 1992), 5–22, while Reynaldo C. Ileto, *Pasyon and Revolution: Popular Movements in the Philippines, 1840–1910*, 4th ed. (Quezon City: Ateneo de Manila University Press, 1995) heightened awareness of the close relationship between religious imagery and thought on the one hand and secular thought and political ideology on the other.

10. The most comprehensive coverage of these plays in their historical context is found in Amelia Lapena Bonifacio, *The "Seditious" Tagalog Playwrights: Early American Occupation* (Manila: Zarzuela Foundation of the Philippines, 1972).

11. The author's thanks go to Laurice Guillen, prominent Philippine actress and director, for reminding me of the importance of her late friend and mentor Rolando Tino's early work as well as that of the Dulaang Sibol theater group.

12. Brief, but comprehensive sources for recent Philippine drama are Doreen G.

Fernandez's pamphlet, *Dulaan: An Essay on the American Colonial and Contemporary Traditions in Philippine Theater* (Manila: Cultural Center of the Philippines, 1994), and Bienvenido Lumbera's discussion in *Revaluation, 1997: Essays on Philippine Literature, Cinema and Popular Culture* (Manila: University of Santo Tomas Publishing House, 1997), 112–151.

13. *Encyclopedia of Philippine Art*, volume 7, published by the Cultural Center of the Philippines, 1994, is devoted to theater and provided a valuable reference tool for some of these plays and their plots.

14. The centennial celebrations were covered by the *Philippine Daily Inquirer*, which can be read online at www.inquirer.net.

15. Some of these early American films from the Spanish-American War have been preserved and are part of the collection of the Library of Congress; copies can be ordered from: http://lcweb2.loc.gov/ammem/sawhtml/sawhome.html.

16. For the early background, see Agustin L. Sotto, *Pelikula: An Essay on the Philippine Film: 1897–1960* (Manila: Cultural Center of the Philippines, 1992), 4–16.

17. Clodualdo A. del Mundo, Jr., *Native Resistance: Philippine Cinema and Colonialism, 1898–1941* (Manila: De La Salle University Press, 1998), 58–60, 53 has an extremely helpful set of statistics for an analysis of the pre-war period. Meanwhile, Nepomuceno's story is told in Joe Quirino, *Don Jose and the Early Philippine Cinema* (Quezon City: Phoenix Publishing House, 1983).

18. The problem of "lost" films is serious. Formerly, some producers even sold old prints to be melted down for their silver content. Even many films made in the 1970s and 1980s are no longer available. Recently, important steps have been taken to preserve the nation's film legacy. The Cultural Center of the Philippines now has a film archivist, and the government's Philippine Information Agency has an active program of restoration. Archives have also been established at the University of the Philippines Film Center and at the ABS-CBN television complex in Quezon City.

19. For this story and a consideration of the link between the country's theater and motion picture traditions, see Nicanor G. Tiongson's article "From Stage to Screen," which is found in the exceptionally good anthology Rafael Ma. Guerrero, ed. *Readings in Philippine Cinema* (Manila: Experimental Cinema of the Philippines, 1983).

20. Edmund L. Sicam's review in the *Philippine Daily Inquirer*, August 15, 1998.

21. A two-part interview of Concio entitled "Bring Back the Passion," by Nestor U. Torre is found in the *Philippine Daily Inquirer*, May 9 and 10, 1998.

22. For a complete overview of the contemporary scene, see Agustin Sotto, "Contemporary Philippine Cinema," in *Contemporary Philippine Culture: Selected Papers on Arts and Education* (Manila: The Japan Foundation, 1998), 113–123.

23. For a recent survey of the Philippine media, see Elizabeth L. Enriquez, "Philippine Mass Media Towards the Close of the 20th Century," in *Contemporary Philippine Culture: Selected Papers on Arts and Education* (Manila: The Japan Foundation, 1998), 33–41, esp. 34–35, for the figures cited here.

24. See Jose Luna Castro, "Philippine Journalism: From the Early Years to the Sixties," in Clodualdo del Mundo, Jr. ed., *Philippine Mass Media: A Book of Readings* (Manila: Communication Foundation for Asia, 1986), 3–13.

25. Two articles are especially informative: Francisco Trinidad, "Philippine Radio: The Early Years," in Clodualdo del Mundo, Jr., ed., *Philippine Mass Media: A Book of Readings* (Manila: Communication Foundation for Asia, 1986), 47–52, and Mario Ampil, "Two Decades of Philippine Radio: A Brief Survey," in Clodualdo del Mundo, Jr., ed., *Philippine Mass Media: A Book of Readings* (Manila: Communication Foundation for Asia, 1986).

26. The Philippine Information Agency reported that ten Pilipino-language newspapers serving Metro Manila and the immediate surrounding provinces had a daily circulation of 2,690,000, while the ten leading English-language newspapers had a combined circulation of only slightly over two million, as cited by Enriquez, 40.

27. Jose Javier Reyes, "Radio Soap Opera," *International Popular Culture* 1, no. 1 (1980): 68–74.

28. Roces, 187–199.

29. See Monina Mercado, *Games Filipino Children Play* (Manila: PAC, 1978).

SUGGESTED READINGS

David, Joel. *Fields of Vision: Critical Applications in Recent Philippine Cinema*. Quezon City: Ateneo de Manila University Press, 1995.

————. *Wages of Cinema: Film in Philippine Perspective*. Quezon City: University of the Philippines Press, 1998.

Fernandez, Doreen G. *Palabas: Essays on Philippine Theater*. Quezon City: Ateneo de Manila University Press, 1996.

Hernando, Mario A., ed. *Lino Brocka: The Artist and His Times*. Manila: Cultural Center of the Philippines, 1993.

Infante, J. Eddie. *Inside Philippine Movies, 1970–1990: Essays for Students of Philippine Cinema*. Quezon City: Ateneo de Manila University, 1991.

Mojares, Resil B. *Theater in Society, Society in Theater: Social History of a Cebuano Village, 1840–1940*. Quezon City: Ateneo de Manila University Press, 1985.

Tiongson, Nicanor G., ed. *Modern ASEAN Plays, Philippines*. Manila: ASEAN Committee on Culture and Information, 1992.

8

Music and Dance

MUSIC AND DANCE in the Philippines defy a simple description because a wide variety of traditions co-exist. Even so-called mainstream contemporary popular Philippine music and dance forms are complex blends of many influences, both indigenous and imported. In their pure form indigenous dances, and the music that accompanies them, has been maintained by numerous ethnic groups who escaped the direct impact of Spanish and American colonialism and whose geographically remote location has helped them sustain traditional dance styles and musical instruments down to the present time. Even the Tagalog people, the country's principle ethnic group, have kept alive pre-Spanish music. So, for example, the Tagalog *kundiman* is perhaps the best known indigenous Filipino musical form and it combines the lyricism with lulling tempos that are evocative of Italian melodies. The *kundiman* is a love song that can be tender and sweet, sometimes passionate, and occasionally even gloomy, but it is always expressive of Filipino life.

Meanwhile, Spanish musicality and the numerous European dances they introduced still thrive in such forums as *rondalla* groups (string instrument ensembles) in towns around the country. Their music is standard fare during annual town fiestas and other festive occasions, along with graceful Iberian folk dances. Similarly, near pure forms of American jazz, ballads, folk, rock, and alternative music can be heard on the archipelago's televisions and radio stations and in urban nightclubs. In fact, the ability of Filipino musicians to master American instrumental and vocal styles has made them famous throughout Asia. Internationally known celebrities from Frank Sinatra to Deep Purple to hip hop rappers all have their Filipino imitators. But much more important, when adopting Western music, Filipinos emphasize lyrical and melodic themes that express their own feelings, longings, values, and dreams. Recently, an increasing number of Filipino performers have incorporated indigenous instruments and musical patterns into their musical arrangements. The resulting mix is a vibrant musical culture that is open to new influences while remaining true to its Filipino self. In the same way, Filipinos have used modern dance set to jazz and electronic music to create lyrical displays interpreting the country's indigenous dances, thereby keeping them alive and vibrant.

INDIGENOUS MUSIC AND DANCE

Pre-Hispanic Philippine music and dance traditions are still maintained by the ethnic groups of the central Cordillera region of northern Luzon, the inhabitants of remote areas of the Visayan Islands, and the Islamic and pre-Islamic peoples of Mindanao and the Sulu archipelago. These people have a song or a dance for every occasion, including secular activities and religious rituals. So, for example, there are songs for birth, childhood, adolescence, courtship, marriage, work, storytelling and joking, teaching, blessing a new house, recounting heroic exploits, curing illness, and burying the dead. The Tingyans of Abra province in northern Luzon sing their *daleleng* at festivities and the *salagintok* to express friendship and love, while the Bontok of the central Cordillera have the *ayegkha* as an evening song or serenade and the *annoay* to accompany themselves while building their world famous rice terraces. For the Hanunoo people of Mindanao, the *panludan* is a two- to three-day social and religious festivity that is accompanied by virtually uninterrupted music and song. Music plays an important role in the social life of the Muslim peoples of the south and also in their religious life, such as the Tausog's *luguh maulud*, which celebrates the birth of Mohammed.[1]

Although singing styles vary from group to group, there are common patterns that emerge whether the singing is solo or by a group. Many songs are improvised and the quality of a performer is often judged by his or her ability to create new lyrics for each song. These are songs that are frequently sung by a couple who are courting or by friends who are gently joking each other. Songs are not limited to specific lyrics or time lengths and can expand as needed. As well, since everyone is expected to sing, there is a great range of vocal quality. The impromptu social nature of musical participation has survived in contemporary Filipino society and frequently catches a foreign visitor by surprise when they are suddenly asked to entertain a group with a song. The foreigner is usually concerned about the quality of their performance, but that is not as important to Filipinos as a person's willing to participate in the shared group activity. Most singers will overcome their sometimes limited range of notes by adding pitches, sounds, trills, tremolos, and other devices to add variety to their performances.

While singing unaccompanied is quite common, Philippine indigenous music also employs a number of instruments made of bamboo, brass, wood, animal skins, and other natural materials. Despite some variations, many of these instruments are very similar from one region and group to another in the Philippines and throughout Southeast Asia. Quite common is the bamboo flute, of which there are a number of styles, including the lip- and the nose-played varieties and the ring flute. Some groups in Luzon's central Cordillera employ the panpipe, although this particular instrument is not common in much of the rest of the country. On the other hand, a wide variety of zithers can be found throughout the country, while two-string lutes are used by a number of groups in Mindanao and northern Luzon. Nearly universal is the "jews harp," which is usually made of bamboo but can also be crafted out of brass. Some ethnic groups also play wood-carved guitars, while many others employ a range of percussion sticks, clappers, bows, percussion beams, shell trumpets, fiddles, rattles, buzzers, scrappers, and conical and cylindrical drums. Perhaps the most impressive Philippine indigenous instruments are the brass gongs used by the peoples of Luzon's central Cordillera and by both the Muslim and non-Muslim inhabitants of Mindanao, as well as some peoples in the Visayan Islands. For instance, the Kalingas of northern Luzon use large and flat hand-held brass gongs that are struck rhythmically while singing and dancing. Meanwhile, the Muslim peoples of Mindanao use a variety of bossed brass gongs including a number of small ones that are laid side-to-side in increasing size to play in xylophone fashion. The Muslims also employ larger bossed gongs suspended from wooden frames and still other bossed gongs that are hand held.[2] Long neglected by the dominant lowland Filipino, these peoples and their music have recently captured the attention of many of the country's best new musicians, who are attempting to integrate modern music with traditional instruments and motifs.

Ethnic groups use dance for a wide variety of purposes, most often for religious life, but also for other social functions, including warfare, work activity, courtship, and the perpetuation of epic tales that are filled with folkloric meaning. Rituals form the core of religious belief for non-Christian Filipinos, and it is believed that through ceremonies led by the shaman harvests are kept plentiful and health is maintained. Sometimes the shaman, or *babaylan*, who is often a woman, will go into a trance and dance according to the nature of the spirits that have entered her or his body. At other times, the shaman will simply sing a chant while the group performs the appropriate stylized dance. An example from Bukidnon province is the *dugso* dance that is performed while the *babaylan* chants an invocation during a *hinaklaran* (offering) ceremony.

For the mountain people of Luzon and the Muslims of the southern islands, the act of war plays a prominent role in their dance tradition. Victories are acted out and martial skills are reinforced for young men in war dances. Of course, war can bring death, so there are dances and songs for the dead, especially if the warrior did not return from battle. In this latter case, the death dance is accompanied by loud music made by hollowed logs and bells so the spirits of the dead can be called home and not left to wander. The tales of warrior deeds and of founding mythologies are told in dance form such as the *Darangan* epic of the Maranaw people of northern Mindanao Island, which is told in the *singkil* dance.

All Filipinos have a variety of dances appropriate to work activities associated with rice culture, hunting or fishing, and with daily mundane tasks, including fetching water, spinning, and basket making. It is also common to use dance for courting, since flirtations can be conducted relatively safely via a dance used to approach and gauge the receptivity of a potential mate. This safety is further increased in dances that mimic the courtship movements of animals, especially the rooster and hen. The imitation of animals is also a feature of dances that are performed simply for fun and in celebration. One frequently mimicked animal is the monkey, which naturally lends itself to human interpretation, but other animals, especially birds, are often mimicked in dance or at least in hand gestures and upper-body movements.[3] And finally, one dance that every visitor to the Philippines is soon introduced to is the *tinikling*, a dance performed by stepping adroitly between bamboo poles as they are rhythmically slammed against each other. The dancer imitates the *tinikling* bird that lives in rice areas and must hop through the farmer's bamboo traps. A delight for all audiences as awkward tourists stumble over the round bamboo poles, this dance has also been used as a leitmotif by N.V.M. Gonzalez (*The Bamboo Dancers*, 1959) and Bienvenido Santos (*The Day the Dancers Came*, 1967) as they analyze the complex nature of the hybrid Philippine society as it steps cautiously into the modern world.[4]

HISPANIC-INFLUENCED MUSIC AND DANCE

The arrival of the first Spaniards to settle permanently in 1565 marked a turning point in Philippine music, which from then onward was exposed to European musicality. Music was especially important for the proselytizing efforts of missionary Roman Catholic priests, who used music and song to teach the native population about Jesus Christ and the church's saints and doctrines. Children were raised singing in choruses in the newly built churches after the scattered population had been relocated within "the sound of the bells," and the young singers were effective agents in spreading the priests' message. By the early seventeenth century, Franciscan and Augustinian missionaries had created a number of boys choirs and founded a seminary to train hundreds of boys in religious music. A little over one hundred years later, a full conservatory of music was established in Manila, and missionaries of the Recollect order set up a school for organ builders. The early years of the nineteenth century even saw the construction of a large church organ constructed entirely of bamboo in the town of Las Pinas, located in today's Rizal province southeast of Manila. After falling into disrepair, the organ was restored in the early 1960s and is a popular tourist attraction.

Despite this strong European influence, pre-Hispanic traditions continued to be evident as in the *pabasa*, a group reading of religious material done in the musical fashion of recitation called *punto*. This form of musicality is used in public readings of the Passion, the story of the life and death of Jesus Christ recounted during Holy Week. Spanish religious music did make its way into a number of Philippine festivities associated with saints that developed independent of priestly supervision. As well, there are religious processions during Easter that are independent of church control, and the practice of *pamumasko*, or Christmas caroling, is frequently employed as a fundraising effort for nonreligious civic activities.[5]

In addition to religious music, the Spanish colonial period also saw the introduction of European secular music and dance. Although secular music dispersed more slowly than the missionary-sponsored hymns and songs of religious praise, profane music embedded itself deeply in the national culture because of its association with dance. A common observation by visitors in the late nineteenth century and in the first years of the American period was the frequency with which Filipinos loved to hold a *baile* (dance party). In the days before electricity, entertainment was only found in theatrical performances or occasional religious celebrations. But, a dance could be held anytime, for any reason, and as often as one wanted. A special enticement for the young men and women of a town was that at dances they could talk to each other and touch hands and, perhaps, even waists.

In the more relaxed atmosphere of the latter nineteenth century, new forms of music and dance, including *jotas*, the *bolero*, or *habanera*, became common as did the *paso doble*, the *balse* (waltz), the fandango, the Polish mazurka, the formal square dance from France called the rigodon, and even the polka. Interestingly, many European music and dance forms were modified when adopted by Filipino society. So, for example, the *habanera* became the more subdued Filipino *dansa* that eventually transformed to include the music of the *harana*, a serenade of courtship. Meanwhile, the indigenous song and dance debate form was expanded to include the gay and lilting manner of the *jota*, a Spanish folk dance and music. This dance was modified in the town of Moncada in Tarlac province and became known as the *jota moncadena*. The waltz was modified into different styles of which the *carinosa* courtship variation was especially popular, and the formal rigodon soon became the *lanceros* and closely resembled the American square dance. The fandango, or *pandanggo*, became modified into a wide variety of dances including one where the woman balances one oil lamp on her head and two more on the backs of each hand while executing complicated cross-over steps. The European polka was introduced by the Spanish ladies and gentlemen of Manila, and soon many Filipino folk songs were fitted into the new dance, which became known as the *polkabal*, a favorite activity in many provincial cities and towns. As well, Filipinos adopted Spanish *marchas* and *valzes* by toning down the tempo from the Hispanic original. In addition to modifying imports, Filipinos invented some new dances of their own such as the *sayaw sa bangko* (bench dance) in which the dancers must perform on a thin wooden bench to the delight of onlookers.[6]

In many cases, new Spanish secular music entered the Philippines through a variety of Hispanic dramatic forms. In particular, the *moro-moros* and the *comedias* of the Spanish colonial period helped the introduction of martial march music, just as the *sarsuela* promoted the *harana* and the development of the indigenous *kundiman* of the Tagalog provinces. New ensembles of European instruments accompanied the introduction of this new music, most especially the *rondalla* and the *comparza*, which were made up of stringed instruments, such as the mandolin as well as the piccolo, bandurria, laud, octavina, guitar, bandola, and the *bajo de unas*. Also gaining in status and importance was the piano. As in Europe and the United States, the piano became a symbol of a family's affluence and culture, and many a young Filipino was induced to practice many hours to master the difficult instrument. Brass bands were also formed in the latter years of the Spanish era for the new marches that were used in parades for religious and civic functions.

The new form of martial march music became especially important in the closing years of the nineteenth century when a new generation of Filipinos began to question and resist Spanish colonial rule. At the request of Andres Bonifacio, founder of the revolutionary *Katipunan* society, Julio Nakpil wrote the first national anthem, and he and other Filipino composers soon wrote a number of patriotic marches for the nationalist cause. Especially notable was the "Marcha Nacional" by Julian Felipe, which has since become the national anthem. The *kundiman* also served the turn-of-the-century revolutionary cause by speaking of patriotism of country even though expressing these feelings allegorically by singing of romantic love. So, for example, the

Music sheet of Constantion de Guzman's 1928 nationalistic
kundiman Bayan Ko, with lyrics by Jose Corazon de Jesus.
Singing this song became a part of virtually every protest action
during the martial law era, and in the 2001 overthrow of
president Joseph Estrada. Courtesy of the Cultural Center of
the Philippines Library Collection.

kundiman "Jocelynang Baliwag" ("Jocelyn of Baliwag") written in about
1896, though dedicated to a real woman, was actually intended to elicit the
patriotism of the audience.[7] The *kundiman* form of love song continued to
be tapped for patriotic purposes under American colonial rule when Jose
Corazon de Jesus's poem "Bayan Ko" ("My Country") was set to music by
Constancio de Guzman in 1928. This patriotic song has continued to resonate strongly and served as the unofficial anthem of the nationalist students
of the 1960s and the martial law period. Later, hundreds of thousands of
Manila's citizens, whose "People Power" revolution toppled the dictatorial re-

gime of Ferdinand Marcos in 1986, sang "Bayan Ko" while defiantly blocking government tanks with their bodies.

AMERICAN SONG AND DANCE

If the Spanish colonial period broadened Filipino music by infusions from Europe, the American occupation of the country in 1898 introduced a flood of cultural influences that included revolutionary new forms of music. Every musical development from the profound to the most superficial that originated in the United States was soon reflected in the Philippines. The music of dance bands, ragtime, blues, jazz, swing, boogie woogie, and, in the post–World War II period, rock and roll, folk, alternative, and rap were all mastered by Filipino composers and musicians. Unlike the Spanish, who introduced European music for religious purposes, but did not actively promote either secular music or social dancing among Filipinos, Americans enjoyed these pastimes and were more than willing to share their rhythmic wealth with their new colonial wards. In the early years, nightclubs, cabarets, and musical variety shows called *bodabil* (Filipino for "vaudeville") were soon in full swing, and Filipino musicians found work and an appreciative audience. From early vaudeville onward, new dances such as tap dancing, buck-and-wing, cakewalk, skirt dance, Charleston, foxtrot, Lindy hop, cha-cha, and mambo made it into the Philippine popular repertoire. The first half of the twentieth century also saw the technological breakthroughs of radio and motion pictures, which transmitted the latest music and dance crazes directly from New York, Chicago, and Hollywood to Manila and then on to provincial cities, towns, and barrios.

Filipinos quickly and enthusiastically adopted this veritable flood of American culture and music. So rapid was this acculturation process that it seemed likely to destroy the Philippine's musical culture that had survived hundreds of years of Spanish colonial rule by slowly and carefully assimilating the new influences. By the 1920s, the *sarsuela* and traveling theatrical companies with their Filipinized versions of European music forms had all but vanished, and young musicians seemed more interested in learning new jazz tunes from Chicago than traditional *awits* and *kundiman* classics. But Filipino culture proved too strong and resilient to succumb entirely to the American juggernaut. The development of the Philippine film industry, for example, provided young musicians and composers with profitable outlets for their work. The songs and music associated with the *sarsuela* survived thanks to Filipino films that used works by local composers. Songs such as Miguel Velarde, Jr.'s "Dahil Sa Iyo" (Because of You), Simplicio Suarez's "Ikaw pa Rin" (It Is Always You), and Constancio de Guzman's "Langit ang Magmahal" (Heaven

Is to Love) are just a few of the many movie tunes that later moved into the mainstream. As well, the nation's few pre-war radio stations broadcast some Philippine music for their audiences thus helping to assure the survival of Philippine music.[8]

The continuing tradition of nationalism of the revolutionary period also exerted a strong influence on musicians of the American era. University of the Philippines president Jorge Bocobo kept the nationalist vision alive, and the school's department of music recorded folk songs and traditional dances, thus saving the memory of these traditional forms for future generations. The university also trained a new generation of composers and musicians who soon labored to keep the country's musical traditions vital by integrating them with the musical sounds of the modern era. In addition to their well-known orchestral works, Nicanor Abelardo and Francisco Santiago wrote a number of *kundiman* songs for which they became famous. Important at the beginning of the twentieth century was the *rondalla*, which first appeared during the preceding Spanish era. Under the direction of Antonio J. Molina, this Hispanic ensemble gained new vitality as it expanded into symphonic forms.[9]

Even the military band reached new heights under Filipino control. Most prominent was the Philippine Constabulary Band first created by Colonel Walter H. Loving. After his death during the liberation of Manila in World War II, the band was later directed by Colonel Antonio Buenaventura. Just as the *rondalla* is found in town after town throughout the archipelago, so too is the marching band, a ubiquitous musical group that plays in town plazas and for fiestas and other occasions such as funerals. The country's bands have served as a training ground for generations of Filipino musicians who would not otherwise have received instrumental music lessons in their cash-strapped elementary and high schools, which could only offer vocal instruction.[10]

The increasing sophistication of Philippine bands and advances in education also led Filipino music into the realm of Western classical music. Filipino musicians soon discovered this new venue through which they could express their artistic sensibilities. One early example of Filipino symphonic writing was a series of compositions based on aspects of the life of Philippine national hero Jose Rizal and performed as early as 1911. By the 1920s, the University of the Philippines Conservatory of Music produced a number of musicians such as Juan S. Hernandez, who wrote the *Simoun Overture* for his 1920 graduation work, and later Hilarion Rubio, whose graduation work was the *Florante and Laura Overture* (1933). Most of this symphonic and chamber music was heavily influenced by its European origins, but even in the pre-World War II period, there were clear indications that the young

Filipino composers were looking to their nation's traditional musical roots for inspiration.

University of the Philippines student Antonio Molina wrote the string quartet piece *Pandangguhan* (1925) based on an Ilokano folk dance, while Buenaventura's chamber work *Igorot Love Song* (1930) also used folks songs and themes. Thanks to postgraduate work in Chicago, Nicanor Abelardo was the first to break from the classical romantic tradition and introduce "modern music," but even his music never veered too far from Philippine folk melodies and tunes. He wrote numerous *awit, kumintang,* and *kundiman* pieces even as he searched for a new form at Philippine music. Following Abelardo's lead, the four-movement *Taga-ilog Symphony in D minor* by Francisco Santiago, premiered in 1939, using a folk melody in its first movement and traditional instruments in the orchestration. Before the outbreak of World War II, the national university was a respected institution, producing numerous new composers who searched for a new Philippine musical foundation that incorporated indigenous music.[11]

SEARCHING FOR MUSICAL IDENTITY

Since gaining independence from the United States in 1946, Philippine music has increased its search for a national/cultural identity, even as the domestic industry has grown. This search for identity is most clearly evident in the realm of symphonic music but is present in popular music as well. Despite the heavy influence of the U.S.-music industry, contemporary Philippine popular music has provided a voice for one generation of Filipino youth after another and has served to inculcate uniquely Philippine cultural values. Clearly, the country's musical development has continued along lines that were present in the prewar period while also developing in new ways.

The continuity in Philippine musical development is especially evident in the thoughtful work of the country's composers, who trained in the earlier American period, plus those who have emerged since then. In a sense, it is only natural that composers should point the way to the nation's musical future, even if their symphonic, operatic, and chamber music will never appear on a Top 40 list of musical "hits." While instrumental musicians and conductors might be content to perform works by European and American composers, the nation's creators of music must pen new works, and their source of inspiration will be the musical tradition of the nation as they write musical descriptions of the country's people, history, and natural environment.

The solid foundation of musical training laid in the prewar period produced a veritable explosion of new music for the contemporary scene. Early in this process was Buenaventura's *Mindanao Sketches* (1947) based on themes from the Mindanao ethnic group, the Manobo, while Lucio San Pedro's use of folk themes in his *Concerto for Violin and Orchestra* (1948) were later seen in his 1992 Republic Cultural Heritage award-winning *Lahing Kayumanggi* (*Brown Race*). An avant-garde indigenous musical composition was Jose Maceda's 1975 production *Udlot-Udlot* (*Fluctuation*), which used over 800 performers with traditional instruments.[12] The influence of Lucrecia Kasilag has been important for Philippine music. Kasilag's *Concert Divertissement for Piano and Orchestra* (1960) combined Western music with the gongs, chants, and rhythms of Muslim Filipinos. Her compositions *Toccata for Winds and Percussions* (1958) and *Misang Pilipino* (1965) won Republic Cultural Heritage awards, and she served for many years as the music director for the Bayanihan Philippine Dance Company, while holding the position of dean of the Philippine Women's University College of Manila. Kasilag's twenty-year leadership role in the Cultural Center of the Philippines; her founding of the Philippine Music Ensemble; and her compositions for Philippine film, theater, and ballet has kept Philippine music directed toward its indigenous roots.[13]

More recently, Philippine music has seen the entrance of a new generation of composers, such as Ramon Santos, whose music incorporates themes from other Southeast Asian nations and China as well as Philippine motifs. Meanwhile, Francisco Feliciano has worked with modern opera productions using local stories and musical scores for productions such as his 1984 *La Loba Negra* (*Black She-Wolf*) that is rich in historical references. These composers continued to work into the 1990s, just as have many of their students, including Bayani Mendoza de Leon, whose 1992 performance of *Sugatang Perlas* (*Wounded Pearl*) combined singers and dancers as well as the chamber musicians.

Beyond the formal concert halls and academic conservatories, Philippine popular folk music maintained itself thanks to the University of the Philippines preservation work. By the 1950s, a number of songbooks were published, which helped to assure the continued knowledge of tunes such as "Bahay Kubo" ("Nipa House"), "Leron-leron Sinta, Atin cu pung Singsing" ("I Have a Ring"), "Si Nanay, si Tatay Namasol sa Dagat" ("My Mother, My Father Went Afishing") and "Ti Ayat ti Maysa nga Ubing" ("The Love of a Young Maiden"). Because of this preservation work, these songs have become part of public school music programs and standard choral singing repertoires. Meanwhile, the Spanish *sasuela* theater form and its accompanying music went through a nationalistic revival in the 1970s thanks to the founding of the Zarzuela Foundation so that Nicanor Tiongson produced *Philipinas Circa 1907* in this almost forgotten format and many other modern *sarsuelistas* soon followed.[14]

Filipino films kept *sarsuela* and *kundiman* songs alive during the American colonial era, but it was the record industry that initiated something of a renaissance in the postwar period. Especially important was the Villar Recording Company that specialized in Philippine music and used new duplicating equipment and the long-playing (LP) record. In the late 1950s and the entire 1960s, Villar fought a battle to sustain local music in the face of popular American and British musical invasions. In that time the recording company released over 500 albums and 3,000 singles of *kundiman,* love songs and folk songs, dance music, and Filipino pop music. The label also featured music from all the major dialects (and some minor dialects as well), rondalla, band, and symphonette recordings. A number of Filipino vocal artists, such as the *kundiman* singer Sylvia Torre, Tagalog love song idols Ruben Tagalog and Cely Bautista, and Ilocano singer Raye Lucero, were given significant career boosts thanks to Villar. Even semiclassical music performers and the more recent "super-star" Nora Aunor had productive careers thanks to the record company. With this solid recording base, radio stations around the country could feature local music as well as the imports on American labels.[15]

Local singers and musicians recorded foreign songs as well. Commonly, the songs chosen by Filipino recording artists were those similar in temperament to traditional Philippine music, lyrics, and sentiment, for example, Nora Aunor's "Pearly Shells." In the 1960s, Aunor also sang other songs in English as well as Pilipino, including "I Made a Mistake" and "Forever Loving You." Active in the same decade were Eddie Peregrina, who had such hits as "What Am I Living For?," "Memories," and "Why Can't I Remember to Forget You." Meanwhile, teen film idol Tirso Cruz III sang "Together Again," and Edgar Mortiz crooned "My Pledge of Love."

Protest Music and Pinoy Rock

Beginning in the late 1960s, Philippine music was energized by domestic political events, and it increasingly served as a vehicle for political protest and social commentary. Closely associated with the new socially committed student movement was a revival of Philippine protest music. Just as the turn-of-the-century revolutionaries used music in their struggles against Spain and the United States, so too did Philippine radical agrarian and labor movements of the 1930s utilize music for recruitment, organizing, and morale purposes. Some of the music of the depression-era Philippines was directed at youth and women: "Gumising Ka Kabataan" ("Wake Up, Youth") and "Babaeng

Walang Kibo" ("Passive Woman"). The lyrics of many of these songs were rather heavy handed, but subtle use was made of traditional musical forms to elicit feelings of sorrow or tenderness. The abrasive nature of these 1930s lyrics were greatly modified during the Second World War when the Philippine Communist and Socialist parties merged and formed an anti-Japanese guerrilla force, commonly known as the Hukbalahap or Huks. Now, music and skits were designed to attract support from the peasantry, and the lyricism of the past became more sophisticated. One memorable song from the war period was "Ing Bie Ding Anac Mu, Balen Cung Alipan" ("The Life of Your Child, My Enslaved Country"), whose lyrics had a broad appeal. In its postwar fight against the newly independent Philippine government, the guerrillas continued to use song as a part of their arsenal to counter claims of national disloyalty. Such was the rationale for the song "Gintong Catimauan" ("Golden Freedom") that denied allegations of banditry while making the claim that their cause was just.

The anti-Marcos protests of the 1960s and 1970s continued this radical tradition as one university campus after another became part of the student movement. Despite strong ideological influence from the contemporaneous Cultural Revolution in China, the music of the Philippine students was not a simple copying of foreign ideological offerings. So, for example, the protest songs of the 1930s were revived and occasionally rewritten to make their messages current, and the beautiful *kundiman* "Bayan Ko," with its slow and melodious cadence, was revived and sung in defiance of Marcos's Metrocom troops, who seemed to enjoy wielding their truncheons on student bodies. A poem by 1896 revolutionary leader Andres Bonifacio, *Pag-ibig sa Tinubuang Lupa* (Love of One's Native Country) was performed in a *kundiman* form and became extremely popular. Still, other than these two songs, most protest music of the era was too martial and energetic to become popular beyond a limited number of dedicated activists.

Once adopted by professional musicians, protest music had a significant impact on mainstream Filipino music. Before then, despite the efforts of Villar Records and their composers, singers, and musicians, Philippine music was barely holding its own against the imported sounds of American and British beats. Protest music helped the local music industry by making feelings of love for country not only acceptable but even popular and necessary for one's self-respect and dignity. Many of the radical songsters of the protest movement showed the way to the future. The first to experiment with a new Filipino protest medium were soon joined by nationalistic, though not necessarily radical, artists such as the popular vocal trio APO Hiking Society. It was APO's slow tempo and poignant song "Hindi Ka Nag-iisa" ("You Are Not Alone"), composed in protest of the 1983 assassination of Benigno

Aquino, that became one of the anthems of the 1986 People Power revolution.[16]

The energy of the student protesters soon transferred to more mainstream Filipino music, especially the rock music of the nation's youth. As early as 1973, the Juan de la Cruz Band performed "Ang Himig Natin" ("Our Music"), widely acknowledged as the first example of "pinoy (slang for Filipino) rock." The band continued to have a number of successful songs until going their separate ways in the late 1970s. Other Philippine "rockers" to emerge included the female singer Sampaguita, the group Anak Bayan, and Mike Hanopol (after he left the Juan de la Cruz Band). Taking the rough edge off of pinoy rock was the group Hotdog, which mixed Western pop with Filipino lyrics to produce what became known as the "Manila sound," as it combined its original music with an irreverent tone and the colloquial language of Taglish (a mix of Tagalog and English popular in Manila and other urban areas).

For a time in the 1970s and 1980s, Filipino folk musicians achieved popularity approaching that of rock stars. Leading the way was Florante de Leon, whose songs "Ako'y Pinoy" ("I Am a Filipino") and "Handog" ("Offering") captured the mood of the period and encouraged others to present their songs. Among those who did so was poet and songwriter Joey Ayala, who fused rock with traditional instruments of Philippine minority peoples to capture the rhythm and soul of the country even while his strong lyrics protested the actions and policies of the martial law government. Ayala and his group Bagong Lumad (which means "new native" although Ayala prefers "alter-native") recorded "Wala Nang Tao sa Sta. Filomena" ("There Are No People in Santa Filomena"), one of his popular songs that assured his staying power. Meanwhile, Heber Bartolome and his band Banyuihay successfully infused rock into his compositions as they produced "Tayo'y Mga Pinoy" ("We Are Filipinos") and "Nena," the latter a song about girls whose poverty drives them to prostitution, both of which became local hits.

Despite the success of these musicians, it was Freddie Aguilar who received the greatest fame, beginning with his hit song, "Anak" ("Child"), a ballad centered on Filipino family values, which became an international hit as it successfully combined Western music with a distinct Filipino style. Philippine music authority Felipe de Leon, Jr. notes that despite "Anak's" basically Western form, the song has a *pasyon*-like quality with which Filipinos could easily identify. Though already many years old, "Anak" endures in Philippine popular culture. In the spring of 2000, a popular film of the same name used that song as its theme and constant refrain. Not originally a political person, Aguilar's thinking evolved during the latter years of the martial law period such that during the 1986 overthrow of the Marcos regime, Aguilar was leading crowds in moving choruses of "Bayan Ko."

Adding to the mix of assimilationist music was the translation work of Roland Tinio, who did for music what he was also doing in theater. Tinio made translations of Cole Porter, Burt Bacharach, and Jim Webb songs to make them accessible to a broader and less English-literate Philippine audience, especially when these classics were sung by Celeste Legaspi. Also expanding the country's musical horizons was the development of Pinoy jazz fusion, which became the "In" thing for young Manila sophisticates in the 1980s. Here too, foreign musical styles were adapted by Filipino composers to fit local tastes and sensibilities. Especially composer Ruben Cayabyab, prominent in the Manila jazz scene, who has penned a number of light pop songs, such as "Kay Ganda ng Ating Musika" ("How Beautiful Is Our Music") and "Tsismis" ("Gossip"). Crucial in gaining acceptance for local music of all types was a 1975 requirement that radio stations play at least one Filipino composition every hour, by 1977 that requirement was increased to three per hour. Once Filipino musicians were assured of airplay, their compositions were heard by local audiences and the industry gained increasing acceptance. This rule was rescinded in 1981, but after agitation by the Filipino music community, President Corazon Aquino issued an executive order restoring the requirement and increasing Philippine music airplay to four songs per hour.[17]

TODAY'S MUSIC

Today's Philippine music scene is alive and well. Indigenous music continues in its native strongholds and remains of interest to musicians and audiences. In the provinces, music in the local dialects continues to be sung while local brass bands and *rondalla* ensembles still make their music. The Philippine recording industry currently reports that almost 60 percent of all music sold is by local artists, which is a reverse of the same statistic only ten years ago. In fact, the vast majority of the repertoire, especially by new rock groups, such as the Eraserheads, (winners of the Asian Viewer's Choice Award at the 1997 MTV Video Music Awards in New York), and by ballad singers, such as Kuh Ledesma, are original Filipino compositions. Meanwhile, the group APO recently entered its thirtieth year of making music, and in 1998, the Juan de la Cruz Band reunited for a performance for their fans. After one decade, the musical ensemble Kontra-Gapi is still active. This group takes traditional ethnic instruments and adapts them for contemporary audiences so that indigenous Philippine music will grow and avoid becoming

Contemporary Filipino musicians in concert; these musicians are in the forefront of creating an alternative to U.S. influence in popular music. Courtesy of the Cultural Center of the Philippines Library Collection.

the exotica of a museum exhibit. Meanwhile, Joey Ayala and Bagong Lumad's CD is readily available in record stores.

In the current Philippine context, the line between 'rock' and 'alternative' music is quite blurry with bands and individuals crossing from one category to another. The country is producing a number of rock/alternative musicians and even rap music has entered the Philippines. Not surprising, these artists do not have the hard edge to their music as the American originals. Philippine rapper Francis Magalona, whose lyrics range from moral appeals to social issues, performs in a style similar to a folk protest singer. Although many Filipino pop stars are not known outside Asia, one exception is Lea Salonga, who won fame on Broadway for her lead role in the 1990s musical *Miss Saigon*, and who sang a number of successful Disney tunes in the movies *Aladdin* and *The Lion King*.

The 1998 centennial celebration also served as a boost to local music and saw the premier of a number of symphonic works by new composers. Among works by established composers featured at the Cultural Center of the Philippines was Lucrecia Kasilag's *Centennial Tribute to Filipino Womanhood*, which combined indigenous instruments with a symphony orchestra plus what was described as "mixed media" to create both "high" and "low" art in her presentation. Her music served as backdrop to dancers from Ballet Philippines, a modern dance company under the direction of Denisa Reyes, who told a Filipino version of the Eve and Adam story. During the performance, Kasilag emerged seated on a throne and then took the baton from conductor Chino Toledo to finish conducting the work herself. Other works aired

Pinoy rap star Francis Magalona in concert. Courtesy of the Cultural Center of the Philippines Library Collection.

during the centennial included a number of repertories by choral groups, and new music based on the poetry of Amado V. Hernandez. Meanwhile, the country's top bands and pop stars, including Sampaguita, Razorback, Cacai Velasquez, Joey Ayala, Ogie Alcasid, and Francis M., appeared in a month-long series of concerts at the Music Museum, playing before packed houses. Record companies also joined in with the release of a small flood of compilation albums of Filipino music.[18]

ETHNIC AND MODERN DANCE

Ethnic and traditional dance is a major Philippine cultural export, but it might not have been so had it not been for the foresighted program of University of the Philippines president Jorge Bocobo to preserve the nation's heritage in music and dance. Especially diligent in responding to Bocobo's call was dance instructor Francisca Reyes Aquino, who began her work in

1931 in cooperation with composer Antonio Buenaventura. She eventually compiled a six-volume sourcebook from her extensive travels throughout the country, and these provided a core of information upon which others could build. Meanwhile, a number of other people made more specialized studies of the dance traditions of various regions of the country. While completing her authoritative body of descriptive knowledge about the country's folk dances, Aquino also founded the University of the Philippines Folk Song-Dance Club in 1937 and a dance troupe and a national society for dance teachers. In 1947, another dynamic woman, Paz Cielo Belmonte of the Philippine Normal College, began the Barangay Dance Company, which also presented dances that were ethnographically faithful to the originals.[19]

A major change was initiated by yet another woman, Leonor Orosa Goquingco, who founded the Filipinescas Dance Company in 1957. Her importance was not as a strict preservationist. Rather, Orosa was a choreographer, and she took the ethnographic dances and brought them to life on stage for modern urban audiences. Orosa's many productions, such as her epic five-part story of the Philippines, *Filipinescas: Philippine Life, Legend and Lore in Dance*, went beyond simple displays of ethnic dances and used techniques of ballet and modern dance to interpret and express the life experience of the Philippine people.[20]

Also in 1957, another young woman, Lucrecia Reyes-Urtula, became the first choreographer of the Bayanihan Dance Company of the Philippine Women's University. After less than one year, the troupe went on its first tour and won rare accolades at the Brussels World Exposition. Under Urtula's guidance, the Bayanihan has always concentrated on remaining true to original dances even while stylizing them for modern audiences. To this end, Urtula continued the work of Aquino by traveling around the country to discover and document Philippine dances. Together with composer Lucrecia Kasilag, Urtula's formula has worked wonders on numerous international tours as well as for home audiences, including a three-year tour held in conjunction with the centennial.[21] The Bayanihan has also been responsible for spawning the careers of a number of dancers, some of whom have gone on to start new dance companies, such as Ramon Obusan, who founded his own Folkloric Group in 1972, or have become choreographers and have further developed the country's wealth of folk dance materials.

As a foreign importation, classical ballet made its mark during the American period thanks to visitors from Europe and the United States. But it has been the modern form of ballet and dance that has exerted the greatest influence on the country. The strongest proponent of modern dance is former Bayanihan dancer Alice Reyes, whose Modern Dance Company, now the Ballet Philippines, has brought the art to new levels. Under her direction, the company not only performed many classical ballets, including *The Nut-cracker*, but also integrated Philippine folklore and historical themes into visually stunning performances. Fortunately, the Philippines has a broad community of talented artists, choreographers, dancers, and composers to support modern dance, and it is upon these people that a successful performance ultimately depends.[22]

Philippine modern dance also retains its relevance for contemporary society by making social commentary, such as Basilio's 1984 *Misa Filipina*, which was a stylized representation of the assassination of Benigno Aquino. Meanwhile, choreographer Douglas Nierras's group, Powerdance, uses a dance style and accompanying music of chants, jazz, and rock that aims at the MTV generation and the *bakya* audience. His themes include humorous looks at street life, marital relationships, and the plight of domestic laborers. A truly amazing young troupe of dancers is the Teatro Silencio, whose members are all deaf and who feel the music's beat through vibrations in the floor on which they perform. In 1997, the group traveled to Paris to represent the Philippines at the World Youth Day, where they impressed their audience and received excellent reviews.[23]

NOTES

1. See Felipe Padilla de Leon, "Philippine Music," in Amparo S. Lardizabal and Felicitas Tensuan-Leogardo ed., *Readings on Philippine Culture and Social Life* (Manila: Rex Bookstore, 1976), 156–162.

2. A concise description of indigenous singing styles and musical instruments is presented by Antonio C. Hila in *Musika: An Essay on Philippine Music* (Manila: Cultural Center of the Philippines, 1989), 4–13, but for a complete study, see Jose Maceda, *Gongs and Bamboo: A Panorama of Philippine Musical Instruments* (Quezon City: University of the Philippines Press, 1998).

3. For a survey of the topic, see Basilio Esteban Villaruz and Ramon A. Obusan, *Sayaw: An Essay on Philippine Ethnic Dance* (Manila: Cultural Center of the Philippines, 1992).

4. See the delightful article by Gertrudes R. Ang, "The *Tinikling* as a Literary Symbol of Philippine Culture," *Philippine Quarterly of Culture and Society* 6, no. 4 (December 1978): 210–217.

5. Hila, 13–15.

6. For more detail, see Lucrecia T. Urtula and Prosperidad Arandez, *Sayaw: An Essay on the Spanish Influence on Philippine Dance* (Manila: Cultural Center of the Philippines, 1992).

7. Hila, 15–18.

8. See Ramon P. Santos, "The American Colonial and Contemporary Traditions," in *CCP Encyclopedia of Philippine Art*, vol. 6, *Philippine Music* (Manila: Cultural Center of the Philippines, 1994), 60.

9. Hila, 30–31.

10. Ibid., 32–34.

11. For complete information, see Mauricia D. Borromeo, "Symphonic Literature," in *CCP Encyclopedia of Philippine Art*, vol. 6, *Philippine Music* (Manila: Cultural Center of the Philippines, 1994), 127–130.

12. Santos, 54–55.

13. A full biographical sketch of Lucrecia Kasilag is found in the honorary publication, *Artista ng Bayan, Lucrecia R. Kasilag* (Manila: Cultural Center of the Philippines, 1989), 9–11.

14. Santos, 56–59.

15. See Elmer L. Gatchalian, M. Carunungan, and Danny Yson, "Industry" in *CCP Encyclopedia of Philippine Art*, vol. 6, *Philippine Music* (Manila: Cultural Center of the Philippines, 1994), 194–195.

16. A wonderfully comprehensive overview is provided by Teresita Gimenez-Maceda, "Protest Songs," in *CCP Encyclopedia of Philippine Art*, vol. 6, *Philippine Music* (Manila: Cultural Center of the Philippines, 1994), 114–122.

17. Maceda wrote "Pinoy Pop," in *CCP Encyclopedia of Philippine Art*, vol. 6, *Philippine Music* (Manila: Cultural Center of the Philippines, 1994), 107–113, and "Popular Music," *International Popular Culture* 1, no. 1 (1980): 24–32. In addition, see Norma L. Japitana, *The Superstars of Pop* (Metro Manila: Makati Trade Times Pub. 1982).

18. This description is based on information gathered from articles published in the *Philippine Daily Inquirer* on June 5, 8, and 22, 1998.

19. Urtula and Arandez, 38–41.

20. Orosa's story is delightfully told by Nick Joaquin in *La Orosa: The Dance-drama That Is Leonor Goquingco* (Pasig, Metro Manila: Anvil Publishing, 1994) while the link between Aquino and Orosa is highlighted by Reynaldo G. Alejandro in "Contemporary Dance in the Philippines," *Crossroads: An Interdisciplinary Journal of Southeast Asian Studies* 1, no. 1 (February 1983): 32.

21. Her biographical sketch is found in the honorary publication, *Artista ng Bayan, Antonio R. Buenaventura, Lucrecia Reyes-Urtula* (Manila: Cultural Center of the Philippines, 1988), 39–43. See also "Bayanihan Moves Guam Audience to Tears," *Philippine Daily Inquirer*, July 19, 1998.

22. Basilio Esteban S. Villaruz, *Sayaw: An Essay on the American Colonial and Contemporary Traditions in Philippine Dance* (Manila: Cultural Center of the Philippines, 1994).

23. Ibid., 42; Marge C. Enriquez, "Dancing to 'Bakya'," *Philippine Daily Inquirer*, August 10, 1998, and Bibsy M. Carballo, "They 'Listen' to the Music with Their Feet," *Philippine Daily Inquirer*, April 25, 1998.

SUGGESTED READINGS

Caruncho, Eric S. *Punks, Poets, Poseurs: Reportage on Pinoy Rock & Roll*. Pasig, Metro Manila: Anvil Publishing, 1996.

Lockard, Craig. *Dance of Life: Popular Music and Politics in Southeast Asia.* Honolulu: University of Hawaii Press, 1998.

Ness, Sally Ann. *Body, Movement, and Culture: Kinesthetic and Visual Symbolism in a Philippine Community.* Philadelphia: University of Pennsylvania Press, 1992.

9

Social Customs and Lifestyle

AS MENTIONED IN OTHER CHAPTERS, in many ways the Philippines is a country where the first-time visitor from the United States can readily feel comfortable. Many people speak English, including folks from small provincial towns and not just the sophisticated urbanites of Manila, Cebu, Baguio, and other major cities. Other aspects of the country's culture, including religion, dress, architecture, music, and dance, are also recognizable, even if subtle differences soon warn the visitor that all is not necessarily the way he or she assumed they would be. However, it is the easy familiarity by which Filipinos deal with Americans and their apparent openness and friendliness that can prove confusing to the newcomer, since many signals that Filipinos send out seem to mean one thing but in fact may mean something altogether different.

A good example of how assumptions are based on apparent cultural similarities is the use of the word *yes*. At first glance, this could hardly be a problem since the meaning of the word is very clear. But *yes* is not a clear concept in the Philippines, and guidebooks written for visiting businessmen make a point of warning their readers about this word and its tricky cultural context.[1] Filipinos, the guidebook warns, will say *yes* when they are not sure and even when they actually mean *no*. This is not done to be duplicitous but, rather, to be hospitable so the foreigner will not be disappointed. Instead of saying *no*, the Filipino will use a variety of ambiguous statements in addition to speech inflections and physical gestures to indicate that the real answer should be seen as something less than what was actually said. While perfectly in keeping with Filipino culture, this practice thoroughly baffles, confounds, and sometimes infuriates the American visitor.

This chapter explores some of the cultural differences that make Filipino social customs so different from what is known in the West, especially the United States. To do so this chapter will pick up from Chapter Six's discussion of the development of Filipinos from birth to adulthood, but with a different focus. While Chapter Six focused on courtship, marriage, and the replication of the Filipino family, the discussion in this chapter looks at the creation of the individual as he or she is made into a representative of Philippine culture and how he or she is expected to act as a Filipino. In addition to this cultural examination, this chapter also examines the formal structure of the Philippine education system and looks at the country's social stratification and how ethnic diversity is managed. Finally, the social problem of the massive overseas migration of many thousands of Filipinos in search of employment is examined.

CHILDREN IN FAMILY AND SOCIETY

As in all societies, the Filipino family raises its young to participate in the wider society and not simply as a member of the basic family unit. Social values are passed on to the child and internalized in a process of socialization. Filipino infants are the object of constant attention by all surrounding adults and elder siblings and are never left alone or allowed to cry. When a child beings to cry, it is immediately picked up and soothed and almost always given something to eat or play with. No matter how tired its parents may be, they drop whatever they are doing to attend to the child. This practice is not seen as spoiling the child, but as an obligation since is considered bad for a child to cry. The child soon learns that human society, especially the family, is a warm and friendly community that looks after his needs and wants even as he is granted freedom to explore the world. Eventually, however, discipline is imposed, usually by scolding and by threats to withhold affection until antisocial behavior is curbed.[2] This form of discipline has the effect of socializing the child into appreciating the relationship between positive social behavior and continued rewards. Only in extreme cases is physical punishment used and then only when other means are exhausted.

As a result of this gentle form of socialization that combines teaching by example and conditioning in addition to instruction, the child soon learns the basic value of group cooperation, respect, and obedience and just how far protests and self-interested acts will be tolerated. From its earliest days, the Filipino child begins to internalize the important Filipino social value of *pakikisama* (to accompany or go along with for the benefit of group harmony), which serves as a guiding principle governing family relationships and interactions in the wider community. Being group focused rather than individualistic, the Filipino instinctively seeks out family members and those with whom special relationships, such as the *barkada* discussed in the Chapter Six, have been carefully constructed.

Because the group is the focus of Filipinos, the coherence and quality of the relationships of its members becomes primary. This focus naturally leads to a concentration of the *amor-propio* (self-esteem) of the individual members of the group.[3] Since the Filipino is raised to consider himself and herself as being at the center of a closely related kin-group, the feelings, and needs of its individual members must be respected so that everyone will participate in the activities of the whole. As a result, the child soon learns that conflict is something that must be avoided at all cost and that the supreme objective of interpersonal relationships is that they be conducted as smoothly as possible. Disagreements are kept to a minimum and are dealt with by negotiations intended to preserve the self-esteem of all parties. Should conflict divide Filipinos, the consequences can be devastating and longer lasting than in American society, which expects an interplay of competition and conflict that will eventually lead to a resolution. In the Philippines, conflicts have the potential of creating permanent ruptures between individuals causing a shame (*hiya*) that cannot be mollified and destroying group cohesion.

A key player in avoiding conflict or even potential embarrassment is the "go-between" who will speak on someone's behalf. In Chapter Six's discussion of the courtship process mention was made of the use of a friend who will speak to the woman on behalf of the suitor. This is a "go-between," and if the young woman is not interested in the young man, she can tell the intermediary without causing either herself or the unacceptable suitor any sense of *hiya*. While children may squabble from time to time, any disagreement that breaks out among Filipinos of adolescence or older will see many others rushing in to restore order and reinforce the childhood lessons of maintaining what anthropologists at the Jesuit-run university in the Philippines, the Ateneo de Manila University, have termed SIR, or smooth interpersonal relations.[4]

The socialization lessons learned during early childhood are continued throughout youth. It is within this process of social growth that the activities of young boys going out with their fathers to work in the fields in rural areas takes on added meaning beyond the simple learning of farming techniques. Farming, especially rice farming, is both individual and communal in that a farmer will own or rent fields to support his family, but the seasonal requirements of preparing the soil, transplanting, irrigation management, and harvesting require cooperation by a number of farmers who share the occasionally intensive labor requirements. A crop cannot be brought in without a close working relationship with neighboring farmers. This shared work ethic is frequently termed the *bayanihan spirit* and is most frequently illustrated by the traditional practice of shared work to erect a house, but the ethic is much more pervasive and deeply rooted than this example of an occasional group activity.

Even during dating, when the adolescent boy consults with his *barkada* mates about which girl he should court and seeks their approval of his selection, he is continuing a group-centered focus for his actions. As well, a young man's cavorting with his male friends as they experiment with adult drinking and other forms of adult social behavior further reinforces the individual male's group orientation. All of these experiences in childhood and adolescence thus constitute an important link between the family origins of behavior to that conducted later in the wider community. Girls and young women also develop bonds with some of their peers, but these ties do not become as well developed because females are expected to stay in the home and learn the skills needed for their future domestic roles as wives and mothers. Still, they too develop strong bonds with close friends that follow them through life, especially if they are in a rural community and do not move far from their birthplace.

Quite unlike the situation in American society, where youth gangs can cause significant social problems, there is rarely a need to enforce conformity and restrain deviant youthful behavior in the Philippines. This is because the individual's bonds to the group and wider community and the need for social approval are so strong that antisocial behavior is simply not an option. The only exceptions to this generalization would be peer groups that become involved in criminal activity, but these are quickly dealt with in rural communities, and even the activities of youth gangs in large cities are quite limited compared to their counterparts in the United States.

Instead of social deviance and rebellion, Filipino youth soon take on the approved values of the wider community. Primary among these values are a sense of obligation (*pananagutan*) that is centered in the family but has implications for the community, especially if one's family is an active participant in a specific activity. Closely allied to this sense of obligation is the need for loyalty (*pagkamatapat*) and a dynamic, ongoing practice of reciprocity (*katugunan*), in which debts and obligations are not calculated but are built into a moral universe controlled by one's sense of gratitude (*utang na loob*) that one accepts within one's inner self. An individual who will not or cannot get along with the group suffers the worst fate possible: being cast out of the group. An individual who isolates himself from others or is ostracized is referred to as *maka-sarili* and is socially unacceptable.[5] Such individuals, or even those who seem to display asocial behavior, will be vulnerable to withering social gossip, or *tsismis*. While *tsismis* about someone's personal life is a favorite Philippine pastime, and everyone is eventually talked about at one time or another, gossip aimed at the asocial individual is powerful and usually has the ability to correct behavior in short order.

The visiting American will, therefore, find a people anxious to please their guest and to incorporate them into their social unit whether a work or social group. But, to be accepted, the guest must also conform to social guidelines that include not seeking a direct answer to a question that might require the Filipino host to say *no*. Not only is it unlikely that the Filipino friend will give that answer, but it will also create a feeling of uneasiness. Instead, the American must be willing to joke around without playing the buffoon and must never ever get angry or short-tempered. In all instances, sensitivity must be shown for the feelings of the individual so his or her self-esteem is never endangered. Even the raising of one's voice, staring, or standing with ones arms akimbo can be seen as aggressive and, therefore, unwelcome. Rather, criticism must be couched so as to encourage and seek improvement and late arrivals or missed appointments should be expected and tolerated. As well, there must be a willingness to socialize either in after hours drinking or on a family-to-family basis.

The foreigner's reward for conforming to socially acceptable behavior is loyal friendship that will last a lifetime and selfless efforts on his behalf, whether that assistance be personal or business related. Though not a social scientist, Douglas MacArthur had a long and extremely personal relationship with the Philippines and seems to have had an intuitive understanding of how to operate within the culture. His warm and deep friendships with numerous Filipinos, and his wartime promise that "I Shall Return" which he conscientiously fulfilled, won him an outpouring of the nation's affections that lasted well into the 1970s. To this day, a portion of his penthouse suite in the prestigious Manila Hotel is still preserved as a monument to the man. While obviously of interest to many people, the hotel treats his former parlor and study with respect rather than as a museum, and interested parties must make individual requests to the management in order to view the rooms.

THE PHILIPPINE EDUCATIONAL SYSTEM

Alphabetic writings on a few bamboo pieces that have somehow survived hundreds of years of the decaying process clearly indicate that at least some Filipinos knew and used a system of writing. This writing system was suppressed by the Spanish friars who attempted to uproot the indigenous Philippine cultures they encountered because they believed them to be backward and unenlightened. In place of what had existed before, the priests substituted religious education, which consisted of stories of saints and liturgical music. For most of the Spanish colonial regime, education was not given or encouraged in the rural areas, and in a reversal of the policy and practice in its South and Central American colonial administrations, there was no conscious attempt to teach Spanish to Filipinos. Instead, the friars attempted to learn the local dialect for daily communication while they celebrated mass in un-intelligible Latin. This aspect of Spain's policy in the Philippines effectively denied the population any knowledge of the colonizer's language, thereby keeping the natives ignorant and more easily controlled.

For most of the nation, the possibility of basic education and literacy was given hope by an educational decree in 1863 that called for the establishment of local schools in every parish of the country. While well intended, the decree did not create a budget to set up such as school system but left affairs up to the local community and the priest who supervised the school. Though le-gally introducing compulsory education, the effect of the law was very lim-ited, and few students in any but the largest of provincial towns regularly attended classes where the level of instruction was woefully limited, supplies nonexistent, and teachers untrained.

In the capital, however, formal educational institutions were established relatively quickly, with the College of Santo Tomas founded in 1610 and raised in status to a pontifical university in 1645. The Philippines, thus, has the distinction of having a university older than Harvard in the United States. In addition, a number of secondary schools were founded, including the Ateneo Municipal and the Colegio de San Juan de Letran, as well as the royal college of San Jose and seminaries in Manila, Cebu, and the provincial capital of Vigan in Ilocos Sur on the northwest coast of Luzon. These insti-tutions were not, however, intended for the general education of the native population, but rather for the children of the Spanish inhabitants and a limited number of offspring of *mestizos* and elite Filipinos. As such, they remained very small institutions until the nineteenth century.[6]

It must be acknowledged that the Spanish reluctance to support a broad-based educational system was a result of their need to control the colony. By the nineteenth century, however, as more and more of successful *mestizos* and the native elite prospered from an expanding international trade and the increased commercialization of the country's hinterlands, these local groups could afford to send their sons to schools in Manila and even to Europe. At the same time, a sophisticated and educated generation of Filipino priests, who formerly served as assistants to the friars, rose in the church and began to threaten the friars' control of the country's religious life. Thus, the spread of education and the introduction of modern ideas proved to be an important a factor in ending Spanish colonialism.

The arrival of the United States at the turn of the century revolutionized the country's inadequate educational system. Schools were opened as soon as hostilities subsided, with common soldiers frequently acting as teachers in hastily erected buildings. Unlike their Spanish predecessors, the Americans used education to firmly implant the English language, which would make the task of governing easier and would develop new social patterns to facilitate the eventual realization of democracy and independence. By 1901, a structure and budget was in place that created a national education system from elementary schools through teacher's colleges. In this structure, each province had an official in charge of that government's educational efforts. Usually, this official was an American. Classrooms were built in every town and many major barrios, and most of the nation's youth were soon in school. It was not much later that teacher's colleges began to produce the nation's first fully trained elementary teachers who fanned out across the country. The University of the Philippines was founded in 1908 as the country's premier educational institution. As the university began to develop its programs, a number of promising Filipinos were sent to graduate school in the United States. When they returned, these young graduates, known in the Philippines as *pensionados*, served an important role bridging the gap between the Spanish and American colonial eras in terms of providing a cadre of well-trained medical doctors and other critical professionals.

American interest in creating an educational system for the Philippines went far beyond the usual government programs and sparked intense public interest. In 1901, a troop transport ship, the U.S.S. *Thomas*, arrived in Manila carrying 540 young American teachers who were assigned to communities across the country where they opened local school houses. The original batch was the single biggest infusion of American teachers, but in subsequent years, many more Americans joined the original "Thomasites," and a significant number of these teachers developed a lifelong relationship with the Philippines, rising up in the ranks of the Philippine Department of Education before eventually retiring. This program that brought American teachers to the Philippines had an eventual impact that went far beyond its origins. For example, John Noffsinger was a young teacher who taught in a rural Philippine school in 1910–1912. Much later he became the executive director of a nongovernment organization known as International Voluntary Services (IVS), which sent young American volunteers to do development work in newly created countries in the Middle East and Asia after World War II. Still later, in 1961, Noffsinger took his Philippines/IVS model for young people's involvement in Third World development work and brought his lifelong knowledge to newly elected President John F. Kennedy's team that created the U.S. Peace Corps, where he served as an advisor.[7]

The American residual imprint on the Philippine's education system remains strong to this day. Although there has been evolution and change, the country's educational structure is still modeled on that originally designed in the early years of the last century. English is still used at the collegiate level and in many private elementary and secondary schools. Whereas as late as the 1970s, English had been the medium of instruction from grade three onward, the country's public school system has since shifted to using the national language of Pilipino while retaining local dialects for the lowest grades of young children who are just socialized into the classroom setting. Though no longer as extensively used as the language of instruction, English is still taught as a second language and the pressure to learn it is very strong. The nation's media is still heavily influenced by English, and Filipinos know that the best jobs go to those with a firm command of the language.

By law, education is free and compulsory for children from ages seven through twelve. Filipino parents are keenly aware that a quality education is crucial to their children's futures, but it isn't always possible, especially for families living in rural areas where there might only be a grade one through six elementary school or, at best, a poorly furnished community high school. The real problem, then, is effective access to quality education as even the most interested rural student usually cannot complete a full course of study because of the distance involved in going on to the next academic level. The result is a serious depletion in student ranks from one level to the next.

Using statistics from the 1995–1996 academic year, there were 11,504,816 children enrolled in the nation's 36,800 elementary schools (public and private), but only 4,883,507 students enrolled in the country's 6,205 secondary schools, which means that only 42.4 percent of the students enrolled in grades one through six will go on to high school. The drop off becomes even more dramatic when institutions of higher education are factored into the calculation. In the same year, there were 2,017,972 students attending 1,286 such institutions, which means that only 41.3 percent of high school graduates continue their education and only 17.5 percent of the original elementary students will probably go to college. Again in 1995–1996, the nation graduated 328,120 students from its institutions of higher learning, which means that the elementary student has only a 2.9 percent chance of getting a college degree that could be his or her means to break out of a continuous cycle of poverty.[8] While the Philippines takes pride in its 94 percent literacy rate and that many of its college graduates are eagerly sought after by international corporations, the fact remains that much more needs to be done to broaden educational opportunities.

Another important factor that does not appear in the preceding statistical calculations is the quality of the education that the students actually receive. The country may have had a 94 percent simple literacy rate as revealed by data gathered in 1994, but this tapers off to an 83.8 percent national rate

Elder passing on lore and values in the provinces.
Courtesy of the Cultural Center of the Philippines
Library Collection.

when "functional" literacy is tested. A further examination of statistical data
confirms what one would expect concerning literacy rate differences between
urban and rural areas. Most revealing are the functional literacy rate differences between metro Manila, which scored 92.4 percent, versus those regions
of the country inhabited by the country's ethnic minorities. Specifically, the
Cordillera administration, which covers the central mountain region of Luzon, had only a 78.6 percent functional literacy rate, while the Autonomous
Region of Muslim Mindanao showed 61.2 percent of its population as func-
tionally literate. In fairness, it should be mentioned that other areas of the
country inhabited by Christian Filipinos were not that much better than the
Cordillera region, and some were actually worse.[9] But, these low statistics
certainly mitigate against the ability of the country to advance itself in the

current competitive global economy where a properly educated workforce is a strong point upon which to build for the future.

Another factor that is even more difficult to calculate in any analysis of the Philippine educational system is the quality of the schools themselves. In the Philippines, it is the national government that assumes the responsibility for basic education, not local communities as in the United States. Of the country's 36,800 elementary schools, only some 2,543 are owned by private schools, usually religious bodies that offer a full religious education from elementary school through college. At the secondary level, the national government still assumes the majority of the burden, but privately owned high schools account for 2,488 of the 6,205 total. It is at the postsecondary level that the government's efforts are dwarfed by private institutions, 1,014 to 272.[10] Since the Philippine government's education budget has been declining steadily, it is not unreasonable to assume that the quality of instruction is being affected severely, especially at the elementary level. But it is at the postsecondary level that a unique Philippine problem emerges. While many of the nation's colleges and universities owned by religious bodies are extremely credible institutions, there is a large number of privately owned trade schools, colleges, and universities that are run as profit-making corporations. Some of these schools are even listed among the country's top 2,000 corporations, and in 1996, one of them, Mapua Institute of Technology, Inc., of Manila, gave its owners a staggering 37 percent return on the school's total sales of 208 million pesos.[11] Other schools also did very well for their owners, but a visit to any of these institutions reveals the need for reinvestments in the facilities and a chat with the faculty about the abysmal student-faculty ratios suggests how these high profits are gained.

SOCIAL STRATIFICATION AND ETHNIC DIVERSITY

The preceding discussion of disparities in functional literacy between urban and rural areas and between the mainstream Christian Filipino population versus ethnic minorities, especially the Muslims in the southern islands, is an indication of the country's problems with social stratification and ethnic diversity that adversely affects the lives of significant portions of the Philippine population. We know from accounts written by the first Spaniards that the Philippines had a stratified social order before European contact, and the population was divided between the local leader and a lesser nobility and the majority of the people plus a dependent servile group.[12] It also seemed possible to move upward in early Philippine society, but the dynamics of the pre-conquest system cannot be determined precisely, since the Spaniards soon introduced a rigidity to the indigenous social structure. To facilitate their rule, the Spaniards identified a leadership group, generally called the *principalia*, who were given rights and privileges denied the rest of the population.[13] This collaborator class was self-perpetuating, since the new rulers also introduced the principle of hereditary rights, an alien European concept. The Spanish era also witnessed the introduction of some new social groups, including the Chinese, who migrated to the colony for economic reasons, and their mixed-blood children who were a product of marriages with local Philippine women. Similarly, many Spaniards also had children by native women, so there soon emerged a class of Spanish *mestizos* as well. Not surprisingly, the resident Spaniards and *mestizos* appeared to hold sway during the Iberian regime's dominance, but their control of the economy was effectively undermined by the Chinese *mestizos* by the latter decades of the nineteenth century. In the end, the Spaniards only had political power, and they soon lost that to the United States.

The arrival of the North American conqueror did not fundamentally alter the existing social structure despite sentiments to assist the poor and create a truly democratic society. Not long after their arrival, American officials realized that they, too, needed a loyal Filipino class to make colonial rule work. Throughout the country, the native and *mestizo* elite who sided with the Aguinaldo government were attracted away from opposition to American rule by direct offers of forgiveness and political positions and the indirect implication of economic benefits that would come with peace. Many Filipino revolutionary leaders took advantage of the U.S. offer, extended through the Federalista Party, an American government-assisted collaborator agency, rather than continuing what they saw as an increasingly hopeless war after the capture of Aguinaldo in March 1901.[14] All but the most irreconcilable of Filipino nationalists were soon serving as provincial governors and town mayors throughout the country.

With their political power continued, and actually enhanced since the U.S. approach to governmental administration was less intrusive than under the friar-dominated Spanish system, the social position of the local native and *mestizo* elite groups was reinforced and could frequently thwart American attempts to introduce reforms.[15] From the early days of American colonial rule to the present, there have been no genuine programs to uplift the poor; land reform attempts were consistently derailed, and political office is still a means to amass great wealth for oneself, one's family, and one's cronies.[16] Unfortunately, this bleak assessment of the Philippine political process is widely shared in the Philippines and is related to the socialization that most Filipinos go through, which gives them a kin and alliance group-centered focus that makes loyalty to a broader more amorphous collectivity such as the 'public good' a difficult concept to put into practice.[17] This characterization of Philippine politics is not intended to dismiss the genuine efforts of numerous individuals in and out of public office who have devoted their lives to reforming the political system. These people have made an incremental difference over time, along with the emergence of a genuine middle class of urban-based professionals, civil servants, and businessmen who are concerned about the direction of their country. Many of these reformers and middle-class urbanite professionals made up the throng that was so crucial in over-throwing Marcos in 1986, and they again mobilized against President Joseph Estrada, whose corrupt practices went beyond the limits of tolerance, even for the very tolerant Filipino people.

Despite genuine efforts to reform the political system, the country is still gripped by a political leadership that cannot seem to focus on programs that would lessen the sharp differences and inequalities that constitute the country's levels of social stratification. The gap between the rich and poor has not lessened but has actually increased since independence in 1946. By 1997, the average income was the equivalent of approximately $5,000 per year. At that time, only 9.8 percent of families enjoyed an annual income between $10,000 and $20,000 (US) while a mere 2.3 percent of Philippine families had incomes greater than that. The existence of a large concentration of urban poor is also seen in the data, where slightly over one half of all urban residents earn below the average income, which is barely enough to keep a family together. In 1997, the metro Manila area was estimated to have 127,873 families living below the poverty line. Meanwhile, the disparity between ur-ban and rural incomes is greater at every level, betraying the concentration of wealth in the cities and the clear advantages urban dwellers enjoy despite their greater costs of living. Simply put, in the nation's rural areas, the vast majority have to struggle to make ends meet, and farmers continue to live in extreme indebtedness to landlords and money lenders.[18]

In all cases, whether urban or rural, the impact of poverty is felt most immediately on women and children who are the human face of economic imbalances and injustice. The disparities between urban and rural are then multiplied to an even greater extent when considering the nation's ethnic minorities who are even further marginalized. American anthropologist Lynn Kwiatkowski's work with the Ifugao peoples of northern Luzon convincingly demonstrates the impact of economic inequality as intensified in an ethnic community, especially among its women and children. Kwiatkowski aug-ments raw economic data with information on nutrition, medical practices, and community belief systems to present an especially damning critique of the efforts of international development agencies. Like their Philippine gov-ernment counterparts, they do not challenge the basic inequalities inherent in the country's social structure that originally created the poverty.[19]

Approximately ten percent of the Filipino people are members of a non-Christian cultural minority group, a categorization that incorporates very diverse groups from the impoverished and primitive Aeta peoples (sometimes referred to as "negritos") in the remotest parts of the country, to the many tribal peoples of Luzon's central mountains, the country's numerous central islands and Mindanao's expansive plains, to the nine highly organized and fiercely independent Islamic ethno-linguistic groups. Most minority groups are very limited in size and live in regions where they comprise only the tiniest part of the local population. These folks are usually sidelined in terms of government attention, but they retain a distinct independence if only by living in remote areas. Though the existence of many cultural minorities is an appealing idea, the reality is that many of the minorities are rapidly becoming acculturated into the dominant Christian Filipino culture at least in terms of dress, popular culture, and employment goals. Old customs are being forgotten, and when the remaining elders go so will the last vestiges of these independent cultures.

Unlike many other minority groups, the people of Luzon's central Cordillera and the Muslims of the south have a sufficient population to perpetuate their culture and live in geographically distinct areas free from most direct outside influences. Because they control significant regional areas, they have also been able to retain a separate and distinct political presence. The non-Christian groups in the central Cordillera and the Muslims were granted autonomous regions in the mid-1970s, and in these areas, they have, at least in theory, control over their own local affairs. In neither case is the situation ideal, and in the southern Philippines this political concession has not dampened the Muslim's desire for some measure of independence from the Manila government.

The situation in the southern Philippines has deep roots, since the Spaniards were never completely able to secure this area of their colony. The United States had more success only because they combined brutal military actions with policies to co-opt the traditional leadership that created a *de facto* autonomous region under their political control. Since 1946, tensions have been fueled in large part by a steady migration of Christian Filipinos into parts of Mindanao that Muslims considered their territory. Questions of land ownership and exploitation of the natural resources and the population only intensified feelings. The corner was turned in the late 1960s, when a radical group of young Muslims led by Nur Misuari formed a new organization, the Moro National Liberation Front, which rejected the traditional leaders and sought complete independence for the Muslim people. Misuari's organization fought the martial law government of Ferdinand Marcos for many years, tying up much of the Philippine Armed Forces personnel and equipment until a series of agreements eventually led to the creation of the current autonomous region. After a period of relative peace in the 1990s, fighting in the southern Philippines flared anew in late 1999, this time under a new Muslim leadership opposed to Misuari's agreement with the government. Once again war raged in Mindanao and the Sulu archipelago, with the government under President Estrada going on the offensive. A number of government military victories in the summer of 2000 gained territory for the government, but peace remains elusive as the current Muslim insurgent leaders are committed to avoiding what they see as the mistakes of the past.[20]

OVERSEAS CONTRACT LABOR

In a sad testimonial to the weakness of the Philippine economy that cannot offer its citizens the prospect of a decent career and livelihood, the number of Filipinos who have migrated overseas on temporary short-term work contracts has mushroomed during the 1980s and 1990s. In Asia's wealthier countries, Filipina maids can be seen tending to the children of their employers as even the graduates of some of Manila's factory universities find that it is better to make a very good wage as a nanny in Hong Kong than search in vain for a job at home. On the weekends in Hong Kong, tens of thousands of Filipina maids can be found socializing with their friends at the terminal of the Star Ferry, the passenger ferry that connects the island of Hong Kong with the mainland peninsula of Kowloon. Their jobs are demeaning, but the pay they can send home is the sacrifice they make for leaving their spouses and children.

This trend in international labor export began in the 1970s when tens of thousands of Filipino construction workers poured into the oil rich nations of the Middle East whose new-found wealth was translated into ambitious building projects. This initial flood was followed by many more Filipinos and the composition of the workforce became largely female as the professions in demand switched to nurses, housemaids, and nannies, although Filipino sailors continue to be employed in high numbers. In 1998, there were 755,684 Filipino overseas workers found in more than 100 countries, with most still working in the Middle East, followed closely by others employed in neighboring Asian nations, followed distantly by the European Union and then the United States.[21]

Currently, the government's Philippine Overseas Employment Administration (POEA) supervises hundreds of private recruitment agencies and collects millions of pesos from the workers in the form of a bewildering number of fees, processing costs, certificates, and required seminars. Even while working overseas, Philippine embassies and consulates collect additional fees from the workers for their services. However, the true value of the overseas worker is found in the money they remit back home through a variety of means. In 1997, the Philippine Central Bank estimated that remittance at $12,460,000 (US), which makes foreign overseas workers the Philippine's greatest single foreign exchange earner.[22]

Despite being a boon to the nation's economy and to some individual families, there are increasing cases of abuse of overseas workers and a number of mysterious deaths. The most dramatic case was that of Flor Contemplacion, a maid working in Singapore who was accused of murdering her employer's child who was left in her care. The local court found her guilty and forensic evidence seems to have confirmed her guilt, but at home Filipinos were incensed at what they thought was the maltreatment of the poor woman. Her execution led to a temporary break in relations between the Philippines and Singapore and resulted in the removal of a number of officials in Manila for failure to protect the interests of the accused maid. In addition, there have been a number of reported rapes of Filipina housemaids in various Middle Eastern countries and a murder case in which a maid killed her employer while defending her honor. In 2000, a popular Philippine movie *Anak (Child)* had the noted actress Vilma Santos in a heart wrenching role playing a poor and abused maid in Hong Kong who finally collects enough money so she could return home only to struggle mightily to repair the damage to her loved ones that her absence caused. In the end, her money is insufficient and she must once again pack her bags and leave for yet another demeaning overseas job.

NOTES

1. The best such book is Luis Francia, *Passport Philippine* (San Rafael, CA: World Trade Press, 1997); see pp. 19–20 for discussion of the cultural use of the word *yes*.

2. See F. Landa Jocano, *Filipino Social Organization: Traditional Kinship and Family Organization* (Quezon City: Punlad Research House, 1998), 78–79, 116–117.

3. This term is discussed in Alfredo Roces and Grace Roces, *Culture Shock! Philippines: A Guide to Customs and Etiquette* (Portland, OR: Graphic Arts Center Publishing 1994), 91.

4. The major voice of the Ateneo de Manila University's Institute of Philippine Culture was the late Fr. Frank Lynch, S.J. Though some of the institute's conclusions have been further refined by subsequent generations of social scientists, many of the original observations form the basis of continuing social analysis. For definitions and an elaboration of SIR and *amor-propio* see Lynch's "Social Acceptance Reconsidered" in Aram A. Yengoyan and Perla Q. Makil, ed., *Philippine Society and the Individual*

(Ann Arbor: Michigan Papers on South and Southeast Asia, no. 24, The University of Michigan, 1984), 23–91, esp. pp. 31–38.

5. Jocano, 153–160.

6. Much of this discussion is based on Isabel S. Panopio, Felicidad V. Cordero-MacDonald, and Adelisa A. Raymundo, *General Sociology: Focus on the Philippines* (Quezon City: Ken Inc., 1994), 286–289.

7. John S. Noffsinger, "A Teacher for Bayombong," *Peace Corps Volunteer*, 3, no. 12 (October 1965): n.p.

8. Republic of the Philippines, National Statistical Coordination Board, *1999 Philippine Statistical Yearbook* (Makati, Philippines: NSCB, 1999), tables 10.3, 10.6, 10.7, and 10.9.

9. Ibid., tables 10.1, 10.2.

10. Ibid., table 10.4.

11. *Ibon Facts and Figures* 21, no. 12 (June 30, 1998), 5, cites data from the country's Securities and Exchange Commission's 1997 report, *SEC Top 2000 Corporations*.

12. E. P. Patanne, *The Philippines in the 6th to 16th Centuries* (Metro Manila: LSA Press San Juan, 1996), 54–75.

13. The best overview and definition of the *principalia* remains Norman G. Owen, "The Principalia in Philippine History," *Philippine Studies*, 22 (Third & Fourth Quarter 1974): 297–324.

14. Ruby Paredes, "The Origins of National Politics: Taft and the Partido Federal," in her edited book, *Philippine Colonial Democracy* (New Haven, CT: Southeast Asian Studies, Yale University, 1988), 41–69.

15. The ability of Filipino political leaders to guard their own interests even during the height of American colonial power has long been recognized. See Glenn A. May, *Social Engineering in the Philippines: The Aims, Execution, and Impact of American Colonial Policy, 1900–1913* (Westport, CT: Greenwood Publishers, 1980), and Norman G. Owen, ed., *Compadre Colonialism, Studies on the Philippines under American Rule* (Ann Arbor: Center for South and Southeast Asian Studies, University of Michigan, 1971).

16. For a superb overview of contemporary political corruption, see Sheila S. Coronel, ed., *Pork and Other Perks: Corruption and Governance in the Philippines* (Pasig, Metro Manila: Center for Investigative Journalism, 1998).

17. See Niels Mulder's thoughtful new book that analyzes a variety of cultural products such as newspapers and textbooks to discover the popular Philippine consciousness of what might be called the commonweal, *Filipino Images: Culture of the Public World* (Quezon City: New Day Publishers, 2000).

18. Republic of the Philippines, National Statistical Coordination Board, tables 2.1 for national averages, 2.2 for a differentiation between urban and rural families, and 2.9 for data on the number of families below the poverty line.

19. Lynn M. Kwiatkowski, *Struggling with Development: The Politics of Hunger and Gender in the Philippines* (Boulder, CO: Westview Press, 1998).

20. Arnold Molina Azurin, *Beyond the Cult of Dissidence in Southern Philippines*

and War Torn Zones in the Global Village (Quezon City: University of the Philippines Center for Integrative and Development Studies, 1996) provides a clear background picture and analysis of the insurgency, while Marites Danguilan Vitug and Glenda M. Gloria take the story up to the present with a commendable clarity in their book *Under the Crescent Moon: Rebellion in Mindanao* (Quezon City: Ateneo Center for Social Policy & Public Affairs and the Institute for Popular Democracy, 2000).

21. Panopio Cordero-MacDonald, and Raymundo, 218–219, and Republic of the Philippines, National Statistical Coordination Board, tables 11.8 through 11.10.

22. "The Philippine Labor Export," *Ibon Facts and Figures* 21, nos. 17–18 (September 15–31, 1998), 3.

Glossary

Adat.   Islamic customary law that sometimes conflicts with Philippine jurisprudence becoming a problem for Muslim-Christian relations.

Adobo.   Stewed dish of either chicken, pork, or a combination that is flavored with vinegar and spices. The Philippine dish resembles a similarly named Mexican recipe.

Amor-propio.   An individual's self-esteem that cannot be violated without an irreparable loss of face; great efforts are always made to ensure that this will not happen.

Anito.   Spirit that is usually friendly if properly appropriated.

Asawa.   Spouse. This term is not gender specific, which reflects the general equality of Filipino kinship structure, if not the daily reality.

Asuang.   Malevolent spirit that acts with seeming capriciousness such that it cannot be appropriated. See also *anito.*

Babaylan.   Intermediary with the spirit world. Very often this person was a woman in pre-Spanish society, but men in this position were not unknown either, especially by the nineteenth century.

Baguio.   Summer capital for American colonial officials anxious to escape Manila's summer tropical heat. Located at a 5,000-foot elevation in Luzon Island's Central Cordillera, Baguio remains a popular Philippine resort city for Filipinos who also appreciate the city's moderate temperatures and low humidity.

Bahay kubo.   Traditional style *nipa* house of the rural Philippines that still forms the basis of contemporary Filipino architecture's aesthetic sensibility.

Bakya.   Derisive term that literally refers to the wooden sandals (*bakya*) worn by the poor. The term is used to describe the audience for lowbrow entertainment or an artistic production that could only appeal to such a low level. It is most often applied to popular Filipino films.

Balagtasan.   Contest in poetic verse waged between debaters.

Barangay.   Boats that brought the first Filipinos to the archipelago. In the Spanish era this name was used for a group of town residents under the authority of a *capitan* who was charged with collecting their taxes. Currently, it designates the lowest level of local government administration.

Barkada.   At a superficial level, this is a mere friendship group. In reality, a *barkada*'s influence is long lasting with bonds that approach, and sometimes surpass, the intensity of familial obligations.

Barong tagalog.   Philippine national shirt that originated during the Spanish regime as a proscribed mode of native dress. The shirt became a symbol of nationalism and is now worn during formal occasions or in a modified casual style for daily office use.

Bathala.   Filipino's pre-Spanish conceptualization for a superior being. However, Filipinos were not monotheistic and this term may only be that applied to the most powerful of a wider range of deities.

Bayanihan.   Shared group activity and willingness to help one's neighbor in a set of reciprocal obligations.

Cebu.   The Philippine's second city located on the island of the same name. It was near Cebu that Magellan landed in 1521 and then lost his life and where the first permanent Spanish expedition later arrived in 1565.

Colorum.   Movement of peasants seeking an end to their poverty through religious release. The original group was formed in the rural area south of Manila and the name has since been applied to similar groups in other parts of the country.

Compadre.   Strong relationship with a ritual co-parent who serves as a sponsor at a child's baptism, confirmation, or wedding. Though associated with religious ceremonies and obligations, the resulting relationship is much deeper and constitutes an extension of the kin group.

Damay.   Quality of compassion seen in Jesus Christ and valued as a social good even at the expense of discipline and retribution.

Datu.   Title for a local Muslim leader.

Hadji.   Religious pilgrimage to Mecca made by the Muslim faithful. Filipino Muslims who make this trip are accorded special religious honor and have become leaders in strengthening and deepening the faith.

Herbolario.   Someone skilled in the traditional science of using combinations of herbs to cure illness and ward off evil spirits.

Hiya.   One's personal sense of modesty or shame that controls social behavior.

Hukbalahap.   Peasant-based guerrilla army that tried to topple the newly independent post-World War II Philippine government. The core of its membership had been a part of a wartime guerrilla army formed by the country's Communist party. At its peak, the Huk movement constituted a serious threat to the government but was not able to seize power due to a number of key arrests, defections, and U.S.-assisted counter-guerilla warfare campaigns.

Ilustrado.   Nineteenth-century educated son of a wealthy Filipino, usually a *mestizo*, who has gone to college either in Manila or Europe. The *ilustrados* created modern Philippine nationalism through their writings and propaganda activities even though others lead the revolt against Spain.

Imam.   Prayer leader in a mosque.

Indio.   Derisive Spanish term for native Filipinos. A turning point in Philippine nationalism occurred when the *ilustrado* sons of wealthy *mestizos* studying in Europe realized that in Spanish eyes they too were little better than the common *indio*, so in response to these Iberian prejudices, they formed an association called *Los Indios Bravos* (the brave/proud *indios*).

Intramuros.   Five square kilometers protected by the walled fortifications of the Spanish city of Manila. Located in the intramuros were the Spanish colony's government offices, the residences of its chief officers, the headquarters of the missionary religious orders, and the country's major churches, and the Manila Cathedral.

Kalayaan.   Interesting Tagalog/Pilipino word with a double meaning that includes independence in a political sense and the freedom one gains from religious redemption. It was often said that Corazon Aquino embodied both values and this made her opposition to Ferdinand

Marcos even more poignant than simply that of the grieving widow out to avenge the assassination of her husband Benigno by Marcos's agents.

Kanin.   Cooked rice. This term forms the root of a number of terms used in Philippine cuisine clearly showing the importance of this grain in the Filipino diet.

Kapatid.   One's siblings. This term has meanings of love and affection reflecting the strong bond of the Filipino family.

Katipunan.   Short version of the name of the revolutionary organization founded by Andres Bonifacio in 1892 that sought to liberate the Philippines from Spanish rule.

Komedya.   Religiously based play featuring a struggle between good and evil often represented by a conflict pitting Christians against Muslims during the crusades or in defense of Spain. Also called the moro-moro.

Komik.   Philippine comic book that has lost some popularity to television but still maintains a significant following as its stories reflect traditional beliefs and the aspirations of common Filipinos.

Kundiman.   Slow and sweet love song popular in traditional music but easily adaptable to more modern and political purposes. The *kundiman* style was used for patriotic songs during the revolution against Spain, and it was this musical form into which the nationalist poem *Bayan Ko* (My Country) was rendered and later sung during the national uprising that removed President Ferdinand Marcos from power in 1986.

Lechon.   Slow roasted pig that is turned over hot coals and served during festivals or special occasions such as a wedding or graduation.

Liwanag.   Light. This word's frequent use refers to "the light of Christ" so it is not as simple as the light from, say, an electric bulb. *Liwanag* was often used by Filipino revolutionaries and by peasants who joined folk religious societies that sought a miraculous deliverance from poverty and oppression.

Madrasa.   Islamic religious schools.

Marian festivals.   Generic term for the variety of festivals honoring the Virgin Mary.

Mestizo.   Progeny of a mixed marriage between a Filipina (or Filipino) and a foreigner, usually a Chinese or Spaniard. The term is used beyond the first generation to identify a family's origins and as a status marker. The *mestizo* group developed and still controls the country's economy and pioneered the independence movement from Spain.

Moro.   Term given to the Muslim population by the colonizing Spanish whose experience fighting the Moors of North Africa tainted their relationship with the Philippine's Islamic population. The term is still used today even by Philippine Muslims.

Mt. Pinatubo.   Volcano in the Zambales Mountain chain that erupted in 1991 destroying the U.S. Clark Air Force Base and rendering the American navy's Subic Bay Naval Base inoperable thereby facilitating the closure of foreign-held military facilities.

Naga.   Stylized serpent used as an artistic motif by the Philippine's Islamic population.

Nipa.   Type of palm used in house construction.

Okir.   Curvilinear designs usually of vine and leaf patterns employed by the Philippine's Muslims.

Pabasa.   Public reading of the story of the life and death of Jesus Christ during the Easter season. The practice passes along social as well as religious values that contribute to the core beliefs of Filipino society.

Pagkamatapat.   Unwavering loyalty to one's kin group.

Pagtitiis.   Perseverance, especially in upholding good morals or in doing well despite overwhelming odds. This is seen as a high virtue usually achieved by the long-suffering wife.

Pakikisama.   Going along with the group to preserve social harmony even if one's own wishes must be sacrificed.

Pananagutan.   Obligation one feels to one's kin group for which the individual will sacrifice his or her own wishes.

Pancit.   Noodle dish made from any of a variety of noodles and other ingredients. *Pancit* entered the Philippines with visiting Chinese merchants and was transformed to suit local tastes.

Parian.   Area created during the Spanish colonial regime for Chinese merchants where they were required to live and set up their shops since they were not permitted to live outside of Manila. This was an attempt to control the foreign population for the benefit of Spain and to monitor their activities.

Pasyon.   Story of the life and death of Jesus Christ. See also *pabasa*.

Pilipino.   Philippine national language. Speakers of other dialects at first resented the imposition of a national language so obviously based on Tagalog, the dialect spoken in the capital city and its surrounding provinces, but over time Pilipino's use in the media, schools, and government offices has increased familiarity with the official language and its acceptance.

Pinoy rock.   Philippine (pinoy is a slang term for a Filipino) adaptation of western style rock music.

Pintakasi.   Contests of fighting cocks where roosters fight to the death. Contests are usually held on Sundays and always in conjunction with festivals.

Poblacion.   Center of a municipality made up of a central plaza, the church, municipal building, public market, additional shops around the plaza and the homes of the town elite, the *principalia*.

Puhunan.   Giving of favors. This term is frequently associated with Jesus Christ who grants favors to those who believe in him while the recipient has a debt of gratitude that can never be repaid.

Pulutan.   Finger food of almost any nature and deemed acceptable to accompany alcoholic drinks.

Querida.   Mistress. This term reflects the Filipino male's practice of attempting to maintain an amorous relationship outside of marriage in a clear double standard since such behavior is not permitted of wives.

Ramadan.   Muslim celebratory month of fasting commemorating the period when Muhammad received the first of the Koran's revelations from God.

Sarimanok.   Legendary bird with a fish in its beak that is often used by Muslim artists.

Sarsuela.   Philippine adaptation of a Spanish theatrical form that combines musical numbers with a popular story, usually about love triangles. The *sarsuela* was very popular and the values it upheld reflected those of its peasant audiences. During the revolution against Spain and the fight against American rule, the *sarsuela* became a propaganda tool for Filipino nationalists. Recently, the form has been revived using modern plays with some success.

Sawsawan.   Custom of using a wide variety of sauces to flavor almost any dish to suit individual taste, reflecting the individuality and creativity found in Filipino cuisine.

Sinakulo.   Religious plays usually staged during festivals and important religious events such as Christmas and Easter.

Sinigang.   Stewed dish of fish or meat that is flavored with a variety of souring agents such as tamarind, green mango, guava, or tomatoes.

Tadhana. Fate, especially that of a woman, which must be suffered and born with dignity.

Taglish. Slang mixing of Tagalog and English, especially in urban areas and among educated sophisticates, that allows for greater linguistic flexibility than either language otherwise. Used especially for humor.

Terno. Traditional dress of the Filipina derived from Spanish notions of fashion and adapted to local materials and sensibilities.

Tinikling. Folk dance in which performers are required to step between bamboo poles being slapped together in time with the music. Said to mimic the bird of the same name, the dance is popular at tourist resorts but has also been seen as an allegory for the Philippine national character.

Tsismis. Gossip. Like in other cultures this is usually harmless but it may be used as a means to evaluate behavior and to enforce group discipline against someone thought to be violating group norms. In this case, the gossip can be quite vicious.

Ulam. Generic term applied to any vegetable, fish, or meat dish that accompanies rice.

Ulamas. Muslim clerics and teachers.

Utang na loob. Debt of gratitude that comes from the inner soul (*loob*) of the recipient of a favor. This debt forms the core of the ties of reciprocal relationships in a Philippine community that keep individuals bound to each other.

Zakat. Religious tithe paid by pious Muslims for the maintenance of charitable and religious institutions.

Zamboanga. Muslim city at the tip of the western arm of Mindanao Island. Early in its reign, the Spanish government established a fort there to monitor Muslim activity to little avail until the American period when the region was brought under control. The city remains a government and religious center for the Sulu Archipelago, which extends southwesterly toward Indonesia.

Bibliography

Alegre, Edilberto N. *Inumang Pinoy* (Filipino Drinking). Pasig, Metro Manila: Anvil Publishing, 1992.

Alejandro, Reynaldo G. "Contemporary Dance in the Philippines." *Crossroads: An Interdisciplinary Journal of Southeast Asian Studies* 1, no. 1 (February 1983): 31–38.

Allen, James S. *The Philippine Left on the Eve of World War II*. Minneapolis, MN: MEP Publications, 1993.

Aluit, Alfonso J. *The Galleon Guide to Philippine Festivals*. Manila: Galleon Publications, 1969.

Alvarez, Santiago V. *Recalling the Revolution: Memoirs of a Filipino General*. Translated by Paula Carolina S. Malay. Madison: Center for Southeast Asian Studies, University of Wisconsin, 1992.

Alvina, Corazon S. "Regional Dishes." In Reynaldo G. Alejandro, ed. *The Food of the Philippines*. Boston: Periplus Editions, 1998, 10–13.

Ampil, Mario, "Two Decades of Philippine Radio: A Brief Survey." In Clodualdo del Mundo, Jr. ed. *Philippine Mass Media: A Book of Readings*. Manila: Communication Foundation for Asia, 1986, 61–71.

Ang, Gertrudes R. "The *Tinikling* as a Literary Symbol of Philippine Culture." *Philippine Quarterly of Culture and Society* 6, no. 4 (December 1978): 210–217.

Anonymous. "Bayanihan Moves Guam Audience to Tears." *Philippine Daily Inquirer*, July 19, 1998.

Azurin, Arnold Molina, *Beyond the Cult of Dissidence in Southern Philippines and War Torn Zones in the Global Village*. Quezon City: University of the Philippines Center for Integrative and Development Studies, 1996.

Bain, David Haward. *Sitting in Darkness: Americans in the Philippines*. New York: Penguin Books, 1984.

Baradas, David. *Sining Biswal: An Essay on Philippine Ethnic Visual Arts.* Manila: Cultural Center of the Philippines, 1992.

Barrios, Joi. *Minatamis at Iba pang Tula ng Pag-Ibig* (*Sweetened Fruit and Other Love Poems*). Pasig, Metro Manila: Anvil Publishing, 1998.

Bonifacio, Amelia Lapena. *The "Seditious" Tagalog Playwrights: Early American Occupation.* Manila: Zarzuela Foundation of the Philippines, 1972.

Bonner, Raymond. *Waltzing with a Dictator: The Marcoses and the Making of American Policy.* New York: Times Books, 1987.

Borromeo, Mauricia D. "Symphonic Literature." In *CCP Encyclopedia of Philippine Art.* Vol. 6, *Philippine Music.* Manila: Cultural Center of the Philippines, 1994, 127–130.

Brands, H. W. *Bound for Empire: The United States and the Philippines.* New York: Oxford University Press, 1992.

Bulosan, Carlos. *America Is in the Heart.* Seattle: University of Washington Press, 2000.

———. *On Becoming Filipino: Selected Writings of Carlos Bulosan.* Edited by E. San Juan, Jr. Philadelphia: Temple University Press, 1995.

Buss, Claude A. *Cory Aquino and the People of the Philippines.* Stanford, CA: Stanford Alumni Association, 1987.

Cabotaje, Esther Manuel. *Food and Philippine Culture: A Study in Culture and Education.* Manila: Centro Escolar University, 1976.

Carballo, Bibsy M. "They 'Listen' to the Music with Their Feet." *Philippine Daily Inquirer,* April 25, 1998.

Carbo, Nick. *Returning a Borrowed Tongue: An Anthology of Filipino and Filipino American Poetry.* Minneapolis: Coffee House Press, 1995.

Caruncho, Eric S. *Punks, Poets, Poseurs: Reportage on Pinoy Rock & Roll.* Pasig, Metro Manila: Anvil Publishing, 1996.

Casal, Fr. Gabriel, et al. *The People and Art of the Philippines.* Los Angeles: Museum of Cultural History, University of California at Los Angeles, 1981.

Castro, Jose Luna. "Philippine Journalism: From the Early Years to the Sixties." In Clodualdo del Mundo, Jr., ed., *Philippine Mass Media: A Book of Readings.* Manila: Communication Foundation for Asia, 1986, 3–13.

Cordero-Fernando, Gilda. "The Festive Board of Landlord and Peasant." In Gilda Cordero-Fernando. ed., *Philippine Food and Life.* Pasig, Metro Manila: Anvil Publishers, 1992, 74–76.

———. ed., *Philippine Food and Life.* Pasig, Metro Manila: Anvil Publishers, 1992.

Coronel, Sheila S., ed. *Pork and Other Perks: Corruption and Governance in the Philippines.* Pasig, Metro Manila: Center for Investigative Journalism, 1998.

Cruz, Andres Cristobal. "Filipino Literature and Commitment." In *The National Artists of the Philippines.* Manila: Cultural Center of the Philippines, 1998, 189–193.

Cruz, Eric V. *The Barong Tagalog: Its Development and Identity as the Filipino Men's National Costume.* Quezon City: University of the Philippines, 1992.

————. *The Terno: Its Development and Identity as the Filipino Woman's National Costume.* Quezon City: University of the Philippines, 1982.

Cruz, Isagani A. "The Gathering Storm." *Philippine Daily Inquirer*, January 19, 2001.

Cullather, Nick. *Illusions of Influence: The Political Economy of United States-Philippine Relations, 1942–1960.* Stanford, CA: Stanford University Press, 1994.

Cultural Center of the Philippines. *Artista ng Bayan, Antonio R. Buenaventura, Lucrecia Reyes-Urtula,* Manila: Cultural Center of the Philippines, 1988.

————. *Artista ng Bayan, Leandro V. Locsin.* Manila: Cultural Center of the Philippines, 1990.

————. *Artista ng Bayan, Lucrecia R. Kasilag.* Manila: Cultural Center of the Philippines, 1989.

————. *Encyclopedia of Philippine Art,* 10 vols. Manila: Cultural Center of the Philippines, 1994.

Dalisay, Jose Y., Jr. *Killing Time in a Warm Place.* Pasig, Metro Manila: Anvil Publishing, 1992.

David, Joel. *Fields of Vision: Critical Applications in Recent Philippine Cinema.* Quezon City: Ateneo de Manila University Press, 1995.

————. *Wages of Cinema: Film in Philippine Perspective.* Quezon City: University of the Philippines Press, 1998.

Davidson, Gary Marvin and Barbara E. Reed, *Culture and Customs of Taiwan.* Westport, CT: Greenwood Press, 1998.

Davis, Leonard. *Revolutionary Struggle in the Philippines.* New York: St. Martin's Press, 1989.

De Leon, Felipe Padilla. "Philippine Music." In Amparo S. Lardizabal and Felicitas Tensuan-Leogardo, ed., *Readings on Philippine Culture and Social Life.* Manila: Rex Bookstore, 1976, 156–162.

De Mesa, Jose. "Holy Week and Popular Devotions." In Rene B. Javellana, S.J. ed., *Morality, Religion and the Filipino.* Quezon City: Ateneo de Manila University Press, 1994, 220–233.

Del Mundo, Clodualdo, Jr. "Komiks: An Industry, a Potent Medium, our National 'Book,' and Pablum of Art Appreciation." In Clodualdo del Mundo Jr., ed., *Philippine Mass Media: A Book of Readings.* Manila: Communication Foundation of Asia, 1986, 179–185.

————. *Native Resistance: Philippine Cinema and Colonialism, 1898–1941.* Manila: De La Salle University Press, 1998.

Elsterio, Fernando G. *The Iglesia ni Kristo: Its Christology and Ecclesiology.* Manila: Cardinal Dea Institute, Loyola School of Theology, Ateneo de Manila University, 1997.

Enriquez, Elizabeth L. "Philippine Mass Media Towards the Close of the 20th Century." In *The Contemporary Philippine Culture: Selected Papers on Arts and Education.* Manila: The Japan Foundation, 1998, 33–41.

Enriquez, Marge C. "Dancing to 'Bakya'." *Philippine Daily Inquirer*, August 10, 1998.

Estepa, Pio C., SVD. "The Myth of Love in Filipino Komiks." In Leonardo N. Mercado, SVD, ed., *Filipino Thought on Man and Society*. Tacloban City, Philippines: Divine Word University Publications, 1980, 42–56.

Estupigan, Ruth V. "Dining at the Filipino Table." *Manila Bulletin, Philippine Centennial Issue*, June 12, 1998, 85–87.

Evangelista, Oscar L. "Some Aspects of the History of Islam in Southeast Asia." In Peter Gowing, ed. *Understanding Islam and Muslims in the Philippines*. Quezon City: New Day Publishers, 1988, 16–25.

Fabros, Wilfredo. *The Church and Its Social Involvement in the Philippines, 1930–1972*. Quezon City: Ateneo de Manila University, 1988.

Fernandez, Doreen G. *Dulaan: An Essay on the American Colonial and Contemporary Traditions in Philippine Theater*. Manila: Cultural Center of the Philippines, 1994.

———. *Palabas: Essays on Philippine Theater*. Quezon City: Ateneo de Manila University Press, 1996.

———. *Panitikan: An Essay on Philippine Literature*. Manila: Cultural Center of the Philippines, 1989.

———. *Tikim: Essays on Philippine Food and Culture*. Pasig, Metro Manila: Anvil Publishing, 1994.

Fernandez, Doreen G., and Edilberto N. Alegre. *Sarap: Essays on Philippine Food*. Metro Manila: Mr. & Ms. Publishing Co., 1988.

Francia, Luis H., ed. *Brown River, White Ocean: An Anthology of Twentieth-Century Philippine Literature in English*. New Brunswick, NJ: Rutgers University Press, 1993.

———. *Passport Philippines*. San Rafael, CA: World Trade Press, 1997.

Friend, Theodore. *The Blue-Eyed Enemy: Japan Against the West in Java and Luzon, 1942–45*. Princeton, NJ: Princeton University Press, 1988.

Gamalinda, Eric. *The Empire of Memory*. Pasig, Metro Manila: Anvil Publishing, 1992.

Gatchalian, Elmer, L. M. Carunungan, and Danny Yson. "Industry." In *CCP Encyclopedia of Philippine Art*. Vol. 6; *Philippine Music*. Manila: Cultural Center of the Philippines, 1994, 194–195.

Giminez-Maceda, Teresita. "Pinoy Pop." In *CCP Encyclopedia of Philippine Art*. Vol. 6, *Philippine Music*. Manila: Cultural Center of the Philippines, 107–113.

———. "Popular Music." *International Popular Culture* 1, no. 1 (1980): 24–32.

———. 1994, "Protest Songs." In *CCP Encyclopedia of Philippine Art*. Vol. 6, *Philippine Music*. Manila: Cultural Center of the Philippines, 1994, 114–122.

Gonzalez, N.V.M. *The Bread of Salt and Other Stories*. Seattle: University of Washington Press, 1993.

Gowing, Peter G. *Muslim Filipinos: Heritage and Horizon*. Quezon City: New Day Publishers, 1979.

Gregor, A. James, and Virgilio Aganon. *The Philippine Bases: U.S. Security at Risk.* Washington, D.C.: Ethics and Public Policy Center, 1987.

Guillermo, Alice G. *Color in Philippine Life and Art.* Manila: Cultural Center of the Philippines, 1992.

————. "The Evolution of Philippine Art." in Joyce van Fenema, ed., *Southeast Asian Art Today.* Singapore: Roeder Publications, 1996, 118–163.

————. "The Popular Arts." *International Popular Culture* 1, no. 1 (1980): 53–59.

————. *Sining Biswal: An Essay on the American Colonial and Contemporary Traditions in Philippine Visual Arts.* Manila: Cultural Center of the Philippines, 1994.

————. *Sining Biswal: An Essay on Philippine Visual Arts.* Manila: Cultural Center of the Philippines, 1989.

Hagedorn, Jessica. *Dogeaters.* New York: Penguin Books, 1991.

Harper, Bambi I. "Quo Vadis, Filipinas?" *Philippine Daily Inquirer,* January 19, 2001.

Hart, Donn V. *Compadrinazgo: Ritual Kinship in the Philippines.* DeKalb: Northern Illinois University Press, 1977.

Hernando, Mario A., ed. *Lino Brocka: The Artist and His Times.* Manila: Cultural Center of the Philippines, 1993.

Hidalgo, Cristina Pantoja. *A Gentle Subversion: Essays on Philippine Fiction in English.* Quezon City: University of the Philippines Press, 1998.

Hila, Antonio C. *Musika: An Essay on Philippine Music.* Manila: Cultural Center of the Philippines, 1989.

Hila, Maria Corazon C. *Arkitektura: An Essay on Philippine Ethnic Architecture.* Manila: Cultural Center of the Philippines, 1992.

————. "Masjid." In *CCP Encyclopedia of Philippine Art.* Vol. 3, *Philippine Architecture.* Manila: Cultural Center of the Philippines, 1994, 150–151.

Hila, Maria Corazon C., and Rene Javellana, S.J. "Kuta." In *CCP Encyclopedia of Philippine Art.* Vol. 3, *Philippine Architecture.* Manila: Cultural Center of the Philippines, 1994, 146–148.

Hines, Thomas S. "The Imperial Facade: Daniel H. Burnham and American Architectural Planning in the Philippines." *Pacific Historical Review* 41, no. 1 (February 1972): 33–53.

Hornedo, Florentino H. *Panitikan: An Essay on Philippine Ethnic Literature.* Manila: Cultural Center of the Philippines, 1992.

Hutchcroft, Paul D. *The Philippines at the Crossroads: Sustaining Economic and Political Reform.* New York: Asia Society, 1996.

Ibon Facts and Figures, various issues, 1998.

Ileto, Reynaldo C. *Pasyon and Revolution: Popular Movements in the Philippines, 1840–1910.* Quezon City: Ateneo de Manila University Press, 1979 (4th printing 1995).

Infante, J. Eddie. *Inside Philippine Movies, 1970–1990: Essays for Students of Philippine Cinema.* Quezon City: Ateneo de Manila University Press, 1991.

Ipac-Alarcon, Norma. *Philippine Architecture during the Pre-Spanish and Spanish Periods.* Manila: Santo Tomas University Press, 1991.

Japitana, Norma L. *The Superstars of Pop.* Metro Manila: Makati Trade Times, 1982.

Javellana, Rene, S.J. "Casa Real," "Eskwelahan," "Fort Santiago," "Munisipyo," "Palengke," and "Sementeryo." *CCP Encyclopedia of Philippine Art.* Vol. 3, *Philippine Architecture.* Manila: Cultural Center of the Philippines, 1994, 136, 138–141, 230–231, 152–153, 153–155 and 161–163, respectively.

Javellana, Rene, S. J., and Fernando N. Zialcita. "Simbahan." In *CCP Encyclopedia of Philippine Art.* Vol. 3, *Philippine Architecture.* Manila: Cultural Center of the Philippines, 1994, 164–178.

Joaquin, Nick. *La Orosa: The Dance-drama That Is Leonor Goquingco.* Pasig, Metro Manila: Anvil Publishing, 1994.

Joaquin, Nick, and Luciano P. R. Santiago. *The World of Damian Domingo.* Manila: Metropolitan Museum of Manila, 1990.

Jocano, F. Landa. *Filipino Social Organization: Traditional Kinship and Family Organization.* Metro Manila: Punlad Research House, 1998.

Johnson, Bryan. *The Four Days of Courage.* New York: The Free Press, 1987.

Jose, F. Sionil. *Dusk.* New York: The Modern Library, 1998.

———. *Don Vicente.* New York: The Modern Library, 1999.

———. *The Samsons.* New York: The Modern Library, 2000.

Jose, Regalado Trota. *Arkitektura: An Essay on the Spanish Influence on Philippine Architecture.* Manila: Cultural Center of the Philippines, 1992.

———. *Simbahan: Church Art and Architecture in Colonial Philippines, 1565–1898.* Makati: Ayala Foundation, 1991.

———. *Sining Biswal: An Essay on the Spanish Influence on Philippine Visual Arts.* Manila: Cultural Center of the Philippines, 1992.

Karnow, Stanley. *In Our Image: America's Empire in the Philippines.* New York: Random House, 1989.

Kerkvliet, Benedict J. *The Huk Rebellion: A Study of Peasant Revolt in the Philippines.* Berkeley: University of California Press, 1977.

Kwiatkowski, Lynn M. *Struggling with Development: The Politics of Hunger and Gender in the Philippines.* Boulder, CO: Westview Press, 1998.

Lacson, Sahlie P. "The Evolution of the Filipino Dress: Then, Now and Beyond." *Manila Bulletin, Philippine Centennial Issue,* June 12, 1998, 60, 62–63, 71.

Larkin, John A. *Sugar and the Origins of Modern Philippine Society.* Berkeley: University of California Press, 1993.

Lawyers Committee for Human Rights. *Out of Control: Military Abuses in the Philippines.* New York: LCHR, 1990.

Lent, John A. "Comic Art in the Philippines." *Philippine Studies,* Vol. 46 (Second Quarter 1998): 236–248.

Lieban, Richard. *Cebuano Sorcery.* Berkeley: University of California Press, 1967.

Lockard, Craig. *Dance of Life: Popular Music and Politics in Southeast Asia.* Honolulu: University of Hawaii Press, 1998.

Lopez, Salvador P. *Literature and Society: Essays on Life and Letters.* Manila: Philippine Book Guild, 1940.

Lumbera, Bienvenido. "A Report on Philippine Writing Since 1986." In Japan Foundation, *Contemporary Philippine Culture: Selected Papers on Arts and Education.* Manila: Japan Foundation, 1998, 83–87.

———. *Revaluation, 1997: Essays on Philippine Literature, Cinema and Popular Culture.* Manila: University of Santo Tomas Publishing House, 1997.

Lynch, Frank S. J. "Social Acceptance Reconsidered." In Aram A. Yengoyan and Perla Q. Makil, eds., *Philippine Society and the Individual. Frank, Lynch, 1949–1976,* Michigan Papers on South and Southeast Asia, no. 24, Ann Arbor: The University of Michigan, 1984, 23–91.

———. "Town Fiesta: An Anthropologist's View." In Aram A. Yengoyan and Perla Q. Makil, eds., *Philippine Society and the Individual: Selected Essays of Frank Lynch, 1949–1976.* Ann Arbor: Michigan Papers on South and Southeast Asia, no. 24, The University of Michigan, 1984.

Maceda, Jose. *Gongs and Bamboo: A Panorama of Philippine Musical Instruments.* Quezon City: University of the Philippines Press, 1998.

May, Glenn A. *Battle for Batangas: A Philippine Province at War.* New Haven, CT: Yale University Press, 1991.

———. *Social Engineering in the Philippines: The Aims, Execution, and Impact of American Colonial Policy, 1900–1913.* Westport, CT: Greenwood Publishers, 1980.

McCoy, Alfred W., ed. *An Anarchy of Families: State and Family in the Philippines.* Madison: Center for Southeast Asian Studies, University of Wisconsin, 1993.

———. *Closer Than Brothers: Manhood at the Philippine Military Academy.* New Haven, CT: Yale University Press, 1999.

McDonough, Lolita W., ed. *United States Military Bases in the Philippines: Issues and Scenarios.* Quezon City: University of the Philippines, 1985.

McKenna, Thomas M. *Muslim Rulers and Rebels: Everyday Politics and Armed Separation in the Southern Philippines.* Berkeley: University of California Press, 1998.

Medina, Belen T. G. *The Filipino Family: A Text with Selected Readings.* Quezon City: University of the Philippines Press, 1991.

Melbourne International Biennial. "Philippines: Gerardo Tan." In *Melbourne International Biennial Program.* Melbourne, Australia: Melbourne International Biennial, 1999, pp. 201–207.

Mendoza, Felicidad M. *The Comedia (Moro-Moro) Re-Discovered.* Makati, The Philippines: Society of Saint Paul, n.d.

Mercado, Monina. *Games Filipino Children Play.* Manila: PAC, 1978.

Miller, Stuart Creighton. *"Benevolent Assimilation:" The American Conquest of the Philippines, 1899–1903.* New Haven, CT: Yale University Press, 1982.

Millie, Reyes. "Eating Out, Filipino Style." In Reynaldo G. Alejandro, ed., *The Food of the Philippines.* Boston: Periplus Editions, 1998, 19–21.

Mojares, Resil B. *Panitikan: An Essay on the American Colonial and Contemporary Traditions in Philippine Literature*. Manila: Cultural Center of the Philippines, 1994.

———. *Theater in Society, Society in Theater: Social History of a Cebuano Village, 1840–1940*. Quezon City: Ateneo de Manila University Press, 1985.

Montinola, Lourdes R. *Pina*. Metro Manila: Amon Foundation, 1991.

Mulder, Niels. *Filipino Images: Culture of the Public World*. Quezon City: New Day Publishers, 2000.

———. *Inside Philippine Society: Interpretations of Everyday Life*. Quezon City: New Day Publishers, 1997.

Ness, Sally Ann. *Body, Movement, and Culture: Kinesthetic and Visual Symbolism in a Philippine Community*. Philadelphia: University of Pennsylvania Press, 1992.

Noffsinger, John S. "A Teacher for Bayombong." *Peace Corps Volunteer* 3, no. 12 (October 1965).

Nofuente, Valerio. "The Jeepney: Vehicle as Art." *International Popular Culture* 1, no. 1 (1980): 38–47.

Noriega, Violeta A. *Philippine Recipes Made Easy*. Kirkland, WA: Paper Works, 1993.

Ong, James P. "Reinventing Silay for 21st Century." *Philippine Daily Inquirer*, July 13, 1998.

Ordonez, Elmer A. *Nationalist Literature: A Centennial Forum*. Quezon City: University of the Philippines Press, 1996.

Owen, Norman, ed. *Compadre Colonialism: Studies on the Philippines under American Rule*. Ann Arbor: University of Michigan, Center for South and Southeast Asian Studies, 1971.

———. "The Principalia in Philippine History." *Philippine Studies*, 22 (Third & Fourth Quarter 1974): 297–324.

———. *Prosperity without Progress: Manila Hemp and Material Life in the Colonial Philippines*. Berkeley: University of California Press, 1984.

Pacific Asia Museum. *100 Years of Philippine Painting*. Pasadena, CA: Pacific Asia Museum, 1984.

Panopio, Isabel S., Felicidad V. Cordero-MacDonald, and Adelisa A. Raymundo. *General Sociology: Focus on the Philippines*. Quezon City: Ken, Inc., 1994.

Paras-Perez, Rodolfo. *Edades and the 13 Moderns*. Manila: Cultural Center of the Philippines, 1995.

Paredes, Ruby. "The Origins of National Politics: Taft and the Partido Federal." Ruby Paredes, ed., *Philippine Colonial Democracy*. New Haven, CT: Southeast Asian Studies, Yale University, 1988, 41–69.

———, ed. *Philippine Colonial Democracy*. New Haven, CT: Southeast Asian Studies, Yale University, 1988.

Patanne, E. P. *The Philippines in the 6th to 16th Centuries*. Metro Manila: LSA Press San Juan, 1996.

Perdigon, Grace P. "Street Foods and the Filipino Family: A Historical Account," In Celia A. Florencio and Flor C. F. Galvez, eds. *Studies on Filipino Families*.

Quezon City: College of Home Economics, University of the Philippines, 1995, 139–152.

Perez, Rodrigo D. *Arkitektura: An Essay on the American Colonial and Contemporary Traditions in Philippine Architecture.* Manila: Cultural Center of the Philippines, 1994.

———. "Kapitolyo," "Malacanang," and "Sabungan." *CCP Encyclopedia of Philippine Art,* Vol. 3, *Philippine Architecture.* Manila: Cultural Center of the Philippines, 1994, 145, 246–247 and 160, respectively.

Pescador, Alex (pseud.). "An Overview of Philippine Church-State Relations since Martial Law." In David A. Rosenberg, ed. *Marcos and Martial Law in the Philippines,* Ithaca, NY: Cornell University Press, 1979, 298–309.

Philippine Human Rights Information Center. *Growth 2000: Selective Prosperity, Human Rights on the Fourth Year of the Ramos Administration.* Manila: PHRIC, 1997.

Pimentel, Benjamin. *Rebolusyon! A Generation of Struggle in the Philippines.* New York: Monthly Review Press, 1991.

Polites, Nicholas. *The Architecture of Leandro V. Locsin.* New York: Weatherhill, 1997.

Polo, Jaime Biron. *Panitikan: An Essay on the Spanish Influence on Philippine Literature.* Manila: Cultural Center of the Philippines, 1992.

Quijano de Manila (Nick Joaquin). "Viva Villa!" In *The National Artists of the Philippines.* Manila: Cultural Center of the Philippines, 1998, 347–372.

Quirino, Joe. *Don Jose and the Early Philippine Cinema.* Quezon City: Phoenix Publishing House, 1983.

Rafael, Vicente L. *Contracting Colonialism: Translation and Christian Conversion in Tagalog Society under Early Spanish Rule.* Ithaca, NY: Cornell University Press, 1988.

Republic of the Philippines, National Statistical Coordination Board. *1999 Philippine Statistical Yearbook.* Makati: NSCB, 1999.

Reyes, Jose Javier. "Radio Soap Opera." *International Popular Culture* 1, no. 1 (1980): 68–74.

Reyes, Millie. "Eating Out, Filipino Style." In Reynaldo G. Alejandro, ed., *The Food of the Philippines.* Boston: Periplus Editions, 1998, 19–21.

Reyes, Soledad S. "The Philippine Komiks." *International Popular Culture* 1, 1 (1980): 14–23.

Rizal, Jose. *El Filibusterismo.* Translated by Ma. Soledad Lacson-Locsin. Makati: Bookmark, 1996.

———. *Noli Me Tangere.* Translated by Ma. Soledad Lacson-Locsin. Honolulu: University of Hawaii Press, 1997.

Roces, Alejandro R. *Fiesta.* Manila: Vera-Reyes, 1980.

Roces, Alfredo, and Grace Roces. *Culture Shock! Philippines: A Guide to Customs and Etiquette.* Portland, OR: Graphic Arts Center Publishing Co., 1994.

Rodell, Paul A. "The 1909 Escalante Murder Case and the Politics of Religion in

Negros Occidental." *Pilipinas: A Journal of Philippine Studies*, no. 28 (Spring 1997): 61–78.

Rosca, Ninotchka. *State of War*. New York: Fireside Book, 1988.

Salanga, Alfredo Navarro. *Writings in Protest, 1972–1985*. Quezon City: Ateneo de Manila University Press, 1993.

Salanga, Alfredo Navarro and Esther M. Pacheco, eds. *Versus, Philippine Protest Poetry, 1983–1986*. Quezon City: Ateneo de Manila University Press, 1986.

Samonte, Elena L. and Annadaisy J. Carlota. "The Mail-Order Marriage Business: A Reconsideration of the Filipina Image." In Amaryllis T. Torres, ed., *The Filipino Woman in Focus*. Bangkok: UNESCO, 1989.

Santiago, Bienvenido C. "Brother Erano G. Manalo at the Helm." In Bienvenido C. Santiago, ed., *75 Blessed Years of the Iglesia ni Cristo, 1914–1989*. Quezon City: Iglesia ni Cristo, 1989, 51–57.

———. "Brother Felix Y. Manalo Remembered." In *75 Blessed Years of the Iglesia ni Cristo* (Diamond Jubilee program). Quezon City: Iglesia ni Cristo, 1989, 49–50.

———. *75 Blessed Years of the Iglesia ni Cristo, 1914–1989*. Quezon City: Iglesia ni Cristo, 1989.

Santos, Ramon P. "The American Colonial and Contemporary Traditions." In *CCP Encyclopedia of Philippine Art*. Vol. 6, *Philippine Music*. Manila: Cultural Center of the Philippines, 1994, 60.

SarDesai, D. R. *Southeast Asia: Past and Present*. 4th ed. Boulder, CO: Westview Press, 1997.

Schirmer, Daniel B, and Stephen R. Shalom. *The Philippine Reader: A History of Colonialism, Neocolonialism, Dictatorship and Resistance*. Boston: South End Press, 1987.

Schumaker, John, S.J. *The Making of a Nation: Essays on Nineteenth-Century Filipino Nationalism*. Quezon City: Ateneo de Manila University Press, 1991.

Scott, William Henry. *Barangay: Sixteenth-Century Philippine Culture and Society*. Quezon City: Ateneo de Manila University Press, 1994.

Seagrave, Sterling. *The Marcos Dynasty*. New York: Harper & Row Publishers, 1988.

Siapno, Jacqueline. "Gender Relations and Islamic Resurgence in Mindanao, Southern Philippines." In Camillia Fawzi El-Solk and Judy Mabro, eds., *Muslim Women's Choice: Religious Belief and Social Reality*. Providence, RI: Berg Publishers, 1994, 184–201.

Sicam, Edmund L. Review, *Biyaya ng Lupa*. *Philippine Daily Inquirer*, August 15, 1998.

Simons, Lewis M. *Worth Dying For*. New York: William Morrow and Co., 1987.

Sotto, Agustin. "Contemporary Philippine Cinema." In *Contemporary Philippine Culture: Selected Papers on Arts and Education*. Manila: The Japan Foundation, 1998, 113–123.

———. *Pelikula: An Essay on the Philippine Film: 1897–1960*. Manila: Cultural Center of the Philippines, 1992.

Steinberg, David Joel. *The Philippines: A Singular and Plural Place*. 4th ed. Boulder, CO: Westview Press, 1994.

Sullivan, Rodney J. *Exemplar of Americanism: The Philippine Career of Dean C. Worcester.* Ann Arbor: Center for South and Southeast Asian Studies, University of Michigan, 1991.

Tan, Michael. "Tuba, Coke and Edu." *Philippine Daily Inquirer,* April 30, 1998.

Tan, Samuel K. *Internationalization of the Bangsamoro Struggle.* Quezon City: Center for Integrative and Development Studies, University of the Philippines 1993.

———. *The Socioeconomic Dimension of Moro Secessionism.* Quezon City: Center for Integrative and Development Studies, Mindanao Studies Reports no. 1. University of the Philippines, 1995.

Tiglao, Rigoberto. "A Better People Power, Yes But . . ." *Philippine Daily Inquirer,* January 21, 2001.

Timberman, David G. *A Changeless Land: Continuity and Change in Philippine Politics.* New York: M. E. Sharpe, 1991.

Tiongson, Nicanor G. *Dulaan: An Essay on Philippine Theater.* Manila: Cultural Center of the Philippines, 1989.

———. "From Stage to Screen." In Rafael Ma Guerrero, ed., *Readings in Philippine Cinema.* Manila: Experimental Cinema of the Philippines, 1983, 83–94.

———. *Modern ASEAN Plays, Philippines.* Manila: ASEAN Committee on Culture and Information, 1992.

Tiongson, Nicanor G., and Ramon M. Obusan. *Dulaan: An Essay on Philippine Ethnic Theater.* Manila: Cultural Center of the Philippines, 1992.

Torre, Nestor U. "Bring Back the Passion." *Philippine Daily Inquirer,* May 9, 10, 1998.

Trimillos, Ricardo D. "Pasyon: Lenten Observance of the Philippines as Southeast Asian Theater." In Kathy Foley, ed., *Essays on Southeast Asian Performing Arts.* Berkeley: Centers for South and Southeast Asian Studies, University of California, 1992, 5–22.

Trinidad, Francisco. "Philippine Radio: The Early Years." In Clodualdo del Mundo, Jr., ed., *Philippine Mass Media: A Book of Readings.* Manila: Communication Foundation for Asia, 1986, 47–52.

Urtula, Lucrecia T. and Prosperidad Arandez. *Sayaw: An Essay on the Spanish Influence on Philippine Dance.* Manila: Cultural Center of the Philippines, 1992.

Vergara, Alex Y. "Seedy Walkway in Quiapo Undergoes Face Lift." *Philippine Daily Inquirer,* July 26, 1999.

Villaruz, Basilio Esteban S., *Sayaw: An Essay on the American Colonial and Contemporary Traditions in Philippine Dance.* Manila: Cultural Center of the Philippines, 1994.

Villaruz, Basilio Esteban S. and Ramon A. Obusan. *Sayaw: An Essay on Philippine Ethnic Dance.* Manila: Cultural Center of the Philippines, 1992.

Vitug, Marites Danguilan and Glenda M. Gloria. *Under the Crescent Moon: Rebellion in Mindanao.* Quezon City: Ateneo Center for Social Policy & Public Affairs and the Institute for Popular Democracy, 2000.

Wickberg, Edgar. *The Chinese in Philippine Life, 1850–1898.* New Haven, CT: Yale University Press, 1965.

Youngblood, Robert L. *Marcos Against the Church: Economic Development and Po-*

litical Repression in the Philippines. Ithaca, NY: Cornell University Press, 1990.

Yuson, Alfred. *Great Philippine Jungle Energy.* Quezon City: University of the Philippines Press, 1996.

Zialcita, Fernando N. and Martin I. Tinio, Jr. *Philippine Ancestral Homes (1810–1930).* Quezon City: GCF Books, 1980.

Index

About the Author

PAUL A. RODELL is an assistant professor in the Department of History at Georgia Southern University and a specialist in Philippine and Southeast Asian history. He is also the executive director of the Association of Third World Studies.